AF662590

Feminism in the Novels of Shashi Deshpande

N.K. Prasad

ATLANTIC
PUBLISHERS & DISTRIBUTORS (P) LTD

Published by

ATLANTIC

PUBLISHERS & DISTRIBUTORS (P) LTD

7/22, Ansari Road, Darya Ganj, New Delhi-110002
Phones: +91-11-40775252, 23273880, 23275880, 23280451
Fax : +91-11-23285873
Web : www.atlanticbooks.com
E-mail : orders@atlanticbooks.com

Branch Office
5, Nallathambi Street, Wallajah Road, Chennai-600002
Phones: +91-44-64611085, 32413319
E-mail : chennai@atlanticbooks.com

Copyright © N.K. Prasad, 2014

ISBN : 978-81-269-1897-3

All rights reserved. No part of this publication may be reproduced, stored in a retrieval system, transmitted or utilized in any form or by any means, electronic, mechanical, photocopying, recording or otherwise, without the prior permission of the copyright owner. Application for such permission should be addressed to the publisher.

Disclaimer

The authors and the publisher have taken every effort to the maximum of their skill, expertise and knowledge to provide correct material in the book. Even then if some mistakes persist in the content of the book, the publisher does not take responsibility for the same. The publisher shall have no liability to any person or entity with respect to any loss or damage caused, or alleged to have been caused directly or indirectly, by the information contained in this book. Hence, the book should be taken as a general guide only.

The publisher has fully tried to follow the copyright law. However, if any work is found to be similar, it is unintentional and the same should not be used as defamatory or to file legal suit against the authors/publisher.

If the readers find any mistakes, we shall be grateful to them to point those to us so that they can be corrected in the next edition.

All disputes are subject to the jurisdiction of Delhi court only.

Printed in India at Nice Printing Press, A-33/3A, Site-IV, Industrial Area, Sahibabad, Ghaziabad, U.P.

Foreword

Women in India have been occupying a prominent position in the literary horizon since the very beginning of our civilization. In the pre-Vedic and the Vedic periods, women held a high place of honour. To give birth to a daughter was considered something honourable. Devahuti, the daughter of Manu, was married to Rishi Kardam. Their union resulted in the procreation of daughters in succession. The nine daughters of Devahuti were the most shining jewels of Indian womanhood. Among them were: Kala, the wife of Saint Marichi; Arundhati, the wife of Vashishtha; and Ansuya, the very epitome of feminine chastity and wife of saint Atri. According to the *Sarvanukramanika,* there were twenty Brahmavadinis who composed the hymns of the *Rig-Veda.* Gargi, Gosha, Godha, Apala, Maitreiyi, Lilavati and others were the women scholars.

Although in medieval period and the period that followed it, women suffered a lot on various counts, yet they excelled in their wisdom and literary activities. In the modern age, they have achieved tremendous success as politicians, writers, novelists, dramatists, scientists, and all other literary genres.

Among the women novelists of the Post-Independence era, special mention must be made of Kamala Markandaya, Ruth Prawer Jhabvala, Nayantara Sahgal, Shakuntala Shrinagesh, Anita Desai, Attia Hussain, Kamala Das, Namita Gokhale, Shobhaa De, Bharati Mukherjee, Gayatri Chakraborty, Spivak and Shashi Deshpande. These novelists have highlighted different problems which emerged in the socio-political scenario of liberated India. Some of the women novelists of India could not help the temptation of writing on the issue of feminism which, as a socio-cultural movement, began in Europe, got strengthened with the help of Marxism, found full echoes in the USA, and like many other similar concepts, spread to the Third World countries.

Feminist writing in Indian English writing originated from the Western feminist movement, but the indigenous factors like freedom movement, independence, spread of education, concern for economic development and stability, employment opportunities, and above all, the resultant new political awareness of women, have also contributed a lot. The Indian women are caught in the flux of tradition and modernity bearing the burden of the past and aspirations of the future. A search for identity and a quest for the definition of the "self" have become the prime features of women in literature under the sway of feminism.

Shashi Deshpande is a renowned name in the arena of Indian English writing. She has contributed a lot to Indian Feminist writing and given it a new dimension. She has nine novels, many short stories, children books and articles to her credit. She is the winner of the Sahitya Akademi Award for her novel *That Long Silence*.

In this book, *Feminism in the Novels of Shashi Deshpande,* N.K. Prasad has critically and minutely analyzed six of Deshpande's novels—*Roots and Shadows, The Dark Holds No Terrors, That Long Silence, The Binding Vine, A Matter of Time* and *Small Remedies*. He has successfully portrayed the undercurrent of feminist concern scattered in her works which sustains her as a bold feminist writer coining her own brand of feminism, different from others to some extent. I hope that the book will be useful for students and teachers of English literature, particularly Indian English literature, and research scholars in these fields.

N.D.R. Chandra

Contents

Introduction

1

This book aims at making a feminist study of Shashi Deshpande as a feminist author of contemporary India. Her novels present the real picture of the middle-class, educated, urban Indian women. At a glance, her novels appear to be products of feminism, thereby lending a fresh perspective for critical analysis. This research book is not only the depiction of the plight of the Indian women as represented in the novels but endeavour to find out the practical solution to the problems faced by Indian women right from the dawn of civilization to the present age. Though Shashi Deshpande has emerged as a leading woman novelist on the Indian literary horizon, and won the prestigious Sahitya Akademi Award for her novel *That Long Silence* in 1990, yet she has not received the critical attention she deserves.

It is true that 'literature lenses the reality of society'. The writer expresses whatsoever he/she experiences in the society. Thus, the social environment contributes much to the writing of the individuals and Shashi Deshpande is no exception. So, before diving deep into Deshpande's literary ocean and fetching the gems of feminism, it is necessary to have a cursory look at the history of Indian English writing including Indian fiction writing and Indian feminist writing in order to forge a clear picture of novelist's mind and art.

Indian English literature emerged as an interesting by-product of an eventful encounter in the late eighteenth century between a vigorous and enterprising Britain and a stagnant and chaotic India. As a result of the encounter, as F.W. Bain puts it "India, a withered trunk...suddenly shot out with foreign foliage" (quoted in M.K. Naik 1997: 1). The original writing in English by Indians took the form of its first foliage. The first task of the historians of this literature is to provide a suitable definition of its nature and scope clearly. This problem got its complication due to two factors: first, this body of writing has, from time to time, been designated variously as 'Indo-Anglian Literature', 'Indian Writing in English and Indo-English Literature'. Secondly, the failure to make clear-cut distinction has often led confusion between categories. For instance, V.K. Gokak, in his book, *English in India: Its Present and Future* (1964), interprets the term 'Indo-Anglian Literature' as consisting of 'translations by Indians from Indian Literature into English'. In his massive survey *Indian Writing in English* (1962), K.R. Srinivasa Iyengar includes English translations of Tagore's novels and plays translated by others in his history of Indian creative writing in English. While H.M. Williams excludes these from his *Indo-Anglian Literature 1800-1970: A Survey* (1976), John B. Alphonso Karkala in his survey *Indo-English Literature in the Nineteenth Century* (1970) uses the term 'Indo-English Literature' to mean 'Literature produced by Indians in English'.

Indian English literature may be defined as literature written originally in English by authors by birth, ancestry or nationality. It is quite obvious that neither 'Anglo-Indian literature' nor literal translations by others can legitimately form part of this literature. The former comprises the writings of British or Western authors concerning India. Kipling, Forster, F.W. Bain, Sir Edwin Arnold, F.A. Steel, John Master, Paul Scott, M.M. Kaye and many others have all written about India, but their work obviously belongs to British Literature. Similarly, translations cannot also form part of Indian English Literature, except when they are creative translations by the authors themselves.

Another problem which the historians of this literature have to face is that of choosing from among the various appellations given to it from time to time—viz., 'Indo-Anglian Literature', 'Indian Writing in English', 'Indo-English Literature' and 'Indian English Literature'. The first of these terms was first used as the title of the *Specimen Compositions from Native Students*, published in Calcutta in 1883. The term 'Indian Writing in

English' has been accused of having a rather circumlocutory air, and while 'Indo-English Literature' possesses an admirable compactness, it has, as noted earlier, been used to denote translations by Indians from Indian Literature into English. The Sahitya Akademi has recently accepted 'Indian English Literature' as the most suitable appellation for this body of writing. The term emphasizes two significant ideas, first that this literature constitutes one of the many streams that join the great ocean called Indian Literature, which, though written in different languages, has unmistakable unity; and secondly, that it is an inevitable product of the nativization of the English language to express the Indian sensibility. Nevertheless, by whatever name Indian English literature is called, it remains a literary phenomenon worthy of serious scrutiny.

The Indo-Anglian fiction made its humble beginning in the last decade of the nineteenth century. Right after its birth, it has passed through three main phases. The first phase is the phase of the historical novel. This phase did not continue for a long time. The second one is the long-lived phase of the socially and politically conscious novel. It was the phase of social realism. The third one is the phase of the psychological novel with a concern for the private. As such, according to trends, the history of the Indo-Anglian fiction has been divided into three periods: from 1875 to 1920; from 1920 to 1950, and from 1950 to the present-day.

The major themes of the Indo-Anglian fiction have been the presentation of the social problems, happiness through sufferings, politics and the confrontation between East and West. Meenakshi Mukherjee says:

> The Indo-Anglians have explored the metaphysical, spiritual, and romantic aspects of the confrontation, each in his or her own way. Even when the novel does not deal directly with the Forsterian theme, the personal crisis in the life of each western educated hero or heroine becomes inter-cultural in nature. (2001: 37)

The Indo-Anglian fiction opens out a strange exotic field of racial inter-mixture and mutual impact of two cultures rooted in two entirely different backgrounds: one very ancient and conservative, the other modern, scientific and progressive; the one surrounding to the supernatural destiny, or the theory of 'Karma'; the other trying to make best the worst of circumstance. The conflict and resolution of these two cultures form an interesting study of the Indo-Anglian fiction. It is, however, strange to note that very few Indians seem to have attempted fiction in English till the beginning of the 20th century. A beginning was made by Toru Dutt, that 'fragile and exotic blossom of song' who wrote an English novel *Binaca or The Young Spanish Maiden* (1878). It was a miraculous performance for a mere girl to whom English was an alien language. But she died young and after her death the novel was published by her father in the column of *The Bengal Magazine.* It was never printed in the form of a book.

The name of another gifted novelist Romesh Chandra Dutt, the former President of the Indian National Congress, is praiseworthy. He translated two of his Bengali novels and published them in English. His first novel *The Slave Girl of Agra: An Indian Historical Romance* (1909) is a picture of Mughal India, and faithfully reflects the social life in the sixteenth and seventeenth centuries. The other novel, *The Lake of Palms: A Story of Indian Domestic Life* (1909) is a live picture of the then Bengal. The scene is set in a village named The Lake of Palms. We come across a host of interesting characters—Bindu, Uma, Kalee, Sarat, Subha and Dhananjay—all of whom are drawn convincingly and portrayed in a life-like manner. There are some occasional glimpses of city life also which make the book all the more interesting. From technical point of view, the novel is quite logically bound together and the events are presented in a most artistic manner.

An another promising writer, B.R. Rajam Iyer wrote an English novel *Vasudeva Sastri* which appeared in *Prabudda Bharata* during the end of the nineteenth century. The novel is now republished in Rajam Iyer's *Rambles in Vedanta* (1905). *Vasudeva Sastri* is an interesting study of the character of a great Vedantic, but even the dry currents of Vedantic thoughts could not make the book dull. There is an undercurrent of humour which enlivens the plot. All the characters are creatures of flesh and blood. All the characters are drawn vividly and convincingly. The book abounds in vivid portraiture. It shows that a great promise could be fulfilled. The thread of Rajam Iyer's life was cut asunder, and he remains like Keats and Toru Dutt, yet one more 'inheritor of unfulfilled renown'.

Another important writer of English fiction from the North is Sardar Jogendra Singh. There are four novels *Nur-Jehan* (1909), *Nasrin* (1915), *Kamla* (1925) and *Kamini* (1931) to his credit. *Nur-Jehan* is a historical romance: *Nasrin* depicts the voluptuous life of Nawabs and Taluqdars. In *Kamla* and *Kamini*, Sardar Jogendra Singh attempts to portray "low" life, although he does not completely shed away the glamour of high romance and philosophy. In his novels we find an artistic blend of philosophy and propaganda. His sympathies are with 'the lowly and the lost' and his heart goes out in sympathy for suffering women. It is worthwhile studying his hill girls and female beauties along with his Nawabs and Rajahs.

At the end of the First World War, India found herself on the threshold of a new era rich with a lot of possibilities. Several Indian writers started writing in English. Among them, one of the most outstanding was K.S. Venkatramani whose *Murugan The Tiller* (1927) is described as "a novel of Indian rural life". Venkatramani's second novel, *Kandan the Patriot* (1934) was inspired by the Gandhian nationalist upheavals of 1930-31. The battle crisis of civil disobedience, prohibition, Swaraj, Satyagraha, and the rest fill the vibrant air of Kandan and the sensitive reader can quickly respond to them all; but all are rendered in terms of poetry and idealism.

Among other novelists of the pre-independence period, special mention may be made of D.F. Karaka, Raja Rao, Kumara Guru, Khwaja Ahmed Abbas, Ahmed Ali, S.K. Chettur, S. Nagarajan and A.S.P. Ayyar. D.F. Karaka's first novel *Just Flesh* (1941) is a novel of English life set in the England of the uncertain nineteen thirties. He has an intimate knowledge of the topography of London and he can easily conjure up a scene of English atmosphere. His second novel, *There Lay the City*

(1942) reflects Bombay. The characters and incidents are not convincing but the style is characterized by charm and facility. His third novel *We Never Die* (1944) deals with freedom struggle and communalism.

Raja Rao's *Kanthapura* (1938) is an attempt to study the response of Indian humanity to the challenge of Mahatma Gandhi's militant programme of Satyagraha and civil disobedience. Although the novel is full of Gandhian politics, yet it remains a creative work of fiction. Raja Rao has not allowed his work to dwindle into a mere propaganda. Raja Rao exploits the age old technique of telling story through the mouth of a grandmother who, after all, is a clever storyteller. Raja Rao himself is quite at home in English. His descriptions are vivid, colourful and sometimes poetical. His characters are real and life-like. His other significant novels are *The Serpent and the Rope* (1960), and *The Cat and Shakespeare* (1965).

Khwaja Ahmed Abbas' *Tomorrow is Ours* is a delicate picture of modern India dealing with real people. Although the creative artist is now and then handcuffed by the screen-writer, yet his portrayal of Paravati, the heroine, is quite natural and convincing. Ahmed Ali's *Twilight in Delhi* presents a fine picture of Muslim life in the twentieth century Delhi, whereas S.K. Chettur's *Bombay Murder* throws light on the ultra-modern and extremely fashionable life of luxurious Bombay. S. Nagarajan's *Athawar House* is done in the manner of Galsworthy's *Forstyle Saga*, as it gives a lasting picture of a south Indian Maratha Brahmin family. The events of the book range over a period of fifteen years and throw light on the many changes that were taking place during the restless post-war period.

A more prolific writer than any of the above-mentioned is Mulk Raj Anand who has contributed a series of remarkable English novels: *Untouchable* (1935), *Coolie* (1936), *Two Leaves and a Bud* (1937), *Lament In the Death of a Master of Arts* (1939), *The Private Life of an Indian Prince* (1953), *The Old Woman and the Cow* (1960), *The Death of a Hero* (1963), *The Big Heart* (1945), *Morning Face* (1968), *The Village Trilogy* (1939). Mulk Raj Anand is a progressive writer and his sympathies are with the 'underdogs' of society. His heart bleeds to see the inhuman and cruel treatment meted out to the sweepers, the labourers, the peasants and the city drudges. They all emerge alive from his novels—anguished and hungry, yet human, superstitious and self-divided, vividly realized, in spite of their thwarted purposes.

A more consistently satisfying artist, R.K. Narayan has a store of novels and collections of short stories to his credit. His first novel *Swami and Friends*, published in 1935, deals with the happy world of young school boys. His next novel *The Bachelor of Arts* (1937) depicts the college life in South India, with a touch of caricature here and there. In his third novel *The Dark Room* (1938), Narayan artistically portrays the family tangles of a middle class South Indian home. After *The Dark Room*, Narayan published *The English Teacher* (1945) that shot him into prominence in the literary world. His other novels are: *Mr. Sampath* (1949), *The Financial Expert* (1952), *Waiting for the Mahatma* (1955), *The Guide* (1958), *The Man-Eater of Malgudi* (1962) and *The Sweet Vendor* (1967). Many of his novels have been translated into many foreign languages. He has been honoured with the Sahitya Akademi Award on his novel *The Guide*, which has been successfully screened.

A more serious and challenging post-independence writer of English fiction is Bhawani Bhattacharya whose *So Many Hungers* (1947) and *Music For Mohini* (1952) have succeeded not only as novels in English, but have been translated into several European languages. His other novels are *He Who Rides a Tiger* (1954), *A Goddess Named Gold* (1960) and *Shadow From Ladakh* (1966). Among the other novelists of the post-independence era, special mention may be made of Dilip Kumar Roy for *The Upward Spiral* (1949), Venu Chitale for *In Transit* (1951), Khushwant Singh for *Train to Pakistan* (1956), *I Shall Not Hear the Nightingale* (1961), Rama Sharma for *The Stream* (1956) and others.

Manohar Malgaonker is one of the most successful and widely read novelists. He wrote six novels—*Distant Drum* (1960), *Combat of Shadow* (1962), *The Princes* (1963), *A Bend in the Ganges* (1964), *Devil's Wind* (1978), and *Spy in Amber* (1971). *Combat of Shadow* deals with races and cultures.

Distant Drum is about the Indian army. *A Bend in the Ganges* deals with the theme at the time of independence. *The Prince* describes the decay of Princely India.

Among the women novelists of the post-independence era, special mention must be made of Kamala Markandaya, Ruth Prawer Jhabvala, Nayan Tara Sahgal, Shakuntala Shrinagesh, Anita Desai, Attia Hussain, Kamala Das, Namita Gokhale and Shashi Deshpande. The most famous novel of Shakuntala Shrinagesh is *The Little Black Box* (1955). Ruth Prawer Jhabvala has to her credit nine novels. The best among these are—*Heat and Dust* (1975), *To Whom She Will* (1955), *The Householder* (1960), *A Backward Place* (1965), and *Get Ready For Battle* (1962). Kamala Markandaya has also some novels to her credit—*Nectar in a Sieve* (1954), *Some Inner Fury* (1957), *A Silence of Desire* (1961), *Possession* (1963), *The Coffer Dams* (1969), *A Handful of Rice* (1966). *Nectar in a Sieve* is a well-written story showing intimate knowledge of South Indian life and portraying India's serenity, despair and tyranny. It has more to tell us of the real India than many more pretentious or embattled works can do. The scene of his second novel, *Some Inner Fury*, is the picture of colourful India, and deals with those momentous days of travail out of which the new India is born. *Two Virgins* is a story of two sisters—Lalitha and Saroja—in a village somewhere in Mysore. There are also some famous novels to the credit of Nayantara Sahgal, viz., *A Time to be Happy* (1957), *This Time of Morning* (1965), *Storm in Chandigarh* (1969), *The Day in Shadow* (1971) and *Rich Like Us* (1985). Santa Rama Rau is known for her novels *Remember the House* (1956) and *The Adventures* (1971). Anita Desai is also a well-known novelist. Her famous novels are *Cry the Peacock* (1963), *Voices in the City* (1965), *Bye Bye Blackbird* (1971), *Where Shall We Go This Summer?* (1975), *Fire on the Mountain* (1980) and *The Village by the Sea* (1982). Attia Hussain's famous novel *Sunlight on a Broken Column* (1961) has created an indelible stamp on the readers' psyche.

Kamala Das, a renowned poetess, has two novels to her credit: *The Alphabet of Lust* (1976) and *A Doll For the Child Prostitute* (1979). *The Alphabet of Lust* is about Manasi, the unhappy and frustrated wife of a government officer Amol Mitra. All the time the husband remains busy with his official work, and denies her love, companionship and warmth. *A Doll For the Child Prostitute*, her next novel, is saga of a child prostitute who struggles all the time for liberation and quest for identity. Mira, the central character, secretly marries her student-client which doesn't last long, and is forced back into the abhorrent profession of prostitution. As an Indian English novelist Shashi Deshpande, daughter of the renowned dramatist and Sanskrit scholar, Shriranga, stands apart, for she writes about certain specific concerns after her own manner. She started her career in the nineteen seventies and has so far published twenty-two books which include nine novels, eight volumes of short stories, four books for children and one collection of essays. She was honoured with the Sahitya Akademi Award in the year 1990. Her important novels are: *The Dark Holds No Terrors* (1980), *If I Die Today* (1982), *Come Up and Be Dead* (1983), *Roots and Shadows* (1983), *That Long Silence* (1988), *The Binding Vine* (1993), *A Matter of Time* (1996), *Small Remedies* (2000) and *Moving On* (2004).

The Indian novel in English made its debut in the last decade of the 19th century. The first striking feature is that the novel is the most dominant branch of Indo-Anglian literature as is the case with American Literature. Though the Indo-Anglian novel came later, the bulk of Indo-Anglian literature is in the novel form. Next to it, we find the emergence of the Indo-Anglian fiction a distinct *genre*. Within a short period of sixty years after independence, it has gained a considerable maturity and separate identity. There are several traits visible of this maturity. The writers are conscious about their technique. They were inspired by varied creative impulses which have changed from time to time because of the writer's predilection for new theme and technique.

EMERGENCE OF SHASHI DESHPANDE

Feminism in Indian Literature, particularly in Indian English Writing is a by-product of the Western feminist movement. But we cannot ignore the contribution made by our freedom struggle, independence, spread of education, concern for economic development and stability, employment opportunities and above all the resultant new awareness of our women. As far as feminism is concerned regional literatures too fall in line with this pattern. The Indian women caught in the flux of tradition and modernity bearing the burden of the past and the aspirations of the future is the crux of feminism in Indian literature. A search for identity and a quest for the definition of the self have become the prime feature of women in literature under the sway of feminism.

Feminist literature highlights the basic differences between a man and a woman in the changed scenario of the contemporary life. One of the major issues recurrently dealt with by feminist writers is the identity crisis. Discreet study of modern Indian English novels reveals that the women serve to reflect the writer's sense of isolation, fear, bewilderment and emotional vulnerability as a symbol not only of growth, life and fertility, but also of withdrawal, regression, decay and death. In the works of the modern novelists, we witness the typical feminist traits—sudden awakening, acute introspection, a straits in time and action, an unthought-of ending with definitive decision. Very often these works do not offer a tangible solution for the feminist. Indian English fiction, poetry and drama are replete with the male-female confrontation, problems of adolescence, and coming of age with special reference to women, explicit and latent pleadings for equality, liberty and self-preservation, even risking the normal self-guarding of man and conventional production of hallowed tradition.

Comparatively, Shashi Deshpande is a new name on the scene of Indian English Writing. However, despite the smaller volumes of her writing, her work has drawn critical attention because of her detailed, sensitive and realistic representation of the Indian middle-class women in the domestic sphere. Her concern for women and their oppression is reflected strongly in all her writings. This is the reason she got eminence as a feminist writer.

Shashi Deshpande was born in 1938 at Dharwad in Karnataka, India. She is the daughter of the renowned Kannada dramatist and Sanskrit scholar, Late Adya Rangachar Shriranga. At the age of fifteen, she went to Bombay where she graduated in Economics; she then moved to Bangalore where she obtained a Degree in Law. She gained her M.A. in English from Mysore University. The early years of her marriage were largely given over to the care of her two sons but she took a course in journalism and for a time worked on a magazine. At present she lives in Bangalore with her pathologist husband. Her writing career began in 1970, initially with short stories, of which several volumes have been published. Besides the novels and short stories, Deshpande has also published some children's books in English like *The Hidden Treasure* (1980), *The Only Witness*, (1980), *The Narayanpur Incident* (1982), etc. and written the screenplay for the Hindi feature film *Drishti.* She began writing rather late in life at her father's insistence. In 1969, inspired by a visit to England, she wrote and published an account of her English experiences. Since then her short stories have been appearing regularly in popular magazines. Her first novel *The Dark Holds No Terrors* was first published in 1980 by Vikas Publishing House Pvt. Ltd. followed by *If I Die Today* in 1982, *Roots and Shadows* and *Come Up and Be Dead* were published in 1983. *Roots and Shadows* won the Thirumathi Rangammal Prize for the best Indian novel of 1982-83. *That Long Silence* published by Virago Feminist Press in 1988 won the Sahitya Akademi Award for 1990. *A Matter of Time* was published in 1996 by Penguin Books, New Delhi. Her latest novel *Small Remedies* appeared in 2000. Her short stories have been collected and published in four volumes: *The Legacy and Other Stories* (1978), *It was the Nightingale and Other Stories* (1986) and *The Miracle and Other Stories* (1986).

THE ART OF SHASHI DESHPANDE

The most challenging task before the Indian English novelist is to write in English language in such a manner which can convey the essence of the Indian socio-cultural ethos without distorting the language. It is very difficult to achieve the goal because of the vast differences between the Indian and the English culture. It is also difficult to overcome the problems of differences which poses to the minds of the writers. Even though, Shashi Deshpande does not seem inhibited by it. She affirms:

> To those of us who write in English, it is neither a foreign language, nor the language of the colonizer, but the language of creativity. Whether the writing is rootless, alienated or elitist should be judged from the writing, not from the language. My writing comes out of myself, the society I live in, it is shaped, as I am, by my family, my ancestry, the place I was born in, the place I live in, the culture I am steeped in, the fact that the writing is in English changes none of these things. (1985: 10)

The fiction of Shashi Deshpande reflects the ethos and milieu of Karnataka and Maharashtra. One can easily find the customs and practices overlapping as are the case in real life. Deshpande herself comes from a middle class, Marathi-Kannadiga background and was educated in English at a local school in Dharwar, Karnataka. These are the influences which have played vital roles in shaping her writings. The language she uses in her writing is "simple", "realistic" and "transparent" (Holmstrom 1993: 22-27). Her primary stress is upon the middle-class ethos and her language reflects this concern. She uses English the way an average, middle-class individual educated in both the vernacular and English would use it. The middle-class language, in fact, proves to be a characteristic quality of Deshpande's work.

Shashi Deshpande feels that writing in English is a drawback in India as it alienates the writer from the mainstream, but she considers English as one of the Indian languages. She says:

> I believe that English writing in this country is a part of our literatures; I consider English as one more of our *bhashas* as Ganesh Devy calls them. I know that our writing comes out of an involvement with this society, out of our experiences here, our readership is now here, and happily our publishers are here as well. Yet, I am disturbed by the recent trend in English writing which in its pursuits of role models outside, is alienating itself from its roots. (1996: 108)

Certainly there are limited readers of English novels in comparison of those Hindi novels, but this does not make her a non-Indian. She is also against being labeled as Indian English writer. She protests: "I am an Indian writer. My language just happens to be English, which cannot be called a foreign language at all because it is so much used in India" (1988: 28). Deshpande is different from the other Indian writers in the sense that she was never educated abroad and is firmly rooted in the Indian soil. She asserts the fact in an interview with Lakshmi Holmstorm:

> My novels do not have any Westerners, for example. They are first about Indian people and the complexities of our lives. Our inner lives and our outer lives and the reconciliation between them. My English is as we use it. I don't make it easier for anyone really. If I make any changes, it's because the novel needs it, not because the reader needs it. (1993: 26)

It is undeniably true that the novel is "the readiest and most acceptable way of embodying experiences and ideas in the context of our time" (Dhawan 1992: 1). The originality or talent lies in the manner a writer uses this genre to bring home his ideas to the readers. Styles and techniques have kept changing with time. In the past much attention was paid to the plot or story overlooking psychological aspects. The modern novelists are doing experimentation, which is far removed from the traditional storytelling.

Deshpande doesn't like the simple technique of straightforward narration and employs the flashback method instead to draw her readers' attention. The narrative technique has earned some criticism from some critics who feel that this leads to confusion in the minds of readers. In novels where the novelist is supposed to present a gallery of characters along with him/her to present things in their chronological order and not indulge in too much experimentation. Shama Futehally remarks:

> This is a device which is useful either when some elements of suspense is needed, or for a novel with a non-narrative

> structure. For this novel chronological clarity is essential, as the reader already has to cope with an abundance of characters and their complex interactions. The first chapter, where we are faced with all of them simultaneously, and without introduction, is rather confusing. (1984: 5)

In *The Dark Holds No Terrors* (1980), the novelist shifts the narrative from the first person to the third person narrative in every alternative chapter. This double narrative helps to lend great authenticity to the portrayal of Sarita's inner self. Deshpande has accomplished the task of giving a real picture of the mental trauma Sarita undergoes. In an interview, she tells how she hits upon the idea of using double narrative:

> The present is in the third person and the past is in the first person. I was doing it throughout in the first. But that is often a perspective I use in my short stories. I wanted to be more objective. So then I tried it in the third. But it wouldn't work at all. Yet I really need not distance myself from the narrative in the present, otherwise it was going to be far too intense. And then I read an American novel by Lisa Alther where she uses this method. And the minute I came across her novel I thought—let me admit it freely—Oh God, this is how I am going to do my novel. (1993: 23-24)

As such, Deshpande succeeds in the portrayal of Sarita's mental state with remarkable objectivity. Besides it, her art lies in her amalgamating the past with the present seamlessly through dream, nightmares, flashback, reminiscences and the simple third person narration.

That Long Silence is very close to real life experience, and achieves its credibility from the fact that the protagonist Jaya is a well-educated lady possessing a literary sensibility corresponding with her fictional role. One must realize that it is a great task to create women characters as they are nurtured in the culture of silence. Y.S. Sunita Reddy has aptly remarked:

> The narrative with its slow unknotting of memories and unravelling of the soul reads like an interior monologue quite similar to the stream of consciousness technique employed by the like of Virginia Woolf. (2001: 136)

In *Roots and Shadows, The Dark Holds No Terrors* and *That Long Silence*, Shashi Deshpande uses a narrative structure which does not progress chronologically. It moves forward thematically, gradually narrating one incident after another till the whole story is revealed. But in *The Binding Vine* the novelist interweaves three individual plots of three different stories about three women of different ages, status and education. Urmi narrates the whole story in the first person. In order to present in a real and objective way of Urmi's mother-in-law Mira's marital experiences, Deshpande has made use of the poetry and writing in her diary and notebooks. She is successful in the reconstruction of Mira's unspoken humiliation and anguish at being subjected to marital rape through the mouthpiece of Urmi.

The narrative art of *Small Remedies* is somehow different from the previous novels of Shashi Deshpande. It is a biography within a biography. The novelist delves deep into the traumatic lives of Savitribai Indorekar, Leela, Munni and Madhu by moving her narrative back and forth between the present and the past. The novel touches different aspects of women's personal and social life. Siddhartha Sharma rightly remarks: "Through the mouthpiece of Urmi, Deshpande has given voice to her own dilemma as a writer—if a biography is an exercise in truth telling, and if it is, whose version must it be?" (2005: 79).

Shashi Deshpande's short stories, especially, reveal her empathy for the victims of oppression, be it a man or a woman. She sensitively explores the taboo realm of extra-marital friendship between the sexes, often concluding realistically that the Indian psyche, especially in the institution of marriage, is not ready for the Western model of co-existence outside marriage. She acknowledges the attraction between the sexes, but does not see an extra-marital relationship as the solution to an unhappy marriage. In fact, the main concern of the novelist in her novels is the man-woman relationship in Indian marriages; she also concerns herself with the exploration of various human relationships within the family.

SHASHI DESHPANDE AS A FEMINIST

Feminist literature in English is certainly not a recent innovation. It has its existence ever since perspectives of life were recorded in literature. Sushila Singh rightly remarks:

> Ever since antiquity, there have been women fighting to free their half of the total population of the world from male oppression. Feminism is neither a fad nor a logical extension of the civil rights movements. The inequalities against which the feminists protest—legal, economic, and social restrictions on the basic rights of women—have existed throughout history and in all civilizations. (1997: 1)

Feminism in the Indian context is a by-product of the Western liberalism in general and feminist thought in particular. The indigenous contributing factors have been the legacy of equality of sexes inherited from the freedom struggle, constitutional rights of women, spread of education and the consequent new awareness among women. The Indian woman caught in the flux of tradition and modernity saddled with the burden of the past but both to cast off her aspirations constitute the crux of feminism in Indian literature. In literary terms it precipitates in a search for identity and a quest for the definition of the self. Indian feminist literature has established a new track, a new vision—a vision that is replete with an unswerving faith and hope, myths and traditions, customs, rites and rituals.

Shashi Deshpande has added a new leaf to the cap of Indian feminine fiction with her novels. She has also given a new dimension to feminist writers in general and Indian feminist writers in particular. She is the only Indian feminist author to have made bold attempts at giving a voice to the disappointment and frustrations of women despite her vehement denial of being a feminist. Besides it she denies any influence of the militant Western feminists like Simon de Beauvoir, Germaine Greer, Betty Freidan and Kate Millet. Her main concern is women's issues in the Indian context. In an interview she tells to Lakshmi Holmstrom:

> It is difficult to apply Kate Millet or Simon de Beauvoir or whoever to the reality of our daily lives in India. And then there are such terrible misconceptions about feminism by people here. They often think it is about burning bras and walking out on your husband, children or about not being married, not having children etc. I always try to make the point now about what feminism is not, and to say that we have to discover what it is in our own lives, our experiences. (1993: 26)

Since her novels are women centred, many scholars have interviewed her to know to what extent she has her feminist temperament. She further denies the charges being labeled as a feminist writer in an interview with Gita Viswanath:

> And as far as readers are concerned, I would like them to read me as a novelist, not as a feminist novelist or women writer or whatever. That's one part, the second part is that when I write, I don't write as a feminist. I keep saying this over and over again and somehow I seem to need to say it again and again. I do not write as a feminist novelist. But my ideology is going to permeate my writing; and my feelings, thoughts and ideas about women are very important parts of my ideology. (2005: 228)

Shashi Deshpande denied the possibilities in her writings being branded as a feminist writing and told that her writings for all human beings. In an interview with Pallavi Thakur, Deshpande says:

> Once you say I am a feminist writer, you are putting some sort of a boundary, an edge around my writing which means that there is nothing else. I deny it very strongly. My writings are not limited in that way. It is all about human beings and it is ultimately universal. You know human beings are the same everywhere. Like I said, feminism has given me a certain perspective, a vision which to some extent is bound to come into my novels. (2003: 66)

In spite of the denials of being called a feminist, a deep study of her novels reveals the undercurrent of concern for the women which they confront in the patriarchal, orthodox Indian society. Indian women have been subjugated to many social malpractices such as child-marriage, *satti*, no remarriage provision for women, dowry, desertion, etc. and such prejudices have been voiced in almost all her novels forging sufficient ground for considering her literature as feminist one. Nowadays she is considered to be the foremost feminist in India to have taken the cudgels against the social norms based upon the ideologies of Manu. Her feminism, sometimes, seems a little uncertain because it is not radical or anti-male. However, she is firm in her conviction that in India, particularly, feminism cannot be 'anti-male' since both man and woman have to communicate and work towards "a better, more meaningful, companionable relationship" (1992: 12). Therefore, although the feminist framework employed to analyze her work is conceptually a Western one, it has been substantially adapted to the Indian socio-cultural milieu to read and analyze Shashi Deshpande's novels.

The Dark Holds No Terrors (1980) is the saga of the traumatic experience the protagonist undergoes as her husband refuses to play a second-fiddle role. Saru, the protagonist faces a lot of humiliation and neglect as a child. Even her marriage with Manohar does not bring any concession to her misery rather it heightens her troubles. The novelist discusses the blatant discrimination based on gender even from the parents' side. Their parents wanted a male child to be born in place of Saru. After marriage, she got a good fame as a doctor and her status surpasses that of her husband, Manohar, an underpaid lecturer. Her husband's inferiority complex and humiliation turned him into a sadist who tried to prove his superiority through sadistic behaviour in sex-relation. Manu's male ego asserts itself through nocturnal sexual assault on Saru who silently bears the pangs of her domestic sufferings. Saru asserts: "I put another brick in the wall of silence between us. May be one day I will be walled alive within it and die a slow painful death" (88). Being annoyed with her husband's behaviour, she started to live with her old father but even there she felt neglected. Her role, however, is a passive one, severely constrained by her womanhood, and further burdened by her familiar and domestic ties.

Roots and Shadows (1983) depicts the agony and suffocation experienced by the protagonist Indu in a male-dominated and tradition-bound society. She undergoes great mental trauma when she refuses to play the straitjacketed role of a wife imposed by society. The man she marries according to her choice is no different from a less educated and conservative husband. It seems, in order to take revenge upon her husband for the misbehaviour and quest for her identity, she develops an extra-marital affair. The novelist thus exposes the gross gender discrimination and its fall-out in the patriarchal society. Indu transverses the road of self-realisation and her destination in the point of comprehension of the mystery of human life. The struggle of such women gives shape and meaning to their individual existence in an insensitive society to women. It culminates in a crisis and ends in a compromise.

That Long Silence (1988) presents the suffocated life story of Jaya who plays the role of a wife and mother. Despite her every sacrifice, she finds herself lonely and estranged. The protagonist realizes that she has been unjust to herself and her career as a writer. The quest for an authentic selfhood by the protagonist finds an artistic expression through her rebellion against the patriarchal dominance in the society. Jaya is an unsuccessful writer. Her creative urge and artistic zeal free her from her cramped domestic and societal roles. She resolves to assert her individuality by breaking that long silence by recording on paper which she had suppressed for seventeen years.

The Binding Vine (1992) deals with the personal tragedy of the protagonist Urmi to focus attention on victims like Kalpana and Mira. Urmila, the protagonist, has just recovered from the sudden death of her daughter, Anu. No sooner had she recovered from her personal sufferings than she got involved in the disclosure of an accused who had raped Kalpana brutally. She further reads the poem of Mira, her mother-in-law. Rape has always been a horrible indignity heaped on woman by man. This violence becomes bad to worse when it occurs in the sanctity of a marriage. Mira's poetry is all about it. In spite of her over-solicitous mother, Inni and her sceptical friend Vanna, Urmila is determined to have these poems published. Throughout the novel, the novelist voices the injustices meted out to women particularly in the matter of sexual exploitation. The most striking fact in this novel, unlike previous ones, is the co-operation she extends to the women of other families. The novel ends with Urmila recollecting the bonds of love that provides the "Spring of Life" to human existence.

A Matter of Time (1996) deals with metaphysical philosophy of Shashi Deshpande. Basically, it presents the traumatic life of three women from three generations from the same family. The novelist succeeds in portraying the ways they adopt to cope with the tragedies in their lives. Sumi is deserted by her husband Gopal, and she faces humiliation with great courage and stoicism. She is struck with immense grief, but tries to keep herself composed for the sake of her daughters. The other important character Kalyani was married to her maternal uncle Shripati. Accidentally, their four-year-old son gets lost at the railway station. Consequent upon it, Kalyani is forced to stay back in her parents' house. After some time Shripati comes back but he maintains a stony silence for the rest of his life. Kalyani's mother Manorama could not beget a male child for her husband. All her life, she was having fear that her husband could remarry for a son. Keeping in view the possibility of passing on property to another family, Manorama gets her daughter Kalyani married to her brother Shripati. In this way, the novelist has revealed the frustration and compulsion of three women from three generations from the same family. Deshpande wants to disclose here the utmost desire for a son and hatred for a daughter. It is also a saga of the painful life of the women who are unable to beget sons for the family.

Small Remedies (2002) is the latest novel by Shashi Deshpande. Her protagonist is still the urban, middle-aged and educated woman, but her canvas has broadened to encompass a cross-section of people who belong to different communities, professions and a level of society. Madhu Saptarishi is not much different from her counterparts Indu, Sarita, Jaya, Urmi and Sumi in age, education and family background. Madhu Saptarishi, the protagonist, has been commissioned by a publisher to write a biography of a famous classical singer,

Savitribai Indorekar, doyenne of Gwalior Gharana who had led the most unconventional of lives. Consequently she had to undergo great mental trauma due to opposition by the society which practises double standards—one for men and other for women. Besides it, Madhu narrates her own life story and also those of her aunt Leela and Savitribai's daughter, Munni.

Through her portrayal of the Indian middle-class woman's existence in India, Deshpande not only presents a feminist insight into patriarchal values, but also prescribes balance between tradition and modernity as a working philosophy for the contemporary woman. By tradition she means those values of security and harmony that symbolize the Indian way of life, while modernity essentially refers to the assertion of the independent, individual self. Her protagonists, at the beginning of their quest, find that they have passively accepted their socially ordained roles. Deshpande advocates that to realize herself, the woman must be true to her own self. The sacrifice and nobility that is expected of the woman is a stereotype that only bogs down the woman in a mire of negation and suppression. The woman needs to venture out of the familial framework, to discover her potential as an individual and give expression to her inner space and self. At the same time, she need not repudiate her marriage or family.

Although Deshpande's primary focus is the man-woman relationship in Indian marriages she also concerns herself with the exploration of various human relationships within the family—for example, the relationship between mother-daughter, father-daughter, sibling, etc. In this way, she progresses from the particular to the universal. The protagonist's recall of traditional precepts from the *Mahabharata* and the *Bhagwad Gita*, emphasizing larger existential question is of a piece with this. The intrinsic alone-ness of human beings in *The Dark Holds No Terrors*, the recognition of responsibility in choice in *That Long Silence*, the meaning of Dharma in one's life in *The Binding Vine* are serious metaphysical that subtly envelop Deshpande's works and take them beyond feminist concern. Deshpande's human-centredness makes her more than just a significant Indian woman writer of our time.

Deshpande writes a variety of Indian English that is rooted in the ambience of regional cultures, those of the states of Maharashtra and Karnataka. For example, her characters have names and pet names that immediately 'place' them for Indian readers as being Maharashtrian or Kannadiga—Saru, Indu, Jaya, Chandu, Kamat. She also uses Marathi or Kannada words to describe various characters and relationships to each other, such as Chandu Mama (rather than uncle Chandu), and Ajji (rather than grandmother). The culturally specific words and sentences set easily and naturally in the body of her work, so that the work reflects a contemporary middle-class Indian-English. Deshpande avoids foregrounding the Indianness of the writing through the self-conscious use of 'local colour', but writes in English with which her readers would be familiar and comfortable.

Shashi Deshpande's literary world, like those of most other contemporary Indian English women novelists, is women–centred. Like them, she concentrates on the theme of meaninglessness and sexual confusion suffered by women in tradition-oriented institutions. For Shashi Deshpande's women, marriage is a serious conflict situation. She deals mainly with theme of marriage. In *Roots and Shadows*, she dwells upon the problems of how a woman brought up in an orthodox, traditional and rural background has to cope up with when she gets modern education and has a choice marriage. In the novel *The Dark Holds No Terrors*, she deals with the psychological problems of how an educated women professionally qualified, earning not only the bread but also the butter for the family, has to face troubles when she marries a person not highly qualified and having a lower financial status. In *That Long Silence*, she depicts two different pictures of women at two parallel levels—the lower strata of women engaged in menial chores to earn their living and educated middle-class women of some financial independence. Women at both these levels prefer to get married and maintain their marriage. In other novels, too, the themes are based upon the aftermaths of marriage faced by the Indian women.

There are many contemporary women writers like Anita Desai, Bharati Mukherjee, Kamala Markanday, Ruth Prawer Jhabvala, Santa Ram Rau, Nayantara Sahgal, Shobhaa De, etc. The themes of these novelists are different but a curious resemblance can be traced out in the novels of Anita Desai, Bharati Mukherjee and Shashi Deshpande. These three novelists belong to urban upper middle class, English educated society, and deal with the world of women. They depict their women character in all their negative and positive traits. For these women novelists, character takes precedence over plot as they depict the inner landscape of their women protagonists. These novelists shatter the myth that women find fulfillment in marriage and portray an honest picture of the Indian women who strive to be true selves.

A study of these three contemporary novelists reveals some interesting similarities and differences among their protagonists, male characters and the society they portray. These three novelists portray a wide spectrum of contemporary Indian women who are true representative of the average urban Indian women of today. Each protagonist strives for an identity of her own, aside from the traditionally ordained straitjacketed roles of daughter, wife and mother. Despite the common traits, these protagonists have their own significant difference from others. The protagonists of these three novels do get marginalized or perform their duties as per the whims and eccentricities of the male members in the family. They all seek their rightful place as human beings in society by refusing to be treated like doormat. They reject the socially defined role models for them. In spite of these similarities, the three novelists make their protagonists function differently. Anita Desai's protagonists seek a harmony that they cannot attain; Mukherjee's Jasmine alone is successful in creating her own harmony. But Shashi Deshpande's greatness lies in fact that her protagonists seek and find harmony within the traditional social setup. In an interview with Pallavi Thakur, Shashi Deshpande affirms thus:

> Men need the support of women and women need the support of men. And we need each other very badly because in this world we are all living together. I would

> not say that women should be active and men should be supporting. No, I think they are both in it together equally together only then it will work. So that it is my kind of feminism.... My feminism certainly does not mean promiscuity. This is not out of any puritan or moral thinking. There are people who are much happier having many relationships. I don't call that feminism. (2003: 67-68)

Most of the critical materials on Shashi Deshpande are descriptive and formalistic in nature. The available literary material can be classified as given below:

(a) There are descriptive analyses which are confined to an examination of the text only. These analyses are not concerned with the socio-cultural or literary context of the work. The anthology *Indian Women Novelists* edited by R.K. Dhawan (1991) contains 15 articles out of which nearly 10 are descriptive in nature.

(b) There are other types of critical analyses which attempt to study Deshpande's literature in a Western feminist framework. For instance, Adele King in her two essays, "Feminist Criticism and Indian Women Writers" (42-49) and "Shashi Deshpande: Portrait of an Indian Woman" (159-69) applies Western feminist theories to her reading of Shashi Deshpande's work.

(c) There are a few essays which place Deshpande's work in Indian context. These essays are focused only on a limited portion of Shashi Deshpande's work. These are not full-length studies. For instance, P. Ramamoorthi's "My Life is My Own: A Study of Shashi Deshpande's Women", R. Mala's "Sexual Predicament and Shashi Deshpande's Women". These articles are sincere efforts to understand the feminist purpose of the writer to depict the subtleties of the social oppression of the Indian woman.

Thus, no full-length study of Shashi Deshpande's work barring a few is available. The present thesis is a modest attempt to use the Indian socio-cultural-specific feminist approach to read Deshpande's novels. These novels have been studied keeping in view the western, Indian and post-feministic theories of feminism. An attempt has been made to unearth Deshpande's implications underlying in her works such as: culture, philosophy and values.

Feminism: Western and Indian

2

FEMINISM: A GENERAL INTRODUCTION

Ever since the dawn of civilization, there has been a struggle to liberate the women from male oppression. Feminism is an expression of resentment at the unjust treatment meted out to any woman. In literature, it refers to any mode that approaches a text with foremost concern for the nature of female experience. The inequalities against which the feminists have raised their voice of protest—legal, economic and social restrictions on the basic rights of women—have existed throughout history across the world in all the civilizations. Naturally the principles of feminism were articulated much earlier and its roots can be traced in the history of human civilization.

Feminism is a diverse collection of social theories, political movements and moral philosophies, largely motivated by or concerning the experiences of women, especially in terms of their social, political and economic situation. As a social movement, feminism largely focuses on limiting or eradicating gender inequality and promoting women's rights, interests and issues in society. Within academia, some feminists focus on documenting gender inequality and changes in the social position and representation of women. Others argue that gender, and even sex, are social constructs, and research the construction of gender and sexuality, and develop alternate models for studying social relations. Feminist political activitism commonly campaign on issues such as reproductive rights, violence within a domestic partnership, maternity leave, equal pay, sexual harassment, discrimination and sexual violence. Themes explored in feminism include patriarchy, stereotyping, objectification, sexual objectification and oppression.

The term 'feminism' originates from the Latin word 'femina' (woman), originally meant "having the qualities of females". It was used with reference to the theory of sexual equality and the movement for women's rights replacing womanism in the 1890s. Its fundamental meaning is in dispute as different scholars have defined 'feminism' differently. *Webster's Dictionary* (1996) defines feminism as "the doctrine advocating social, political, and all other rights of women movement for the attainment of such rights for women". Similarly, the *Oxford Dictionary* (1985) defines feminism as "Movement for recognition of the claims of women for rights (legal, political, etc.) equal to those possessed by men". *The Dictionaire de Philosophe* (1906) defines feminism as "a position favorable to the rights of women". Ellen Du Bois found in her research on feminism and suffrage that the term 'feminism' was in general use around 1910 to describe that political movement, and the usage originated in France. Linda Kealey found the term used by 1890s to refer new woman. She also says "recent women's history has refined the term, distinguishing between the different strands of feminism, all of which recognize the right of woman to a public role and also her right to define her autonomously" (Kealey 1979: 6). Toril Moi says: "The words 'feminist' and 'feminism' are political labels indicating support for the aims of the new woman's movement which emerged in the late 1960s" (1986: 20).

Whatsoever may be the definition of 'feminism', but it must be understood in its broadest sense as referring to an intense awareness of woman identity and interest in feminine problems. Its area should not be limited only up to advocacy of women's rights. Its area of concern is vast, viz., the history of women's oppression, differential treatment of girls and boys, women's role in children books, male sexual fantasy, anthropological studies of women, politics, and so on. Feminist studies aim at to analyze the reasons for and dimension of women's oppression and to achieve women's liberation. Expressing the same view Teresa Billington Grieg wrote:

> Feminism is a movement which seeks the reorganization of the world upon a basis of sex-equality in all human

> relations; a movement which would reject every differentiation between individuals upon the ground of sex, would abolish all sex privileges and sex burdens, and would strive to set up the recognition of the common humanity of woman and man as the foundation of law and custom. (1911: 158)

These days feminism is not confined to any particular nation or continent, rather it is a global phenomenon. It has various connotations and shades of meanings. Besides it, there are different kinds of feminism—the American feminism, the English feminism; there are several kinds of feminist theories and practices. The feminists enormously differ in their approaches and perspectives. Some critics prefer to use the word "feminisms" instead of mere "feminism". However there is one common strand, i.e., feminism is a movement against patriarchal ideology. It is a movement of reforms in the interest of women.

In the 1960s and 1970s, feminism and feminist theory largely represented was concerned with problems found by western, white, middle-class women while at the same time claiming to represent all women. Since that many feminist theorists have challenged the assumption that "women" constitute a homogenous group of individuals with identical interest. Feminist activists emerged from diverse communities, and feminist theorists began to focus on the intersection between gender and sexuality with other social identities, such as race and class. Many feminists today argue that feminism is a grass-root movement that seeks to cross boundaries based on social class, race, culture and religion; is culturally specific and addresses issues relevant to the women of that society; for example female circumcision in Sudan, or the glass ceiling in developed economies; and debate to the extent to which certain issues such as rape, incest and mothering are universal.

The feminism of the 19th and the early 20th centuries focused on the acquisition of a few basic political rights and liberty for women, such as the rights of married women to own property and enter into contracts, the right of defendants to have women on juries, and the crucial right to vote. A campaign lasting a century ensued and culminated in winning of the right to vote in England in 1918 and in America in 1920.

Without the significant role played by Mary Wollstone Craft (1750-87) and John Stuart Mill (1806-73) in this crusade, this could not have been possible. Ironically, Mary Wollstone Craft, one of the earliest crusaders for the emancipation of women is remembered by literary historians as mother-in-law of the poet Shelley. Her whole life and her works were one long protest against the institutions that denied women any other identity except the one they acquired through men. She knew through better experience the hardships women were exposed to simply by virtue of their sex. Influenced by the revolutionary fervour of the time, and by her association with a group of radical writers, artists and philosophers including William Godwin and Thomas Paine, the author of *The Rights of Man*, she wrote *A Vindication of the Rights of Woman* (1792). This book aroused wide and violent response. Horace Walpane resolved never to read it and attacked the author as a "hyena in petticoats". Other writers also attacked and burlesqued it with strong objection to its contaminating influence. Ironically, *A Vindication of the Rights of Woman*, which anticipated virtually all the demands of the woman's movement—education, legal representation, the right to vote, the right to property and admission to professions—was read by very few in the 19th century. Hers is an extreme ironic example of the treatment posterity accords to a feminist writer.

Similarly, the singular contribution made by John Stuart Mill to the arousal of feminine consciousness cannot be over looked. He was one of the most extraordinary men of his century. Son of the utilitarian philosopher, James Mill, the younger Mill was a precocious genius. He matured to become a political economist and social reformer, the author of a number of books, and an ardent supporter of liberal causes ranging from universal education to population control and Negro emancipation. Of all his work, *The Subjection of Women* (1869) was the most controversial and provoked strong hostility. He concentrated in this book on the abilities of women and made a vigorous plea for their right to enter any trade or profession. He also pleaded for their right to practise arts, and for their right to vote. Mill's sympathetic attitude towards feminism was one aspect of his belief that the liberty of the individual is absolutely necessary for the development of the society. As he says, he wrote *The Subjection of Women* to show:

> That the principle which regulate the existing relations between the two sexes the legal subordination of the sex to the other is wrong in itself, and now one of the chief hindrances to human improvement; and that is ought to be replaced by a principle of perfect equality, admitting no power or privilege on the one side, nor disability on the other. (3)

Mill held the views that women's position is not natural but the result of political oppression by men. This analysis of the effects of this use of power has had on both men and women is exceptionally persuasive, yet the crux of the book, and the reason for the hostility is provoked, is its radical criticism of the family. He maintained that the masculine domination of the family was a corrupting influence, making boys selfish and girls abject.

When elected to the parliament, Mill introduced a motion to get women's suffrage included in the second Reform Bill of 1867. Although the motion was ridiculed and defeated, it won increasing support in subsequent years because of his influence. With his stepdaughter, Helen Taylor, he formed the women's suffrage society in England and persuaded many prominent women to join it. Before his death, he left more than half of his fortune for women's education.

However, the credit for an organized movement for women's rights goes to America beginning with the Seneca Falls Declaration of Sentiments and Resolutions, drawn and signed at the obscure Village, Seneca Falls, New York, in the summer of 1848. The radical demand for suffrage at Seneca Falls carried the social and political revolution for women's rights into a new era. Special support for this historic event came from Elizabeth Candy Stanton. After a hot debate, the convention agreed to acknowledge the right of American women to elective franchise.

A final clause to the resolution was added by Lucretia Mott urging men and women to work for professional and vocational equality. The Seneca Falls Declaration of Sentiments and Resolution went far beyond the expectation of most of the feminist present at the convention. Viewed on the correct historical perspective, the insistence upon the right to vote proved to be a matter of crucial importance, determining the course of later developments.

Even more basic to women's future than the pursuit of suffrage was the long struggle for the elimination of economic and social injustice to which they had been subject for generations. America matured during an era affected by three great wars. Working women advanced in respect of their better representation in the professions and in the labour force. Even though they gained an improved legal status in 1960, the psychological wound as a result of the grievances of 1848 continued to cause pain. This decade was a period of protest movements—civil right peace the New Left, anti-poverty. But the revival of feminism was a startling event. People with traditional views stood aghast, feeling that these must be sick, unbalanced women or at best, just bored housewives. They were puzzled as to what these women meant by "liberation" or "oppression". Describing the reaction to the new feminist movement, Maren Lockwood Carden writes:

> The press and the other mass media had a field day making fun of the 'women's libbers'. The reaction they reported were often highly charged emotionally, negative and frequently contradictory. These women were sexually promiscuous, deprived. They hated men, wanted to take over the world, or wanted to subordinate men to women. They were portrayed variously as rejecting both marriage and motherhood, they were unhappily married or divorced or single. Physically unattractive they were compensating for their 'failure' as women. Strident, hostile, hysterical and maladjusted they lacked human compassion and perspective. (1974: XVIII)

By now it had become clear that women liberation was not just a fad. It had come to stay. A realization dawned that behind the bizarre elements played up by the media lay a serious reform movement.

> The New Feminism is not about the elimination of differences between the sexes; nor even simply the achievement of equal opportunity; it concerns the individual right to find out the kind of person he or she is and to strive to become that person. (Carden 1974: 2)

Broadly speaking, the contemporary feminist movement worked for female equality as the earliest nineteenth century feminism had done. But the two movements are different significantly in the basic arguments regarding the nature of the biological differences between sexes. The 19th century feminists saw far great differences between the "male" and "female" nature than their present counterparts do. They were convinced that women's biological inheritance included many feminine characteristics and that their natural instincts suited them primarily for home making and childcare. They argued, however that these differences do not justify the unfair treatment meted out to them by society. For contemporary feminists, different processes of socialization account for a larger part of the observed differences in men's and women's inequitable system promotes the assumption that such differences are basic. Today, feminists protest against the way the social institutions, supported by cultural values and normative expectation, force women into an unreasonably narrow role. They object not to marriage and motherhood, but to the excessive restraints these roles involve. They argue that in a society with real equality women would be in a position comparable to that of men who at the present time are able to combine occupational and other roles with those of husband and father. Consciously or unconsciously, almost everyone co-operates in this oppressive socialization or 'conditioning'. Parents, teachers, toy manufacturers and writers of children's book encourage girls to be 'feminine'.

BASIC TENETS OF FEMINISM

The feminist literature of today is the product of the 'woman's movement' of the 1960s. This movement was literary from the beginning of the images of woman promulgated by literature, and saw it as vital to combat them and question their coherence. The feminist studies in 1970s started to expose what might be called the mechanisms of patriarchy—the cultural 'mind-set' in men and women which perpetuated sexual inequality. Kate Millet's *Sexual Politics* (1971) presents a distinction between 'sex' and 'gender'. 'Sex' is determined biologically whereas 'gender' is culturally or socially constructed through sex-role stereotyping and historical conditioning. Millet argues that women as much as men are responsible in perpetuating the sex-role image, she analyses the representative role of male and submissive role of the female.

The foremost task of the feminist theory is to rethink the principles, aiming at the analyses of text written by women. It is also important to examine the representation of women. A feminist analyst must raise the question whether men and women are 'essentially' different because of biology, or are socially constructed as different. Peter Barry has presented a crystal clear picture as to what critics should do:

(a) Rethink the cannon, aiming at the rediscovery of text written by women.
(b) Revalue women's experience.
(c) Examine representation of women in literature by men and women.
(d) Raise the question of whether men and women are 'essentially' different because of biology, or are socially constructed as different.
(e) Explore the question of whether there is a female language an *ecriture Femimine,* and whether this is also available to men.
(f) Make clear the biological base of supposedly 'neutral' or 'mainstream' interpretations. (1999: 134)

Thus, the feminist analysis includes various fields like the history, styles, themes, genres and the structures of writing by women, the psycho-analysis of female creativity, the trajectory of individual or collective female career and the evolution of laws of a female tradition. The feminist literary criticism has developed as a component of the women's movement and its impact has brought about a revolution in literary studies. Its wide range is evident from the fact that it flourishes in combination, and not in isolation, with every other critical approach from formalism to semiotics, and can be effectively applied to the literary study of every period and genre. Since antiquity, it has been taken for granted that the reader, writer and critic of literature are male. Feminist criticism has shown that women readers and critics bring different perceptions and expectations to their literary experiences. Elaine Showalter has drawn attention to this critical revolution in the following words:

> While literary criticism and its philosophical branch, literary theory, have always been zealously guarded bastions of male intellectual endeavour, the success of feminist criticism has opened a space for the authority of the woman critic that extends beyond the study of woman's writing to the reappraisal of whole body of texts that take up the literary heritage. (1985: 3)

Feminist criticism operates in three ways (1) it unfolds the literary representations of sexual difference; (2) it brings out the ways that literary genres have been shaped by masculine or feminine values; and, (3) it shows the exclusion of the female voice from the institutions of literature, criticism and theory. Thus, feminist criticism establishes gender as a fundamental category of literary analysis.

In articulating feminist literary theory, clarity of thought regarding 'female', 'feminist', and 'feminine' as three categories is essential. The strength of feminist theory is its very openendedness, which has very often been mistaken for its weakness. It can use the existing critical theories, and ideologies with advantage. Thus, it is pluralistic, and the term 'appropriation' is of special significance in the contexts. Anglo-American and French thinkers, initially conflicting groups, are now entering into open dialogue, accepting the alternative perspective to 'define' and articulate feminist literary theory, leading to a meaningful reading of the sign—reading of the text.

This will lead to the deconstruction of the opposition between traditionally 'masculine' and traditionally 'feminine' values confronting the full political force and reality of such categories. As Toril Moi says, "We must aim for a society in which we have ceased to categorise logic, conceptualization and rationally as 'masculine', not for one from which these virtues have been expelled altogether as 'unfeminine'" (1986: 220). This decoding of the meaning of text will certainly go on till the objectives are achieved.

DIFFERENT WAVES OF FEMINISM

The first wave feminism emphasized on social and political emancipation of women. The maiden eminent voice of feminism was echoed in Mary Wollstonecraft's *Vindication of the Right of Women* (1792). Before Mary Wollstonecraft, the woman who explored and asserted ideas about woman was Mary Astel. In her first published book *A Serious Proposal to Ladies* (1694), she argued that women should take themselves, work to develop their own mind and skills, rather than always deferring to masculine judgement. The nineteenth century women struggled and finally gained the right to hold property in 1880. Further they presented the idea of gender equality. Theoretical analysis of woman was produced by the arrival of twentieth century. Charlotte Perkins Gilman's *Women and Economics* (1898) and Oliver Schreiner's *Women and Labour* (1911) talked about vote for women, for property rights, for fairer legislation concerning divorce and certain other issues. Two main feminist works of the first Wave Feminism were Virginia Woolf's *A Room of One's Own* (1928) and Simon de Beauvoir's *The Second Sex* (1949).

Virginia Woolf has been declared as irrelevant by some contemporary feminists. For example, Sheila Rowbotham remarks that her demand, in *A Room of One's Own*, for £500 a year and space to oneself was simply aimed at a minority of the educated middle class. That is true; but she is read still, and by women and men who would never so much as glance at most feminist writing. Woolf was certainly ambivalent about the term 'feminism'; she admitted that she was anxious, when the book was first published, that she might be 'attacked for a feminist'.

She clearly asserts that the woman's cause is also the man's cause and true happiness cannot be achieved by trying to marginalize each other. She realizes that both men and women are human resources to be used for the development of the culture, but these genders cannot be dissociated from each other. Her feminism does not confine a woman to the relations she bears to man, but at the same time, does not deny these relationships to her. The belief that there is no fundamental juxtaposition between man and woman unfolds in the thematic structures of her novels with a poetic intensity, and is shared by many other feminist thinkers.

The 'second wave' feminism emerged after the second world war in several countries. In 1947, a commission on the status of women was established by the United Nations, and two years later it issued a Declaration of Human Rights, which acknowledged that men and women had 'equal rights as to marriage, during marriage and at its dissolution', as well as women's entitlement to 'special care and assistance' in their role as mothers. This feminism is identified by breaking down the barriers by the feminists prevalent between the private and the public issues such as domestic violence and sexual abuse of children. Pornography was strongly opposed. Some prominent issues on the women's agendas were fight against violence meted out to women, struggle for child-care facilities, abortion on demand, protection from sexual harassment and discrimination on the basis of gender. Some prominent works of this period are Betty Friedan's *The Feminine Mystique* (1963), Germaine Greer's *The Female Eunuch* (1971), Kate Millet's *Sexual Politics* (1971), Sundra Gilbert and Susan Gubar's *The Madwoman in Attic* (1979), Patricia Spack's *The Female Imagination* (1975), Ellen Moer's *Literary Women* (1976) and Eline Showalter's *A Literature of Their Own* (1977).

Post-feminism is also known as the third wave of feminism because first two phases of feminism have already passed with achievements, success and failures. It is a general assumption that 'Post-feminism has arrived, feminism is passe'. With the arrival of post-feminism, it has become a matter of scholarly discussion whether it is a saga of victory or a narrative of defeat. As a matter of fact there are many feminist theories, each having several theoretical approaches and positions. Its two primary concerns are power and freedom. Both have traditionally been denied to women, placing them on the margins. It is these margins which are being redefined or shifted through a shift to post-feminism in literary aesthetics. Gayatri Spivak in her essay "Marginality and the Teaching Machine" has observed:

> There can be no universalistic claim in the human sciences. This is most strikingly obvious in the case of establishing "Marginality" as a subject position in literary and cultural critique. The reader must accustom herself to starting from a particular situation and then to the ground shifting under her feet. (1985: 53)

Thus post-feminism emerges not merely as a 'post' phase but perhaps part of feminist strategy to renegotiate the margins, to prevent feminist aesthetics from reaching a dead end and from being trapped in confessional and victim-centred narratives. It defines the readership and confines it to the level of 'sharing' and 'consciousness-raising' writing. Its evaluation and critiquing are still largely male centred and dispute its very validity. It is not just the discovery of the self, the exploration of the past, the correction of history, the shaping of the epistemological systems which are of significance, but also the participation in the present and the acceptance of new definitions of space and freedom, so that the centre and margins do not appear as antagonistic, hostile, mutually exclusive categories but acquired sufficient fluidity to enlarge each other. Feminism is about the self, about rights and about difference; post-feminism is a move towards reciprocal change, and expresses a need to look anew at the harsh political realities. Post-feminism, in its impact on literary aesthetics, shifts the issue from identity to relationships, from a concern with oppression to one with the concept of freedom. By refusing to be constrained by the label of feminism, women writers are foregrounding a message that to be a feminist is not to be non-human.

POST-FEMINISM

Feminist movements have crossed several phases; one phase has been the need to be equal with the men, meet the challenges of the male dominated society. This theory was followed by emphasis on differences and introspective relationship with the female body and mind prevailing of female experience and motherhood. The literal meaning of the word 'post' is 'after'. It is a prefix according to the rules of grammar. The term 'Post-feminism' is made of 'Post' and 'Feminism'. So, we can understand it as a theory after feminism. Webster's *Encyclopedic Unabridged Dictionary of the English Language* (1996) defines the term post-feminism as follows:

1. Pertaining to or occurring in the period after the feminist movement of the 1970's.
2. Resulting from or incorporating the ideology of the movement: a post-feminist household in which both partners share all tasks equally.
3. Differing from or reflecting moderation of this ideology.
4. A person who believes in, promotes, or embodies any of various ideologies springing from the feminism of 1970's.

This understanding further gives birth to several complex questions such as (a) Have the feminists succeeded in bringing complete victory over centuries old gender discrimination? (b) Is post-feminism a jubilation after achieving the goals of feminism? (c) Is post-feminism a new wave of feminism replacing the old ones as they did not achieve success partially or impartially? In her article "Manufacturing Post-Feminism", Susan J. Douglas has expressed the opinion:

> What the hell is post-feminism, any way? I would think it would refer to a time when complete gender equality has been achieved. That hasn't happened, of course, but we (especially young women) are supposed to think it has. Post-feminism, as a term, suggests that women have made plenty of progress because of feminism, but that feminism is now irrelevant and even undesirable because it has made

> millions of women unhappy, unfeminine, childless, lonely and bitter, prompting them to fill their closets with combat boots and really bad India print skirts. (2007: 1)

As a matter of fact there are many branches of feminism and these are culture specific. The nature of feminism in Indian context is different from that of the European countries. Even the feminist theories are also not the same. Jasbir Jain opines:

> Feminist theory is not one, it has several different theoretical approaches and positions but whether it is socio-economic, psychological or literary, its two primary concerns are power and freedom. Both have traditionally been denied to woman, placing them on the margins. It is these margins which are being redefined or shifted through a shift to post-feminism in literary aesthetics. (2001: 82)

Thus, we can conclude that the earlier waves of feminism could not completely dismantle the centuries old discrimination being practised in the name of gender. We cannot completely negate the achievement of feminist movements as well. It has changed, though partially, the psyche of male counterpart to consider the female as the equal partner in all walks of life. Post-feminism is also not a publication over feminism rather it is something different.

Toril Moi has used the term "post-feminism" to cover the different configurations of feminism and post-modernism prevalent these days. Present day feminist theorists believe that strictly speaking feminism is an impossible position. The agonistic definition of feminism sees it as the struggle against all forms of patriarchal and sexist oppression. Such an oppositional definition keeps feminism as the necessary resistance to patriarchal power. Logically, the aim of feminism as an emancipatory theory becomes to abolish itself along with its opponent. "In a non-sexist, non-patriarchal society feminism will no longer exist" (Moi 1988: 5). As such feminism is an impossible undertaking. Feminism is committed to the struggle for equality for women, an effort to make women like men. But the struggle for equal rights historically and politically emphasizes the value of women as they are. The very argument rests precisely on the fact that women are already as valuable as men. But in the situation of women's lack of equal rights, this value must be located as *difference,* not as equality. Women are of equal human value in their own way. When feminism asserts the value of women as women, then it truly and efficiently counters the systematic devaluation of women under patriarchy.

Thus, equality and difference are not antithetical. But a disclosure of female difference, articulated in isolation, runs the risk of echoing the very patriarchal prejudices against which the champions of equality are struggling. Accepting the constraining logic of sameness and difference, Julia Kristeva suggests a third space for feminism to operate—the space which deconstructs all identity, all binary oppositions. But again in deconstructing patriarchal metaphysics, the risk of deconstructing the very logic that sustains the two forms of feminism—of sameness and difference—cannot be avoided. Therefore, the three "spaces" of feminism are logically and often strategically incompatible. In the 1980s, feminism emerged as a thought system, a point of view to reorganize the world realities, a positivist holistic approach to life, a step towards sanity in human relationship, and perhaps the only mode for preservation of human existence on this earth. Moreover, women have been the custodians of humane values for centuries. The primary value is reverence for life. This ethic must become the world ethic.

WESTERN-FEMINISM

Feminism as a socio-cultural movement began in Europe, got strengthened with the help of Marxism, found its full echoes in the U.S.A. and like many other similar concepts spread to the countries of the third world. It was Alexander Dumas, the nineteenth century French dramatist, who first used the term 'feminism' for the movement of women's political rights. Later it spread in almost all the countries of the world to secure complete right for woman: political, social, economic and educational. The movement got momentum and finally by the end of the twentieth century, compelled the complacent society to think in a new direction.

Credit goes to Simon de Beauvoir's book *The Second Sex*, first published in French in the year 1949, which sowed the seeds for a women's movement. It won great acclaim as a feminist book, when its English translation was made available to the world. She succeeds in shattering the myth of femininity and shows how, deprived of their social, economic and political rights, they remain relegated to the background. Despite their equal contribution in the society, they are treated as the weaker sex. Simon de Beauvoir says:

> All agree in recognizing the fact that female exists in the human species; today as always they make up about half of humanity. And yet we are told that femininity is in danger; we are exhorted to be women, remain women, become women. It would appear, then, that every female human being is not necessarily a woman; to be so considered she must share in that mysterious and threatened reality known as femininity. Is this attribute something secreted by the ovaries? Or is it a platonic essence a product of the philosophic imagination. (1983: 13)

She contributed a lot to the women's liberation movement in the mid-nineteenth century. "Drawing heavily on disciplines like biology, psychology and history, she discusses girl's education, love, sex, marriage, prostitution and domestic drudgery as well. She frankly talks about sexual exploitation and sexual pleasure for women, and does not give way to sentiments while discussing 'maternity'" (Sharma 2005: 5).

Betty Friedan is second to none in providing a new momentum and dimension to the feminist movement. She is known as one of pioneers of the 'second wave' feminism which emerged after Second World War. Her book *The Feminine Mystiques*, published in 1963, sparked off the movement. She interviewed many housewives in the affluent, white, American suburbs. She discovered the falsity of a woman's achieving happiness and contentment in marriage and motherhood although they had been blessed with all the comforts of life. All were merely trying to seek fulfillment by playing the role of a devoted wife and caring mother. Friedan says:

> For a woman, as for a man the need for self-fulfillment—autonomy, self-realization, independence, individuality, self-actualization is as important as the sexual need, with a serious consequence when it is thwarted. Women's sexual problems are, in this sense, by-product of the suppression of her basic need to grow and fulfill her potentialities as a human being, potentialities which the mystique of feminism fulfillment ignores. (1971: 282)

Kate Millet is another pioneer of the 'second wave' feminism. In her book *Sexual Politics* (1970), Millet set out to analyze 'patriarchy as a political institution'. Politics, she insists, refers to all 'power structured relationships', and one between the sexes is a 'relationship of dominance and subordinance' which has been largely unexamined. She found out a surprising fact in two of her studies on female children. Most of them preferred to be born a boy if they were given a choice. She explains very minutely the sense of insecurity in women. She writes:

> The phenomenon of parent's parental preferences for male issues is too common to require such elaboration. In the light of imminent possibility of parent's actually choosing the sex of their child, such a tendency is becoming the cause of same concern in scientific circles. (1971: 56-57)

Germaine Greer's lively and provocative *The Female Eunuch* (1970) challenged the 'sense of inferiority or natural dependence' which women have too often accepted placidly, passively, allowing it to distort and impoverish their lives. She, being a militant feminist, goes to the extent of saying that "If woman are to affect a significant amelioration in the condition it seems obvious that they must refuse to marry" (Greer 1976: 319).

There are many other feminist writers who contributed to the feminist movement. Margaret Drabble, Doris Lessing, Iris Murdoch, Marilyn French and Margaret Atwood have also contributed greatly in the movement, and have been internationally acclaimed as great feminist novelists. Just two centuries back women writers dared not express themselves honestly by defying the rigid norms laid down by society, inviting social censure. However, there were many spinster writers like Jane Austen, Emily Bronte, Stevie Smith, Charlotte Mew, Mananne Moor and Elizabeth Smith. But the freedom to express themselves from the core of their heart was sought at the price of giving up the so-called "womanliness"—sex, marriage, children and the social status of a wife.

The western feminist movements have achieved a lot for the women of the West in particular and across the world in general. This is the reason almost all the constitutions have made provisions to remove the inequalities which the women had suffered. They are equal before law. Now they cannot be discriminated on the basis of gender. They have been guaranteed equality of opportunity in public employment and education. But on the ground of reality, still some discriminations are prevalent.

INDIAN FEMINISM

Feminism in Indian English literature is, of course, a by-product of the western feminism. To a great extent it is like the feminism in literature of other countries of the world. However, it cannot be called the replica of the western feminist literature. Though the feminist of all shades and nationalities share the basic paradigms of feminism with the western feminists, they have been conscious of maintaining their own identities independent in their own respective ways.

Such differences are quite natural due to socio-cultural reasons. Western feminists have taken into account the problems of marginality created by gender-discriminations but they did not take seriously the effect of class and race in the context of the Third World. The Third World countries, too, have their own reasons to differ among themselves. Even within India there are differences and divergences. A peasant woman from the rural area cannot have a common bond with her metropolitan, middle-class sister from Delhi. Charu Sheel Singh endorsing the view of Tharu and Lalita points out:

> Our problems are not the same as those concerns; we cannot, and should not, imbibe, impose and practise what is alien to our social conditions and psyche. (1998: 49)

Besides the neglect of class and racial factors dominant in the Third World countries, the first world feminist had not been able to free themselves from the complex of "white and black" or "imperialist design". Therefore, Gayatri Chakravorty Spivak, Chandra Talpade Mohanty, Susie Tharu and K. Lalita have strongly objected to the western feminist move of global sisterhood against patriarchy. Chandra Talpade Mohanty observes, "Beyond sisterhood", of the first world feminists, "there is racism, colonialism and imperialism" (Qtd. Palker: Pathak 1996: 192). Gayatri Chakravorty Spivak also notices a "colonialist move" in the white feminist criticism and clearly points out that it "celebrates the heroines of the first world in a singular and individualist, and the collective presence of woman elsewhere in a pluralized and inchoate fashion" (*ibid*: 193). The Indian feminists have a strong desire to fight against oppression and injustice suffered by woman in India, at the same time, they suspect any kind of sympathy or help extended by the British Colonists for liberation of women from traditional practices in India.

The post-independence Indian women are caught in the flux of tradition and modernity—the burden of the past as well as the aspirations of the future. Traditionally, the role of the woman in Indian society has been regulated and determined by age old conventions. During the pre-British Indian society women were assigned a position subordinate to men. Describing the traditional norms prevalent in Indian society, Dube comments:

> According to the traditional norms of the society a husband is expected to be authoritarian figure whose will should always dominate the domestic scene.... The wife should regard him as her master and should serve him faithfully...the husband is superior, the wife is his subordinate. (1955: 141)

Law and religion did not recognize equal rights for men and women. Women had to depend on men for protection and survival, and thus men were considered their protectors and much superior to them. Manu declares:

Pita Rakshti Kaumare Bharta Rakshti Yauwane
Rakshanti Sthvire Putrah Na Stri Swatantraymar Hati
(*Manusmriti*, ch-9, Hymn 3: 347)

(Father protects the woman in her childhood, husband in the youth, Son in the old age. She must be kept in subordination because she doesn't deserve freedom.)

Women were denied the right to study the Vedas, and were treated no better than sinners and slaves. The code of Manu was so strictly observed that the role of women was confined to the family, and they were denied the rights equal to men. It is undeniably true that their lot in the family kept changing with the time, but it always remained an inferior one. The same idea can be traced out in the *Ramcharitmanas*. Tulsidas says:

Dhol Gawanra Sudra Pasu Naree
Sakal Tadana Ke Adhikari (1990: 396)

(Drums, illiterates, Sudras, Animals and Women—they all deserve beating.)

Shanta Krishnaswamy's views on the subjugation of the Indian women are quite remarkable:

> She is a creature who as a child is sold off to strangers for a bridal price, or when she grows up, serves as a supplier of dowry for her husband's family, or who as a widow, in a final act of obliteration immolates herself on her dead husband's funeral pyre to be acclaimed as 'Sati-Savitri' as an immortal.
>
> (Quoted in Sandhu, 1991: 8)

A glance at the cultural history of India proves that the position of women was not subordinate to men. Women were treated as Goddesses and harbingers of all kinds of prosperity in life. Manu says:

Yatra Naryastu Pujyante Ramante Tatra Devata
(*Manusmriti*, ch-3, Hymn 56: 101)

(Where women are worshipped, there abode gods.)

In the Pre-Vedic and Vedic periods, women held a high place of honour. To give birth to a daughter was considered something honourable. Devahuti, the daughter of Manu was married to

Rishi Kardam. Their union resulted in the procreation of daughters in succession. The nine daughters of Devahuti were the most shining Jewels of Indian womanhood. They included Kala, the wife of Saint Marichi; Arundhati, the saintly wife of Vashishtha; Ansuya, the very epitome of feminine chastity and wife of the illustrious Saint Atri. According to *Sarvanukramanika* there were twenty Brahmavadinis who composed the hymns of the Rig Veda. Gargi, Gosha, Godha, Vishwakarma, Apala, Maitreiyi and Lilavati were the woman scholars.

During Vedic times, women were still held in high esteem in society. The Vedas are religious books written by the Aryan Brahmins around 1200 B.C. to record earliest Indian history. Clara Nubile in her book *The Danger of Gender* has presented a clear picture of the Indian women during the Vedic period:

> Vijayalakshmi Seshadri (1995) explains that during the Vedic period there was no discrimination on the basis of gender and women were allowed to perform the Upanayan ceremony, which was the prerequisite for pursuing Vedic studies. Education was important in society and twenty women composed hymns of the Rig Veda. The Rig Veda is a collection of 1028 hymns which the Aryans sang to their gods. These hymns were probably composed between 1500 and 900 B.C. In this period, there were even the *brahmavadinis*, who remained unmarried in their quest for knowledge and wisdom. (quoted in Nubile 2003: 4)

In the sixteenth century, the Mughals conquered India and consolidated Islamic power. They remained in power till the eighteenth century. The women were forced to live within the four walls of home. "Under the Mughal rule, women's lowly position in the upper castes of both Muslim and Hindu communities were reinforced. In particular, purdah spread in area where Hindu Muslim conflict was strongest, based on the fear of abduction and rape from the opposing side" (Nubile 2003: 9). It was Mughal rule, which gave birth to so many evil practices, viz. sati system, child marriage, purdah system, prohibition of women from getting education, etc. This period is the darkest period in the history of Indian women.

When the British started ruling India, the status of woman was very pathetic. Even though, the British government made some reforms in order to improve the lot of the Indian women. For example, in 1829 William Bentic abolished the practice of sati, in 1856 the Widow Remarriage Act was enforced, and in 1872 the Civil Marriage Act raised the age of marriage for girls to fourteen years. Another important act was passed in 1874; the Married Woman's Act; it widened the scope of *streedhana* to include earnings of a woman by exercise of her artistic and literary skills. So many odd and inhuman restrictions on women rights, though not completely, started to break. The woman started to get education in schools, colleges and universities. The impact of woman education was obvious when India got independence in 1947. The women who had got education in the early 20th century during the British rule rendered their services as politicians, writers, bureaucrats, etc. in the nation building after independence. In the post-independence India, the lot the woman has changed. K.M. Panikkar in his essay "The Awakening of Women" has rightly remarked:

> There was no suffragette movement in India, no feminism for the share of women in the battle of freedom gave them this position of equality without their having to fight for it separately.... The legislative reform establishing the equality of women has been one of the most significant political achievements in the period of partial self-government. Their right to independent property, to freedom of marriage, to education and employment has been recognized by law. Many important pieces of legislation, especially the raising of the age of consent for marriage and the prevention of the dedication of women to temple services, have helped to change their status. (2003: 17)

Despite all the possible steps taken by government for the upliftment of the Indian women, much more is required on the ground reality. No doubt India is dreaming to stand in the queue of advanced nations of the world, but yet the age-old social evils are present even today. Women are burnt alive for the sake of dowry. Girl babies are killed in the wombs. Girls are not allowed to get education in lower middle class families in rural areas, which constitute a major portion of our population. Even in suburban areas women are deprived of getting higher education. Though not often, yet rarely the self-immolation of widows with the dead husbands appear in the newspapers and the media. Thus, we can conclude that much more is required to eliminate the discrimination being meted out to women in the Indian society.

In the Pre-independent India, womanhood was stale and perverted. It was either exaggerated or neglected. Woman did not occupy any important place in most of the Anglo-Indian novels. In E.M. Forster's *A Passage to India* Indian women are sketched, not drawn. The Indo-Anglican novels of this period present women as romantic, charming, cultured, graceful, wise and courageous. The novels of this period treated women's lives, experiences and values as marginal. They assumed that literature was serious about public events than about the private life. They thought literature by and about women was inferior to that of men.

Bankim Chandra Chatterjee, Raj Lakshmi Debi, Toru Dutt, Krupabai Sutthiannadhan and others have written about the suffering women. For them woman was either a Devi or a doormat. She was a stereotype of the 'Pativrata' and had no identity. Their ideal was to obey the elders and follow the traditions which made them submissive and dependent. Women in early fictions suffered mostly due to the infidelity of her husband or the stigma of childlessness. Mulk Raj Anand, R.K. Narayan, Kamala Markandaya and Manjeri Isvaran have portrayed women in their novels as the traditional image of the Pativrata. She is nothing more than an object of pity and has no will of her own. To suffer in silence is the destiny of Indian women.

The ideal of womanhood was to attain motherhood—the marvellous, unselfish, all suffering, ever forgiving mother. The Indian woman had to wait for a few decades to assume an existence and an identity. With the spread of education, there was a gradual erosion of faith in the traditional customs and values, but it took some time for the modern ideas and western culture to fill the vacuum so created. The mingling of Indian and western cultures has created a transitional society neither fully modern nor fully traditional. Bhabani Bhattacharya says:

> I think the women of India have more depth, more richness than the men. The transition from the old to the new, the crisis of value adoption strikes deeper into the lives of our women than our men folk. (1974: 2)

The post-colonial India has shown much emphasis on education, which has in turn benefited women at least in finding good employment and good matches in marriages. It is true with the women belonging to well to do and highly educated families. But the condition of average women has not improved upto expectation. It is true that many women have successfully discharged their duties as high dignitaries, but the lot of under-privileged women forging the majority has not changed much. There are so many hindrances in the path of women liberation such as female infanticide, feticide, dowry, gender-discrimination and violence against women. They are humiliated even in the 21st century in homes as well as workplaces. A woman in Indian is entrapped into the inescapable cage of "being a woman, wife and mother". A woman cannot exist outside the boundaries of married life and motherhood. She is perceived as useless and unworthy according to traditional views. Indian woman does not appear to have few independent roles in society. Moreover, she must be a male appendix in order to have a role.

Feminism in Indian English poetry is by and large an upshot of the various gender-based social taboos which suppress the freedom of women and compel them to adopt to the given situation. Much reaction is evoked by such stereotyping as idealization of domesticity and sexualization, and objectification of women as mere object of male's sexual and sadistic pleasure; humiliation and harassment of women both at home and workplace, sexual violence, crime and ill treatment done to women and male despotism.

The modern feminist thought came into Indian English poetry with Kamala Das, who emerged as a staunch rebel against the customary patriarchal arrangement in the Indian society. Sunita Jain, another prominent figure among Indian women poets, writes extensively on the various vicissitudes of love and man-woman relationship. Her poems are characterized by intense feminine feelings and female urges. But, she rarely prefers to revolt against the domination of patriarchy in such a bold and overt manner as Kamala Das and Gouri Deshpande do. She rather seeks her pleasure and redemption in cultivating the sense of sharing and mutual understanding with her man. She often wavers between romance and reality. The frequent use of irony and contrast makes her articulation forceful and compelling.

Indian women novelists can be said to be highly conscious of the woman's liberation movement. By and large they have portrayed women and their stories with consciousness of the injustices being meted out to woman by society. These novels have a feminist undercurrent. If we look at these fictional female characters, a large number of them rebel against the existing social set up. They discard the idea of being submissive, suffering and sacrificing. The protagonists in the novels of the Indian women novelists have often come up to paying the prize of their rebellion rather than submitting and dying through suffocation.

Bhabani Bhattacharya is one of the novelists who dominate the post-independence scene of the Indo-English fiction. The themes of Bhattacharya's novels differ from those of the predecessors. His women characters are tender, charring virtuous; and play a significant role in effecting social changes. Kajali in *So Many Hungers* (1947) undergoes immense suffering and misery, but her spirit remains invincible. The next novel *Music for Mohini* (1952) presents a changing situation of the independent India. Mohini, a Calcutta born girl and a radio star, marries Jayadev who lives in a village. Jayadev's sister, Rooplikha, marries a Calcutta born gentleman. That gives a chance to Bhattacharya to present a conflict between the rural and the urban, the tradition and the change, the old and the new. The other novels *He Who Rides a Tiger* and *A Goddess*

Named Gold also describe the tyranny meted by society to the cultured women.

In her novels Anita Desai has graphically presented the turbulent psyche of the modern Indian women. Her protagonists are intelligent, sensible and sensitive, but competent enough to manage home and children, and attain emotional fulfillment. Being unable to cope with the crisis, they resort to drastic steps. Maya in *Cry, The Peacock* kills her husband Gautama by pushing him from the roof. In *Where Shall We Go This Summer?* the author lays bare the void in Sita's life as a woman, wife and mother. It is a poignant tale of a middle-aged woman torn between her desire to abandon her comfortable, albeit boring existence, and the realization that the bonds that bind her to it cannot easily be broken. Desai has been acclaimed as a feminist of high order in the Indian context. She, however, does not provide any suitable solution.

Nayantara Sahgal is also an eminent woman writer. She has dealt with issues concerning women that later become major issues in the feminist movement. With delicate sensibility, she exposes the prejudices which women face in a male-dominated society. *The Day in Shadow* is about the prejudice faced by the divorced heroine Simrit. Sahgal, being a divorcee herself, presents in a realistic and vivid manner how Simrit tries to square her equation with her growing children and her ex-husband. Her other novel *Rich Like Us* is about Sonali, the daughter of a Marathi father and a Kashmiri mother. She goes to Oxford to escape the Indian world of arranged marriages. Though Sahgal has a limited world of feminist ideas, she presents a sensitive study of her elite women characters.

Kamala Das is both a poetess and novelist. Her novels *The Alphabet of Lust* and *A Doll for the Child Prostitute* are the true depictions of Indian women's problems. The protagonists are in quest of their identities in the male-dominated society. Manasi, the protagonist in the novel *The Alphabet of Lust* is an unhappy and frustrated wife of a government officer who is old enough. All the time he remains busy with his work and never loves his wife. Out of frustration, despondency and diminished status, she longs for emancipation and identity. Kamala Das' next novel *A Doll for the Child Prostitute* is about the child prostitute who struggles for liberation and quest for identity. Mira, the child prostitute, secretly marries her student client, which does not last for a week, and is forced back into the abhorrent profession of prostitution. Thus Kamala Das' novels are clear manifestations of a woman's quest for identity.

Shashi Deshpande is a novelist who is rising like a star feminist among women novelists of India. Her women characters are educated; stay conscious and sensitive. Their revolt against the rigid social and family set up comes out of Neurosis. Saru in *The Dark Holds No Terrors* pays the prices in terms of being brutally insulted by her husband simply because she is superior to him mentally as well as socially. She has traumatic experiences because she is woman and highly skilled. Likewise, other women characters of Deshpande's novels, Saru also suffers a lot. Their pain and tortures are too much which cannot be exactly explained in words. A deep and sincere analysis of her novels leaves no doubt about her genuine concern for women. Her protagonists are acutely aware of their smothered and fettered existence in an orthodox male-dominated society. They, being caught between tradition and modernity, search for their identity within marriage.

In theory all men and women are equal but in practice women are subject to all sorts of discrimination. India is a vast country and the inhabitants range from the highly sophisticated to illiterate primitive people. There are diverse religions with diverse beliefs and conventions. The Hindus, forming the majority, are caste-ridden and there are classes within the castes. Obviously, the country is teeming with complex problems. In a country where about fifty per cent people live below poverty line and are illiterate, the condition of women can better be imagined than described. All these points should be taken into consideration when we compare the writings of women novelists of India with those of European countries. Women novelists are working with an increased speed and efficiency, and they have created new possibilities for themselves. An author is influenced by his/her social milieu. Conditions being different in India and western countries, the novelists like Doris Lessing, Irish Murdoch, Margaret Drabble, Kamala Markandya, Anita Desai, Nayantara Sahgal and Shashi Deshpande discuss the feminism from their own point of views. In European countries, an average woman does not struggle for sheer survival. Under such varying conditions, we cannot expect the Indian women revolt against the men following the footprints of the western feminists.

These are some of the important points of divergence in the approach of Indian women novelists. But, in spite of all these divergent issues, the basic similarly doesn't diffuse. The exploitation of women in various ways, male chauvinism, patriarchal ingrate, relegating women to second class citizenship in practice, stultification of woman in marriage and their loss of identity, all these pertinent practices and experience remain. The following chapters will examine how the problems are perceived and communicated in the novels of Shashi Deshpande.

Feminism in *Roots and Shadows* and *The Dark Holds No Terrors*

3

The literary world of the Indian English fiction has spread red carpet for women writers. Increasingly more and more women are articulating anxieties and concerns focusing on women's issues and creating a body of 'literature of their own'. Feminist issues transcend all limits of nationality, race, creed, etc. Women writers have been echoing the feelings of marginality and expressing their revolt against the purely masculine world. One of the major concerns of the contemporary literature all over the world has been to highlight the plight of women, their increasing problems, their physical, financial and emotional exploitation, and their mental anguish in the male-dominated society, in every sphere of life. In almost all the countries, in the academic fields, in women forum, the main focus these days is to bring into light the oppression faced by women in various forms. The enforcement of the feminist movement, the establishment of various women studies centres, the formation of various women's welfare organizations, and the best sale in the market of writing dealing with women and their problems, are indications of the fact that the voice of women is being heard. In order to reach the stage of being listened to, the women writers had to struggle much, and through their writings they have been projecting their viewpoints, pleading and fighting for a change in the attitude of society towards women. In her article, Parvati Bhatnagar mentions:

> Values need to be redefined, so also human relationships, especially within the family. Such is the dilemma of the middle class. Adherence to traditional values has become

> difficult. New values have yet to be evolved. It requires tremendous amount of courage (and thoughtlessness?) to break away from the tradition. So despite western education, psychology remains tradition oriented. (2001: 50)

Many female writers such as George Eliot, Sylvia Plath, Margaret Atwood, Dorris Lessing, Anita Desai, Shashi Deshpande, Dalip Kaur Tiwana, Bharati Mukherjee, Shobhaa De and many others, and a few male writers like Thomas Hardy, Mulk Raj Anand and R.K. Narayan, in their many writings, have analysed the female psyche, the inner turmoil of women, the culture and context-specific problems of women and have expressed the need for a transformation in the age-old negative attitudes of the society towards women.

A name that tops the list of contemporary Indian feminist writers who have shown their serious concern with the depiction of women in literature and have expressed restlessness with the traditional positioning of women is that of Shashi Deshpande. In almost all her writings including *Roots and Shadows* (1983) and *The Dark Holds No Terrors* (1980), her concern with the social and cultural construction of gender, her open protest against the treatment of women as sexual object, her defiance of the stereotyped roles assigned to women, her bold efforts to project the prejudiced attitude of society towards women, are obvious. She not only forthrightly articulates a thematic and technical maturity but also effectively communicates an intensely apprehended feminine sensibility. She has apparently injected a new consciousness, offering varied interpretation of imperishable Indian values as well as highlighting our cultural heritage. She has added a new dimension to Indian English feminist literature. Ramesh Kumar Gupta's remark in this context is noteworthy:

> Shashi Deshpande's novels are concerned with a woman's quest for self; an exploration into the female psyche and an understanding of the mysteries of life and the protagonist's place in it. (2002: 42)

This chapter proposes to examine and explore the feminine note in first two novels of Shashi Deshpande *Roots and Shadows* and *The Dark Holds No Terrors*. The women protagonists in these novels achieve "personhood" yet do not negate the family or the society. They go beyond what Elaine Showalter calls the "female phase" which is a phase of self-discovery, a turning inward freed from the dependence of opposition, a search for identity (1977: 13). They, no doubt, discover themselves but the quest does not end there. It seems they are not feminist in the *Prima facie*, but they prove their identity later. The second stage cannot be viewed in terms of the separate personhood or equality with men.

ROOTS AND SHADOWS

Roots and Shadows (1983) is Shashi Deshpande's first full length novel. Indu, the protagonist, represents the educated, middle class women. The story of the novel is about the struggle of the protagonist who has a lot of hurdles to cross and achieve freedom. Being smothered in an oppressive male-dominated and tradition-bound society, she attempts to explore her inner self to assert her individuality. "...Indu, a rebel, often wished to be free and unrestrained. Thus, she is presented as a model against women belonging to the older generation" (Gupta 2002: 43).

Indu, the protagonist in *Roots and Shadows* shares the fate of Sisyphus. Her crime is to reveal long hidden inner world of women in general and Indian in particular. In an article, G.D. Barche opines:

> She is suffering in our world and her suffering is deeper and deadlier than Sisyphus' as he was to roll up only one stone, while she is rolling up many, viz. the ideal of Independence and completeness, the concepts of self, sin, love the ideal of detachment and freedom, and so on. (1989: 48)

Indu comes back to her parental home after a gap of eleven years, which is occasioned by her cousin Mini's marriage being performed in the traditional manner in their ancestral home. She had left home at the age of eighteen to marry the man she loved. She represents new generation and reviews everything with reason and new visions. In his article "Image of Women in Shashi Deshpande Novel *Roots and Shadows*: A Critical Study," Ramesh Kumar Gupta aptly remarks:

> She explains the ideal of detachment and liberation and tries to achieve them. She tries only to listen to the voice of her conscience and revolts. But unfortunately, she fails, in all her efforts, miserably either due to the impact of culture and tradition, or fear of stigma, or timidity, or all these combined together. (2002: 43)

She returns on being called by Akka, the domineering matriarch, as she is on her death bed. Akka has made her the sole heiress to her property, and the household atmosphere becomes charged with resentment by the family members for being excluded from the will. Deshpande has presented very clearly the details of a large Maharashtrian Brahmin household, and the myriad women characters, their greed, jealousy, hopes, fears, disappointments, and anguish. In a book-review of *Roots and Shadows*, C.W. Watson has opined:

> This novel which was first published in 1983 succeeds magnificently in its haunting description of the decline of a once prosperous middle-class family in South India. Much of the material of modern Indian writing, especially Indian writing in English, is drawn from this social milieu of one has only to think recent novels by Anita Desai, Amitav Ghosh, and Amrit Chaudhuri—but where the strength of this novel lies is in the marvelous evocation of character and mood. (1995: 75)

Besides, the problems faced by the girls of the new generation have also been paid special attention. Indu, Mini and Akka belong to this series of girl-children. Mini possesses in her character all the traditional feminine qualities since her childhood. Devoid of any fixed aim in her life, she devotes herself to her family members. Her obedience, silence and submission never allow her to cross the boundary line of rules and regulations set by the family for girls. As she was brought up under strict supervision, guidance and restrictions, she became acquainted with the real duties of a girl at an early age. This is the reason, Indu, her cousin, recalls Mini as a child.

> Mini had always been very much of a girl, the way a girl was expected to be, helping the women with small odd chores from a very young age, waiting on her father and brothers and being generally docile. Our words had rarely touched. (122)

Indu contemplates on the existence of inner strength in the women of her family who have spent their whole life slavishly without a word of appreciation for their services. While following their footsteps Mini also accepts that the life of a girl is devoid of 'choices', Indu could find the reason behind Mini's submission before her parents' decision of getting her married to a man who was neither properly educated nor mentally sound. Indu remarks:

> A woman's life, they had told me, contained no choices. And all my life, specially in this house, I had seen the truth of this. The women had no choices but to submit, to accept. And I had often wondered...have they been born without wills, or have their will atrophied through a lifetime of disuse? And yet Mini, who had had no choice either, had accepted the reality, the finality with a grace and composure that spoke eloquently of that inner strength. (6)

Mini's father, Anant, faces a financial crisis. He, being in no job, has to depend on the cultivation of the parental land. His sons having inclined towards office jobs were reluctant to look after the lands. Anant was aware that with his weak financial position, he won't be able to get his daughter married. Finally he agrees to marry Mini to a distant relative of Akka as she promises to pay for Mini's wedding. In India, a girl's marriage is consummated only after satiating the demands and choices of the groom whereas the bride's demands and choices don't matter. Vrinda Nabar writes about the dowry system of India in *Caste as Women*:

> The bride's father gives according to his means, frequently out of proportion to them, borrowing if necessary, since he believes that his daughter's prestige and happiness are at stake. Ironically, no one who is party to such a

> transaction appears to wonder what happiness measured in these terms implies, or whether it exists at all, or is worth acquiring at that price. (1995: 160)

Anant accepts the proposal as he had no other option left before him. Mini's lackadaisical face makes Indu understand that she found the match incongruous. But in order to save her father from further complexities of her marriage, she poses a semblance of agreement and decides not to show her disagreement. Indu, on perceiving the displeasure in Mini towards her own marriage, requests her uncle to look for a better match. Anant rejects the idea stating:

> May be the boy is a little ugly, may be a little stupid... but everything else is fine. The family is good, it's known to us, they have money, she'll be quite comfortable. And Akka has promised she would pay for their wedding expenses as well as the dowry if this came through. What else could I ask for? (51)

Women, like Mini, who are always involved in the fetishes of traditions and household work, have no other option but to remain satisfied with the things provided. Women are also conditioned to merge their aspirations and desires with those of their aspirations and desires with those of their family. Mini, too, absorbs the trend established by the elder women of her family. She has been prepared for looking after the house and Akka's desire to educate her was not because of giving her an independent stand but because she feels that educated girls get a good match. Mini accepts:

> Of course I'm marrying him because there's nothing else I can do. I'm no good at studies. I never was. I went to school because...I had to. And then to college because Akka said I must go. Boys prefer graduates these days, she said. So I went. But I failed and it was a relief to give it up. There's only one thing I'm really good at...looking after a house. And to get a home, I have to get married. This is not my home, is it? (125)

As a matter of fact, Mini did not welcome this proposal of marriage wholeheartedly, but gave mute consent considering the problems of her father. Her parents' growing concern to settle her marriage fills her guilt—guilt for being a girl, guilt for remaining unmarried, guilt for being a burden on her family. She also feels humiliated when people rejected her on the pretext of her physical appearance or the manner of her dressing. After being interviewed and rejected several times she loses all her buoyance and enthusiasm towards marriage and her only wish is to get married at the earliest in order to save her parents from the imbroglio of groom hunt. She says:

> Any man, Indu? Yes, any man. Any man who says "Yes". You don't know what it has been like watching Kaka and Hemant and even Madhav Kaka running around after eligible men. (126)

Mini describes to Indu the efforts made by her *Kakas* and *Kakis* as well as her parents to wheedle and lure the boy and his family. Every time they rejected her, she felt downcast and blamed herself for putting her parents in distress. Mini expresses the reason behind her resolute silence and her inability to refuse the match fixed by her parents. She says:

> And finally, if everything was fine, there was the dowry. You know nothing of this, Indu. You're lucky. You escaped all this. And now, when someone has agreed, can I refuse and make Kaka go through all of it all over again? Just because the man isn't.... (126)

Mini perceives her husband's house as her final abode and her husband as an oracle. The Indian women have been accepting their husbands with their flaws and trying to live upto their desires and demands by transforming and moulding themselves. Their predecessors act as archetypes for them. They absorb the trends set by them which dictate the feminine qualities to be performed by women. Although these feminine qualities are imposed on them yet they find it difficult to free themselves from its bondage. Indu analyzes:

> What choice do I have, Indu? She asked me, resuming her snipping.... Millions of girls have asked this question millions of times in this country. Surely it was time they stopped asking it. What choice do I have? Surely it is this,

> this fact that I can choose, that differentiates me from animals. But years of blindfolding can obscure your vision so that you can no more see the choices. Years of shacking can hamper your movement so that you can no more move out of your cage of no choices. (125)

Among the myriad women characters, the old tyrannical matriarch Akka deserves special mention. She is rich and childless, and decides to stay in her brother's house after her husband's death. She wields absolute control over her brother's household, and her venomous tongue reduces Indu's grandfather *Kaka* into a tongue-tied, submissive character. Akka, representative of old order, is so obsessed with untouchability that she refuses to move into a hospital for fear of getting polluted by the touch of nurses belonging to lower castes. She is very particular about how a girl should conduct herself in society, and reprimands Indu for talking to a boy in the library. She is also dead against the idea of Naren's mother willing to learn music. She says:

> What—learn music from a strange man! Sit and sing in front of strangers! Like those women? Are we that kind of a family? Isn't it enough for you to sing one or two devotional songs, one or two *aarti* songs? What more does a girl from a decent family need to know? (50)

Only after her death Indu came to know about Akka's life from Narmada *Atya*. Akka was married at twelve and her husband—tall, bulky with coarse features—was well past thirty. On the contrary Akka was small, dainty, and pretty with round face, fair skin, straight nose and curly hair. She went to her husband house after six months. By the time she was thirteen, she made two unsuccessful attempts to run away from her husband's house. Her mother-in-law whipped her and kept her starved by locking her up in a room for three days. Then she was sent to her husband's room. Narmada *Atya* narrates the story of panic-stricken *Akka* trying to escape from her husband's and mother-in-law's brutal behaviour.

> But I heard that twice she tried to run away...a girl of thirteen. Her mother-in-law I heard, whipped her for that

> and locked her up for three days. Starved her as well. And then, sent her back to her husband's room. The child, they said, cried and clung to her mother-in-law saying, "Lock me up again, lock me up." But there was no escape from a husband then. I remember her telling me before my own marriage was consummated, "Now your punishment begins, Narmada. You have to pay for all those saris and jewels." (70)

Those days sex was a kind of punishment for child brides against which they could do nothing and continued to suffer in silence. Tara Ali Baig aptly observes: "Arch traditionalists that women are it is they who have successfully and brutally established man's ascendancy over women in society" (qtd. in Shirwadkar 1979: 26). Thus Deshpande, unlike a militant feminist does not put the blame squarely on man's shoulders but reveals the contradictions in a woman's character also.

Akka's husband was a wealthy man and he kept mistresses. She as a married woman was expected to bear children but she had many miscarriages due to the uncomfortable life she led. Her mother-in-law makes her life miserable for her inability to give birth to a living child. The chains of traditional marriage are heavy and the escape routes are not available to a wife, who often seeks consolation and refuge in obsessions, masochism or mental slavery often leading to her physical decay or death. She is supposed to bear her exploitation and sufferings with willing fortitude. Akka, too, has to endure and submit to insults, injuries and humiliations with a stoic patience and never complain.

A change in Akka's personality appears when her husband faces a stroke. The other side of her character is manifest in the way she controls her husband after he is struck by total paralysis. Although she takes every care of her sick husband for two years, but avenges herself of all that she had to forbear by not allowing his mistress. The situation has brought a change in her position. Earlier Akka was feeble, fragile and timid and so he saddled her but now he was dependent on the mercy of Akka. This is the reason she is not ready to succumb before his demands. She declares:

> It's my turn now. I've listened to you long enough. She came here. Twice. She wanted to see you. She cried and begged to be allowed to see you just for a short while. I threw her out. You'll never see her again. (71)

Thus, Deshpande makes a strong statement towards women. A husband can have a mistress with impunity for his physical and mental needs, whereas a wife cannot take another man—her act is branded as adultery. Another aspect of Akka is also manifest. She had undergone great mental and physical tortures. Even though she did not turn militant. Like an ideal Indian wife she forgives her tyrant husband and serves him day and night; but she is not all the time timid. She took the cudgel for her right over the husband by forcing the mistress run away.

Although Akka has undergone great suffering at her husband's house, on her return to her father's house after her husband's death, she enforces a rigid code of conduct on women in the household. She insists that a woman should never utter her husband's name because it is not only disrespect towards him but also shortens his lifespan. But Indu, an educated upper middle-class woman, reacts as to what connection there was "between a man's longevity and his wife's calling by name? It's as bad as praying to the *tulsi* to increase his lifespan" (32).

Indu, the protagonist of the novel has an estranged relationship with Akka. Like Mini, Indu was also advised by the elderly women as a child to inculcate in her the cherished feminine qualities as it was the only way to survive in male-dominated families. But Indu has her own dreams and promises herself not to become their replica. She recalls:

> As a child, they had told me I must be obedient and unquestioning. As a girl, they had told me I must be meek and submissive. Why? I had asked. Because you are a female. You must accept everything, even defeat, with grace because you are a girl, they had said. It is the only way, they said, for a female to live and survive. And I...I had watched them and found it to be true. There had to be, if not the substance, at least the shadow of submission. But still, I had laughed at them, and sworn I would never pretend to be what I was not. (158)

Indu's mother belonged to a different caste which was not appreciated by her father's family. Consequently, Govind, her father, developed revulsion and resentment towards them. After the death of his wife, he left the motherless daughter at the disposal of his family. Indu is shocked to see the rigidness in his fatherly duties. She gauges her father as a callous person:

> How else could he have parted leaving me, a fifteen-day-old motherless baby, with the family he hated and despised? He had not even come to see me until I was more than a year old. But that, perhaps, was because I was a girl. If I had been a son.... (163)

Indu "resented" her womanhood as she was made conscious of her femininity by the elder woman of her family. The onset of puberty perplexes her and makes conscious of her own body. Almost all the women protagonists of Shashi Deshpande's novels endure the restrictions of puberty imposed on them. She also focuses on the customs and rituals meant for women who expect them to perform 'fasts' and 'prayers' to earn eternal wifehood as well as peace and harmony for their family. Indu, too, perceives the women of her family involved in various rituals to perform them to secure good fortune. Indu, too, accepts life as a curse without a husband but she does not believe in the superstitious rituals supposed to save oneself from the widowhood. She is always accused of questioning the established norms and of being cleverer and more educated than her predecessors. She remarks: "It had always been thrown at me like an accusation. As if it was a disgrace to be clever. I had sobbed out my hurt to old uncle one day. And he had said, "For a woman, intelligence is always a burden, Indu. We like our women not think" (33).

Indu went ahead with her education and went for an inter-caste marriage with Jayant, who was of her choice. Like her mother, she was segregated from the family for transgressing the traditional mode of settling marriages. Deshpande has given us the glimpse of the rigid system of marriage in India which is decided not on the basis of compatibility but on caste, religion and dowry. Indu speaks against the traditional mode of settling marriages when she sees Mini being pushed into an incompatible marriage by their elders. In her marital life, Indu could not free herself from "the shadow of submission" (158).

In her march towards emancipation and self-hood, the contemporary Indian woman has to struggle against the insensitive fatality of options and the indoctrination of centuries which silently yet persistently endeavours to fashion her into the mould of "womanhood" as defined and defiled by the society. Simon de Beauvoir rightly remarks: "'The true woman' is an artificial product that civilization makes, as formerly eunuchs were made. Her presumed 'instincts' for coquetry, docility, are indoctrinated, as is phallic pride in man" (1997: 428). Indu moulds herself of satiate Jayant and prevents herself from retaliating as it will certify her marriage as a failure. Indu foresees it and decides to hide the frictions of her marital life from her family. She analyzes herself:

> The hideous ghost of my own cowardice confronted me as I thought of this...that I had clung tenaciously to Jayant, to my marriage, not for love alone, but because I was afraid of failure. I had to show them that my marriage, that I, was a success. Show whom? The world. The family, of course. And so I went on lying, even to myself, compromising, shedding bits of myself along the way. Which meant that I, who had despised Devdas for being a coward, was the same thing myself. I had killed myself as surely as he had done. (159)

Indu is interested in creative writing—a means to articulate her feminine voice, to forge moments in art that are arresting and original. To this Jayant says 'No' because they need money and they have a long way to go but "To go where?" (18), Indu could not ask for she had no rights to ask. Jayant betrays her hopes for harmony and integration, for peace and happiness. He fails to be her 'alter ego'. Neither is he 'a sheltering tree' to protect her in weal and woe. Instead she finds that she has relinquished her identity by surrendering before Jayant's masculinity, by becoming his wife. Willingly she yields to the demands of marriage and moulds herself upto the dictates of her husband. But she never blames him for it is women who 'tear' and who 'bear'. Indu exists and yet does not exist. There are women in our society who hate rearing of a child. They are simply sex objects who produce children and leave them to their lot. Indu is one such woman who does not believe in mothering. She is a woman who 'bears' and not the one who 'rears'. In an act of unreflecting defiance against patriarchy, she believes that a woman should deprive herself of the satisfaction that comes from not only bearing a child but playing a major role in his/ her personal development. In this sense she is an anti-radical. She says: "Having children...it isn't something you should think and plan about. You should just have them. And yes, I smiled to myself, end up like Sunanda-Atya. Pure, female animal" (115).

Marriage subjugates and enslaves woman. It leads her to "aimless days indefinitely repeated, life that slips away gently towards death without questioning its purpose" (Beauvoir 1997: 428). Women pay for their happiness at the cost of their freedom. Beauvoir emphasized that such a sacrifice all the part of a woman is too high for anyone since the kind of self-contentment and security that marriage offers woman trends her soul of its capacity for greatness:

> She shuts behind her the doors of her new home; when she was a girl, the whole countryside was her homeland, the forests were hers. Now she is confined to a restricted space, Nature is reduced to the dimensions of a potted geranium; walls cut off the horizon. But she is going to set about overcoming these limitations. (1997: 469)

Indu, true to her feminine virtues, plays the role of a wife. It restricts rather circumscribes her self development—firstly by taking away her freedom of thought and expression and secondly by denying her the scope of giving free play to her artistic potentiality. Regarding a woman's role playing, Rose Marie Tong observes:

> Sometimes women play their roles not so much because they want to be, as because they have to in order to survive economically and/or psychologically. Virtually all women engage in the feminine role playing. (1993: 208)

Even in her professional life, Indu has to curtail her freedom and submit to the dictates of the editor. She cannot give up her job which fails to be self-satisfactory. Jayant wants her to compromise with the profession of a writer. But could she compromise? The uncompromising Indu surrenders at times before Jayant just for show only. She is the embodiment of the feminist principle which is an uncompromising pledge and an antidote to exploitation and oppression of women. This uncompromising stance that Indu assumes is ventilated through her dialogic imagination. Women like Indu are alienated from the product upon which they work: their body. Tong further observes:

> A woman may say that she diets, exercises, and dresses for herself, but in reality she is probably shaping and adoring her flesh for man. A woman has little or no say about when, where, how or by whom her body will be used. (1993: 187)

Whatever Indu does, it is only to please Jayant, and to please him is her way of life:

> 'Now I dress the way I want. As I please'. As I please? No, that's not true. When I look in the mirror, I think of Jayant. When I dress, I think of Jayant. When I undress, I think of him. Always what he wants. What he would like. What would please him. And I can't blame him.... It's the way I want it to be. (49)

A woman's responding and relating to other's needs may detract her from her own sense of identity, of her becoming so fluid as to assume any shape. Indu feels as if she had become so fluid that she has no tangible shape, no form of her own. Without wants of her own, what is her identity in the family? Indu minus 'I' of course renders her an ideal woman—"A woman who sheds her 'I', who loses her identity in her husband" (49), a woman who bears everything without a drop of tear. Marriage has reduced into a state of "total surrender" (52). Through Indu, Deshpande voices her views of marriage:

> It's a trap...that's what marriage is. A trap? Or a cage? May be the comic strip version of marriage...a cage with

> two trapped animals glaring hatred at each other...isn't so wrong after all. And it's not a joke, but a tragedy. But what animal would cage itself? (60-61)

"Women's experience is primarily defined through interpersonal, usually domestic and familial relationship: serving the needs of others. Her identity exists largely on being-for others (needing to please: narcissist vanity and deriving security from her intimacy with others) rather than being-for-itself" (Wough 1989: 43). Indu experiences herself as a woman given to physical narcissism in her self-reflexive concern with the body often looking in the mirror, thus trimming of herself to please Jayant, to please her narcissist self. She loves being "looked at". In this context, it is quite relevant to note what Berger says:

> A woman must continually watch herself. She is almost continually accompanied by her own image of herself.... She has to survey everything she is and everything she does.... Her own sense of being in herself is supplanted by a sense of being appreciated as herself by another.... Men act and women appear. Men look at women. Women watch themselves being looked at.... The surveyor of women in herself is male: the surveyed female. Thus, she turns herself into an object—and most particularly an object of vision: a sight. (1972: 46-47)

Indu loathes womanhood for it is thrust upon a girl and for its association with the idea of "Uncleanliness" (79). In order to assert her rights to an independent existence, she longs to escape from the burden and responsibilities of womanhood. She fears her becoming a mother and hence her "introduction to the beautiful world of being a woman" (79):

> "Tell me Indu, why do you fight against your womanhood so much?"
>
> "Do I?"
>
> My womanhood...I had never thought of it until the knowledge had been thrust brutally, gracelessly on me the day I had grown up.
>
> "You're a woman now," *Kaki* had told me "You can have babies yourself."

> I, a woman? My mind flung off the thought with an amazing swiftness.... Felt an immense hatred for it. (78-79)

Indu fails to establish emotional rapport with Jayant for "it shocks him to find passion in a woman. It puts him off" (83). She confesses to Naren:

> When I'm like that, he turns away from me. I've learnt my lesson now. And so I pretend. I'm passive. And unresponsive. I'm still and dead. And now, when you tried to kiss me, I thought...this is Jayant. So that's all I am, Naren. Not a pure woman. Not a too faithful wife. But an anachronism. A woman who loves her husband too much. Too passionately. And is ashamed of it. (83)

Such is the paradoxical situation in which Indian women are enmeshed. Like Indu they lead ambivalent lives. They cherish within their hearts deep and profound love but when the occasion comes for expressing it they react. Willing to wound, they hesitate to strike. They are loyal and obedient women who have been nourished and reared by traditionally bogged society. Indu says:

> As a child, they had told me I must be obedient and unquestioning. As a girl, they had told me I must be meek and submissive. Why? I had asked. Because you are a female. You must accept everything, even defeat, with grace because you are a girl, they had said. It is the only way, they said, for a female to live and survive. (158)

Indu's problematic of "becoming" expresses Deshpande's feminist polemics against sexual and gender roles imposed upon women in a patriarchal malist culture. Such 'relative identity' or rather the 'received role models' distort and problematize her self-perception. Such a world reduces women like Indu to a mere thing or a mindless body. With her peremptory and subjugating voice, her feminine instinct for articulation is suppressed. Even ready to please Jayant, Indu acquiesces to his wills and desire and does everything to reflect his image. Indu gradually realizes that she does not exist for her but for Jayant, that archetype male, imperialistic and subjugating. She feels in her a sense of existential angst and insecurity. Look at a fear-stricken and lacerated woman railing at her family in a malist world, where a girl is never claimed but is set apart from others. She says:

> This is my family. These are my people. And yet...I hate them. I despise them. They're mean and petty and trivial and despicable. I had always told myself.... I won't be like them. I won't live like them. And I thought...I have got away. But to what, Naren? To what have I got away? Is that any better than this? Is there no more to life than this? Are we doomed to living meaningless, futile lives? Is there no escape? I'm afraid, Naren...I'm afraid.... (159-60)

Indu ultimately realizes that she has been chasing shadows, leaving her roots far behind in the family and in Jayant. Naren with whom she develops an adulterous relationship is a mere shadow to her. Naren has no permanent place in her memory. Hence, she decides to go back to Jayant whom she feels is totally innocent. It is she who is to be blamed for the marital discord in their lives. She has created a hell out of a heaven. She, the narcissist who "had locked herself in a cage and thrown away the keys" (85), has forgotten the roots, feeding on only dreams and shadows. She has failed in love. She has escaped from familial responsibilities of the home, chasing after oneirodynic and uncrystallising shadows. She realizes that marriage had stunted and hampered her individuality for she saw it as a 'trap' and not a bond and the home where the family is housed, she saw it as a 'cage'. Now she realizes that all those were mere illusion not reality and all struggles of her life was an act of futility:

> But what of my love for Jayant, that had been a restricting bond, tormenting me, which I had so futilely struggled against? Restricting bond? Was it not I who had made it so? Torment? Had I not created my own torment? Perhaps it was true.... There was only one thing I wanted now... and that was to go home.... The one I lived in with Jayant. That was my only home.... I would put all this behind me and go back to Jayant.... I knew I would not tell Jayant about Naren and me.... That had nothing to do with the two of us and our life together. But there were

> other things I had to tell him. That I was resigning from my job. That I would at last do the kind of writing I had always dreamt of doing. (186-87)

Indu resorts to freedom not only intellectually but sexually too. For, her sexual starvation forces her to seek recourse to extramarital sex-relation. Since her sex hunger is unfulfilled, she strives for expression through sexual relationship or affair with a man other than her husband. The solution given by Deshapande to the sexual predicament is ambiguous and argumentative particularly in the Indian context. The novelist's credo is "take refuge in the 'self' which means that the 'self' is not metaphysical but psychological". In her article "Sexual Predicament and Shashi Deshpande's Women," R. Mala has expressed her views:

> By this assertion to the self, Deshpande certainly takes her heroines to the pole of feminism, though she may not have aimed at propounding any such "ism" and there women have certainly begun their protest as indicated by their sexual emancipation. (1991: 57)

To some extent the similar idea has been expressed by Madhu Singh in her book-review:

> Having broken the sexual norms imposed on women, Indu is able to analyze her marriage and herself. She has lacked courage and in order to be loved has, has submitted to her husband: It is not "nothing" that she wanted from Jayant, "but to live without fear of being unloved, misjudged, misunderstood, displeasing, without the fear of failure" She has wronged her husband long before the act of bodily betrayal, by giving him less than her true self—"that was more dishonourable and dishonest". (1993: 21)

Thus Indu's uncompromising and paradoxical feminine self that frantically longed for self-expression for the articulation of her feminine voice, finally finds its root in the home and with her husband. Shadows disappear from vision and she sees the clear light of day with the realization and discovery of her authentic female self. Her experiences teach her that one should listen to the voice of one's conscience and be faithful to it. Freedom within marriage is possible if one dares to do what one believes is right and tenaciously follows it. This alone can bring harmony and fulfillment in life.

The meek, docile and humble Indu finally emerges as a bold, challenging, conscious and rebellious woman. She resigns her job, thus defying the male authority, hierarchy and the irony of a woman's masked existence. Her self-discovery is the frightening visions of the feminine self's struggle for harmony and sanity. She comes out of her emotional upheaval to lead a meaningful life with her husband Jayant. Her 'home-coming' is ironical since the home she had discarded becomes the place of refuge, solace and consolation. It is Akka's house which makes her realize many things and offers ample opportunities to know herself, her inner life. It is true that she is able to discover her roots—an independent woman and a writer and what the shadows are—a daughter, a mother and a commercial writer. She begins to see life in a new light. She remarks: "Yes, the house had been a trap too, binding me to a past I had to move away from. Now, I felt clean, as if I had cut away all the unnecessary, uneven edges off myself" (186).

Indu, now, feels a sense of hope for life for existence. She negates the ideas of non-existence. She says:

> No, there is no such thing. To accept it will be to deny the miracle of life itself. If not this stump, there is another. If not this tree, there will be others. Other trees will grow, other flowers will bloom, other fragrance will pervade other airs.... I felt as if I was watching life itself...endless, limitless, formless and full of grace. (184)

Indu's liberation is a biological-revolution. She detests the idea of woman as a 'rearing machine', a caretaker of the child. In playing such a role she yields herself, though reluctantly, before patriarchy—"the systematic subordination of woman" (Firestone 1970: 01). She seems to question herself as to why women should take care of the offspring. Why not men? Perhaps she wants to eliminate division of labour based upon sex—the sexual caste system.

Indu struggles hard to experience the realities of life. She analyses the actual cause of her distorted married life. She holds Jayant, her husband, responsible for it. Whenever she tried to share the troubled feeling with him, he called it only "nonsense" and nothing else. This becomes the crux of the problem. Jayant never bothers to understand what she really wanted. To be precise, we can say that there is no real communication between them. Finally she took the decision to leave Jayant when she found that there was no mutual understanding between them. But, the execution of this decision did not bring any relief to her. On the contrary when she went back to her parental home, she felt alienated though family comprised so many members. She felt void in her life there in absence of Jayant. Though the novelist does not mention any specific reason for her extra-marital sex relation with Naren, her cousin, yet it might be the lack of conjugal relation with her husband for a long time that is the biological and the psychological need for the young couple. The other reason might be the westernized education of Indu. She might have developed this contemptuous relation in order to teach Jayant a lesson. Whatsoever may be the cause of her rebellious behaviour, she realizes the ground realities of life. She recognizes her roots that are the homes of her father and husband. The impact or interference of Naren is just the temporary shadow.

The predicament of Indu represents the larger predicament of women in contemporary India where the new concepts of western education, economic independence and globalization have completely shaken the roots of old Indian culture and social values. The breaking up of the joint family—the school of inculcating dedication, sacrifice, moral values, etc.—is the immediate visible impact upon the Indian culture. It has adversely affected different relationship at different levels in general and husband-wife relationship in particular. In the old family pattern, there were no conflicts in the relationship of wife-husband, there was mutual understanding among the different members of the family, and there was a deep sense of respect for the elders, husbands; love and compassion for the children and special care for the disabled and orphans. These attributes were considered to be the essence of the Indian socio-cultural life.

No one could have imaged the extra-marital sex relation of Indu with Naren—none but one of her cousins. The novelist seems to have justified this incident by providing the equal liberty for women in having extra-marital sex relation as a few men have without any special social censure or contempt. The readers never find Indu indulged openly in this relation, rather in the darkness of night stealthily. This indicates that she is misguided or confused by the Western thought. The inner consciousness never allowed her to do so, it was just an act to taking revenge upon her husband, but she soon realized the ground realities of life. She realized that the plant of Western feminism can never survive or bear fruits in Indian soil as it is in the European countries. So, we can conclude that the love marriage of Indu with Jayant and extra-marital relation with Naren are the products of Western education as well as Western way of feminism. The other incidents in which Indu comes to terms with Jayant, her husband, and the decision not to tell Jayant the sex-relation with Naren proves the maturity of her mind leading to the Indian way of feminism and post-feminism. The novelist has very subtly conveyed the message of mutual understanding and co-operation between wife and husband. The Indian women need not to be rebellious like the Western feminists nor like the legendary meek and submissive Indian wives. The Indian women must seek their freedom within the periphery of marriage through mutual understanding without disrupting the Indian socio-cultural values.

The novel ends with a positive note with the hope of a new dawn. The novel depicts the permanent mark carved on the psyche of women by traditions, norms and conventions of the male-dominated society which prohibits them from exhibiting their true self. The mode and style of their development inculcates in them submissiveness; silence and passiveness which holds a strong hold on their psyche. Even modern, educated women consciously drape themselves with these traits and find themselves in a fix. Thus, Shashi Deshpande conveys the message that the modern Indian women should learn to conquer their fears and assert themselves. The novel comes to an end with a note of compromise rather than revolt and revenge which is the basic attribute of Indian feminism.

THE DARK HOLDS NO TERRORS

The Dark Holds No Terrors (1980) is Shashi Deshpande's second novel. This novel presents the condition of the women in the Indian society—her role model—and how the different types of women play their roles with their silence. The protagonist Sarita alias Saru is an educated, economically independent, middle class lady. She has been very much conscious of her gender as a child and loveless relationship with her parents and strained relation with her husband. These incidents lead to her agonizing search for herself. The novel begins with Saru's return to her parents' home after fifteen years of her marriage with the man she loved. Unfortunately, her relations with her husband Manu become unbearably strained and she comes back to her father's home for some solace. Here she gets a chance to think over her relationship with her husband, her children, her parents and her dead brother Dhruva. Saru being a girl and unwanted child becomes more unwanted due to her brother's death. She is on a perpetual war with her mother who could never forgive her for being alive when her brother died.

As Saru remembers her childhood experiences in the familiar surroundings of her parents' home, the novelist, through deft manipulation of the narrative, reveals the origin of her identity crisis. Whatever opportunities her middle class background provided for happiness and personal expression were spiked by the oppressive dominance of her mother who insisted on her conforming to the traditional way of life. She did not show any interest in Saru's education and personal advancement. Instead, she constantly snubbed Saru for one thing or the other, denied her the love and attention which Dhruva was given. Even her birthdays were never acknowledged whereas Dhruva's birthdays were celebrated nicely. She was not allowed to go around freely like her brother. Her mother made very unkind remarks about her dark complexion without considering how her words would hurt Saru's sentiments. Consequently, Saru grew up feeling herself an unwanted, unloved and insecure child. She remembers an incident:

> Don't go out in the sun. You'll get even darker.
> Who cares?
> We have to care if you don't. We have to get you married.
> I don't want to get married.
> Will you live with us all your life?
> Why not?
> You can't.
> And Dhruva?
> He's different. He's a boy. (45)

This type of blatant discrimination between Saru and her brother creates a sense of insecurity and hatred towards her parents, particularly mother. It causes the rebellious nature of Saru. Y.S. Sunita Reddy observes: "In this connection, Saru's mother's attitude is typical of most Indian mother and a common enough phenomenon in the Indian context" (2001: 51). Regarding the rebellious nature of Saru, Malashri Lal in the book-review "Good Luck to Entrepreneurs", expresses the possible reasons in the following lines:

> The deaths of two members of the family—Sarita's mother and little brother—are mysteriously linked with her; and suddenly the placidity of Baba's eyes begins to seem like hostility and Madhav's affectionate "Sarutai" sounds like an insistent reminder of her neglect of her dead brothers. Thereby hangs another tale of self-accusation and guilt-consciousness liberally sprinkled with flashback scenes juxtaposing the nightmares of childhood and nightmares of sexual brutality in wifehood. (1982: 169-70)

The accidental death of her brother by drowning brings a turning point in her life. She is haunted all her life by the memories of her mother accusing her of intentionally letting Dhruva die by drowning: "You did it. You did this. You killed him" (191). She, too, on her part has a guilty conscience as she considers herself responsible for having remained a mute spectator to her brother's death by drowning. She never denied the charge labelled against her by the mother. As G. Dominic Savio observes: "Dhruva's demise had always been her subconscious desire and there is a very thin demarcation between her wish and its fulfilment" (2001: 61). Shashi Deshpande thus reveals the social aspects of keen sibling jealousy born of a mother's undue fondness for the son.

As a growing girl, Saru had known the community rituals, customs, social and religious ceremonies, but her need of love and security had remained unfulfilled. As Muriel James and Dorothy Jongeward remark:

> At a deeper level of human encounter with rituals, pastimes, games and activities lies the potential that each person has for intimacy. Intimacy is free of games and free of exploitation. It occurs in those rare moments of human contact that rouse feelings of tenderness, empathy and affection.... Intimacy involves genuine caring. (1978: 64-65)

Even when studying medicines Saru felt some parts of her years for love and affection, the satisfaction that comes from close emotional contact. This explains why she felt pulled towards Manu when she happened to meet him in the medical college canteen one day. True, she looked at Manu through the dreamy eyes of a young girl who had wished that one day a fairy tale prince would appear and marry her in spite of her dark complexion. In the intermediate college where Saru had studied, Manu was "one of the known Names then" (50). She admired him for his debating and dramatic talents, and was the centre of talk in the ladies' room. Besides, he was a budding writer and poet. The chances of meeting flowered into a mutually fascinating friendship, and when Manu proposed to Saru, she could hardly believe it. She deserted her parents to marry him, but she was still troubled by the fear that the loving words might turn out to be untrue and then she would know she was never loved.

Saru, unloved and unwanted, develops hatred towards the traditional practices during her impressionable years. Her hatred towards her mother is so acute that she becomes rebellious just to hurt her. "I hated her, I wanted to hurt her, wound her, make her suffer" (142). This hatred makes her to leave home for Bombay to seek medicine as a career. In the Medical College she falls in love with Manu, a College mate and marries him against her parents' wishes. Her orthodox mother was dead against marrying her daughter to a man of lower caste:

> What caste is he?
>
> I don't know.
>
> A Brahmin?
>
> Of course not.
>
> Then cruelly...his father keeps a cycle shop.
>
> Oh, so they are low-caste people, are they?
>
> The word that her mother had used, with the disgust, hatred and prejudice of centuries had so enraged her that she had replied.... I hope so. (96)

It seems if her mother had been a loving mother, Saru could have dropped her idea of marrying Manu, a man of lower caste. Her marriage had hurt her mother's feelings deeply; but she (mother) herself was responsible for it by neglecting her daughter. Saru later recollects:

> If you hadn't fought me so bitterly, if you hadn't been so against him, perhaps I would never have married him. And I would not have been here, cringing from the sight of letters, fighting with terror at the sight of his handwriting, hating him and yet pitying him too. (96)

It is remarkable here that she was deprived of parental love and security. It was her utmost desire to be loved. She gets the fulfilment of this deprived love when she gets attention from Manu. She wonders, "How could I be anyone's beloved? I was the redundant, the unwanted, an appendage one could do without" (66).

The demand of the time was a relation for her with someone who could give her love and an assurance of security. She thinks: "The fisherman's daughter couldn't have been more surprised when the king asked her to marry him, than I was by Manu's love for me" (66). Later when her relations became strained with Manu she regrets for having tied herself in the wedlock unconditionally: "The fisherman's daughter was wiser. She sent the king to her father and it was the father who bargained with him, while...I gave myself up unconditionally, unreservedly to him. To love him and to be loved" (66). The circumstances which forced her taking such a step are the products of her parents' rigidness and orthodox beliefs. Sunita Reddy has aptly remarked: "If her mother had provoked her by her blatant hostility, her father had contributed to her present predicament by remaining a mute spectator in the family drama" (2001: 51).

Saru considers herself the luckiest woman on the earth, as the early years of her marriage are sheer bliss. Manu is her savior because he saves her from the hostile environment in her parents' house. He proves himself the romantic hero who rescues Saru —a damsel in distress. She marries to regain her lost love in her parental home and her identity as an individual. As S.P. Swain writes: "Her marriage with Manu is an assertion on and affirmation of her feminine sensibility" (1990: 35-36). Though Saru is educated in the Western style, she refrained herself from any kind of pre-marital relation with her lover; but, after marriage, she reveals the pleasure and pain of sex relation with Manu in detail and wild abandon:

> I became in an instant a physically aroused woman, with an infinite capacity for loved and giving, with a passionate desire to be absorbed by the man I loved. All the clichés, I discovered, were true, kisses were soft and unbearably sweet, embraces hard and passionate, hands caressing and tender, and loving, as well as being loved, was an intense joy. It was as if little nerve ends of pleasure had sprung up all over my body. (40)

The initial years of marriage were full of joy for the young couple as their physical lust got satisfied; but with the passage of time both experienced the ground reality of life. Even her dingy one-room apartment with "the corridors smelling of urine, the rooms with their dank sealed in odours" (40) is "a heaven on earth" for her. Soon she realizes that happiness is temporary. She remarks how a particular incident becomes a turning point in their blissful marital relationship. One night she returns home late in her bloodstained coat as she had helped the victims in a fire accident in a nearby factory. In this way the people of the locality came to know her identity, and she gained recognition. Thereafter, people started to come to her for medical treatment and other related matters. This social recognition of hers generates a sense of inferiority complex and jealousy in Manu. In the beginning she does not realize it. Her success as a reputed doctor becomes the cause of her strained marital relations with Manu. She says: "He had been the young man and I his bride. Now I was the lady doctor and he was my husband" (42). Manu feels uncomfortable with his wife's growing popularity. Since Saru was a doctor, people used to visit her almost all the time; but Manu feels ignored as he is not greeted and paid attention. On the other hand, he also felt ignored by his wife because she had not enough time to spend with him. Manu and Saru want to move out to some other place for their own reasons. While Manu feels humiliated and embarrassed, Saru is no longer happy in that compound and stinking apartment and wants to move into something more decent. Earlier she was happy and contented to live on Manu's salary but in her new role as earning women she becomes discontented. She says:

> For me, things now began to hurt...a frayed sari I could not replace, a movie I could not see, an outing I could not join in. I knew now that without money life became petty and dreary. The thought of going on this way became unbearable. (92)

Manu does not love her as he used to love earlier. Saru, too, begins to hate this man-woman relationship, which is based on need of attraction and not love. She hates the word "love" now. She realizes that there is no such thing between man and woman. With the passage of time, some new circumstances emerged in which she felt gradual disappearance of love and attachment towards husband and children. One night Manu behaved as if he had desperate need of conjugal relationship, but when he tried to possess her he failed. All efforts of Saru at rationalizing away the event as "It was his failure. It had nothing to do with her" (87) failed to calm her troubled conscience. Earlier in the day she had told Manu that her boss whom they called Boozie had offered her a loan and now she could have her own consulting room. She had expected Manu to say something, to ask "why", but he kept silent. As Saru grew in social esteem and became the main economic support for the family, Manu's behaviour began to change.

It is true that Boozie is flirtatious in nature and Saru has no aversion towards flirts. Their relation comes to a stage when Boozie helps her financially to set up her own practice in a posh area. Saru, blind in love, is unscrupulous in her relationship with Boozie and consoles herself by treating it as a mere teacher-student relationship. She tells herself:

> It was just a teacher-student relationship. If he put his hand on my shoulder, slapped me on my back, held my hand or hugged me...that was just his mannerism and meant nothing. It had nothing to do with me and Manu. (91)

Both had their vested interests in sustaining such a relation. Boozie openly flaunts his relationship with Saru to hide his homosexual nature and Saru wanted to exploit him through her feminine tricks to achieve her much coveted goal of becoming an established, reputed doctor. Even at the inauguration of her consulting room, when Boozie flaunts her by his side openly before the invitees to the programme, she feels resentful towards her husband:

> I could feel the stares. Everyone's except Manu's. Who would not look at us. And I should have hated him then... not Manu, for he had done nothing then for which I could hate him, but this attractive, ravishingly masculine man who was doing this deliberately. Attracting attention to the two of us. But, funnily enough, it was not him I hated. It was Manu for doing nothing. (94)

But Saru's rise in social and financial status in contrast to Manu's status of an underpaid lecturer sets in great discomfort in their conjugal relation. Her contentment in career is no match to her discontentment at home. As Saru grew in social esteem and became the main economic support of the family, Manu's behaviour began to change. The warmth between them cooled off. Saru is assailed by feelings of guilt. It was she who had persuaded Manu to give up writing poetry, abandon the plan of starting a journal, and instead take up the job of a lecturer in a local college, thinking that it was more respectable job for the husband of a doctor. Her professional work kept her away from home for the better part of the day and she knew she was neglecting her home, her husband and children. It was a tactless remark of a friend of Saru which finally precipitated a crisis in the married life. Saru and Manu met her in a store and told her they were planning a holiday in Ooty. And she quipped they could think of Ooty because Saru was a successful doctor. She asks: "How does it feel when your wife earns not only the butter but the bread as well?" (35). A psychologically hurt Manu, smarting from a sense of being dominated, tried to assert his manliness by assaulting her that night. It is the sense of an emotional togetherness that validates the sex act. Earlier Saru had treasured the moments in bed with Manu. "I was insatiable, not for sex, but for love. Each act of sex was triumphant assertion of our love. Of *my* being loved. Of *my* being wanted. If I ever had any doubts, I had only to turn to him and ask him to prove his love for me" (40).

But now the marital life becomes a nightmare for Saru. She can no longer stand the mighty assault, a savage Manu at night, and a normal-looking Manu during the day. She asserts the cruel behaviour meted out to her at night by her frustrated husband in the following lines. "He attacked me like an animal that night. I was sleeping and woke up and there was this...this man hurting me. With his hands, his teeth, his whole body" (201). She tolerated everything. She says: "I could do nothing against him. I couldn't fight back. I could not shout or cry, I was so afraid the children in the next room would hear. I could do nothing. I can never do anything. I just endure" (201).

It is undeniably true that she has achieved economic independence, but her condition is miserable, as she has to perform double roles. Besides practising medicine she has to fulfil the assigned duty of a housewife. Once she proposed to give up her medical practice, but Manu dissuaded her from doing so, as it would be difficult to maintain their standard of living on his meager income. She is not well satisfied with her small salary and Manu's uncertain income as a journalist. Apart from it, she felt humiliated as the wife of an unemployed man. Only on her persuasion, he managed to get the job of a lecturer in a private college. Manu protested fearing it would stifle his aspirations. But to her "My husband teaches a college" sounded more respectable than "My husband is a Journalist" ultimately both of them are caught in the money web. Parvati Bhatnagar holds Saru equally responsible for the strained relation in the married life.

> When Saru had got married she had sworn that she would never dominate over her husband because there is something about female domination which ultimately destroys the man. It baffled in doing that which she had shorn never to do and destroyed Manu's manhood. She had actually murdered him. It hurt Manu to be pushed into a corner of insignificance and he reacted by becoming over aggressive so that she shuddered at the very thought of his touch. (2001: 55)

Manu's beastly behaviour with Saru at nights became intolerable for her. At this juncture she comes to know about her mother's death. Though she had taken a firm decision not to return to her parents' home, yet she went back to her parental home. It is not so that her heart was purged of the hatred for her dead mother. It was just a pretext to go there and get rid of Manu who behaved like a beast, like a rapist, like a sadist at nights but pretended to be normal during day times. She also seems to be ready for giving explanations for elopement. At her father's house she objectively mulls over the reasons of her disastrous marriage. She blames herself for it as she easily identifies the consequences of the shattered male ego. She seems to suffer from guilty feelings: "My brother died because I heedlessly turned my back on him. My mother died alone because I deserted her. My husband is a failure because I destroyed his manhood" (217). But what Shashi Deshpande wants to reflect is the gender discrimination by parents towards their children, and the compulsion to perpetuate male-dominance if the marriage is to be kept going. As such, she has successfully portrayed the gross gender discrimination prevailing in our society.

When she comes back to her parents' home in detached condition of mind, she feels strange despite the fact that nothing had changed in the house, not even the seven pairs of large stone slabs leading to the front door upon which she used to play hopscotch during her childhood. Her father also appeared to be strange when he talked like an unwilling host to her as if she were an unwelcome guest. As a matter of fact she needed sympathy at that juncture of time but he did nothing to console her. She remembers the fate of a sister of her friend's who had come home after her disastrous marriage. She remembers how she had received care and sympathy from her parents because her marriage was an arranged one; the parents too shared her misfortune. As Saru's marriage was not an arranged one, she holds herself solely responsible for her ill fate. She suffers from guilty feelings. She is completely confused and feels that she has done great injustice towards her brother, mother, husband and children.

Though Saru was against the social norms framed for women by the male-dominated society, yet she seems to have come to terms with them. Once she presented a perfect recipe for a successful marriage. On being asked by her friend Nalu to talk on medicine as a profession for women, to a group of college students, she remarks:

> A wife must always be a few feet behind her husband. If he's an M.A., you should be a B.A. If he's 5′4″ tall, you shouldn't be more than 5′3″ tall. If he is earning five hundred rupees, you should never earn more than four hundred and ninety-nine rupees. That's the only rule to follow, if you want a happy marriage. Don't ever try to reverse the doctor-nurse, executive-secretary, principal-teacher role. It can be traumatic, disastrous. And, I assure you, it isn't worth it. He'll suffer. You'll suffer and so will the children. Women's magazines will tell you that a marriage should be an equal partnership. That's nonsense. Rubbish. No partnership can ever be equal. It will always

> be unequal, but take care that it's unequal in favour of your husband. If the scales tilt in your favour, god help you, both of you. (137)

Saru also introspects her relationship with Padmakar, her classmate in medical college. After a few meetings she dissuades him for attempting to develop a deeper relationship with her. She does so because she had experienced that such a relationship was not sufficient enough to provide any comfort in her life. Now she had no illusions about romance or love for these two words had lost relevance in life: "Love? Romance? Both, I knew too well, were illusions.... And for me, sex was now a dirty word" (133). She could not achieve any happiness and fulfilment through her relations with Boozie and Padmakar. These extra-marital relations are not any kind of substitute and compensation for her strained married life. Kamini Dinesh's remarks are noteworthy: "There cannot be an 'escape route' from the tension of married life. The woman seeking a crutch has, finally, to fall back on herself" (1995: 200).

The novelist contrasts Saru's life with the lives of her two school friends—Sunita and Nalu. Sunita leaves effort to pose as a happy married woman. All the time she talks about her intimacy with her husband as if she were a non-entity without him, which only invokes pity in the eyes of the reader and hatred of her two friends. Nalu also questions her as to why she let her husband change her name from Sunita to Anju: "Do you have to surrender so easily?" (117). Nalu is contemptuous of Sunita's constant references to her husband and hates her for her submissive attitude of satisfying every whim of his. She tells her, "Well, I refuse to call you Anju or Geetanjali or whatever. To me you are Smita and will always be Smita"(118).

On the other hand, Nalu, a spinster, is a teacher and lives with her brother and his family. Saru contrasts Nalu with the Nalu of her college days who was full of enthusiasm. But bitterness has crept into her, and Saru does not blame her bitterness on her spinsterhood. Saru feels that it would be wrong to say that Nalu "is bitter because she never married, never bore a child. But that would be as stupid as calling me fulfilled because I got married and I have borne two children" (121).

Deshpande contrasts the lives of Saru, Sunita and Nalu and shows that a wife, a mother and a spinster had their own share of joys and sorrows, and it is almost difficult to conclude as to who is the happier or the more fulfilled.

Saru tries her level best to keep the married life smooth, by proposing to her husband that she might give up her profession. But Manu likes to live in comfort and without her money that is not possible. If Saru had accepted his double behaviour, the marriage would continue, and Manu would be happy. But Saru does not like the self-deception, and that is why she has to find out a way. As Saru herself says her marriage would have continued its normal way, if she would have been different, "would it have happened in any case, what happened to us later, he being what he is and I being what I am?" (42). It might have been so. What really matters is that man's image of himself as a superior being. It is the wife who has to break away from old images of womanhood and assert her ways, shape her life fearlessly without feeling any guilt for deviating from the tradition rooted role models of Sita, Gandhari or Savitri. Deshpande avoids on the one hand, the obsession what the Western feminists feel and on the other hand presents the Indian version of the modern woman who searches for the whole of her identity—not fragmentations of herself. Out of the swirling restlessness Saru emerges a whole woman who is not dependent on anyone outside her. P. Venugopalan, in an article, rightly remarks:

> She undertakes to educate herself on how to live a trauma free life. Sarita's education, spread through girlhood, wifehood, and motherhood culminates in her becoming the 'Woman'. That is, at the end of the novel, she emerges as a confident individual who is no more afraid to live like a woman in the Indian conservative society characterized by overriding patriarchy the practitioners of which can surprisingly be women themselves, as Kamala, Sarita's mother proves in the novel. (2002: 16)

The novelist carefully and cautiously avoids the pitfall of feminist separation, in order to deny female dependence on male culture that is historically inaccurate. An existence without relation to society, a life in isolation is no existence. Saru, in the final scene, displays courage, her commitment to herself, and an affirmation of life and society. In her book-review, Meenakshi Mukherjee has remarked:

> Saru's consciousness is not untouched by her experience as a doctor. She analyses her own physical and psychological trauma with the detachment of an analyst. Her dilemma is not miraculously resolved at any point though there is a hint at the end, confirmed by epigraph from *Dhammapada*—of Saru's realization that one has to be sufficient within oneself because there is no other refuge elsewhere. (1981: 33)

Ragini Ramchandra in a review expresses almost the same opinion:

> From the final hinting of a possible reconcilement between the rebel protagonist and her husband, (despite it somewhat 'forced' appearance), it could be argued that the novelist is after all in the mainstream of Indian tradition. The realization at the end of the novel that "the only thing is to go on as if it real knows all the while it is only an illusion" supports the view, not to speak of the promise of hope in the title. (1986: 121)

Gur Pyari Jandial, in an article, mentions:

> *That Long Silence* is a scathing critique of our social system which stifles the growth and free expression of the individual. Women are put into slots—wife, daughter, sister, mother. Like Indu, Jaya is also a writer, but social and family pressures never allow her talent to flower or her identity to blossom. (2003: 119)

Deshpande has successfully and artistically presented the situation the modern Indian woman faces, and presents her as a person not crucified individual but a purposeful, conscious being. The present day Indian woman is neither like the typical Western liberated woman nor like an orthodox Indian one. Deshpande does not let herself get overwhelmed by the Western feminism or its militant concept of emancipation. In quest for the wholeness of identity, she does not advocate separation from the spouse but a tactful assertion of one's identity within marriage.

III

Both the novels *Roots and Shadows* as well as *The Dark Holds No Terrors* reflect the pictures of the inner world of women who are striving towards self-realization. Protagonists of these novels are actively engaged to trace out their identity as an independent being. Both Indu and Saru try to find meaning in marriage and try to retain at the same time their own individuality. In an article "On the Writing of a Novel", Deshpande herself has remarked:

> Marriage invariably takes you to the world of women, of trying to please, of the fear of not pleasing, of surrender, of self abnegation. To love another and to retain yourself intact—is that possible? To assert yourself and not be aggressive, to escape domination and not to dominate? (1991: 35)

Indu, the protagonist of *Roots and Shadows*, is highly sensitive, intelligent and educated lady who can be the role-model of modern young women. On being hated, suppressed and neglected in the family, she breaks the boundary line of the family prestige and marries Jayant. She affirms: "I had felt that in marrying him, I had become complete. I had felt incomplete, not as a woman, but as a person. And in Jayant, I had thought I had found the other part of my whole self" (114). But this realization does not last long and comes to realize that marriage makes one dependent. She loses her identity in marriage with Jayant. She does not find herself different from her mother. It is undeniably true that she loves Jayant and wants him at all times. But the self-same love seems to be shacking. She says:

> What I feel for Jayant...can I compress all of it within this world? It is so much more, so overwhelming a response of the whole of me to him. Sometimes I wonder if I will leave him one day and live by myself. The only way in which I can be myself, my whole self again. (88)

Indu finds herself stifled and suppressed when she failed to come to terms either with her love for her husband or her true self. She realizes that her marriage is robbing her of her identity as a being apart from her husband. Her realization that she is also being moulded into the very image of woman which she had tried to break away from, worries her. In the first phase of her youth, she wanted to prove herself the pioneer of the new generation. It would not be an exaggeration to say that it was the sole reason of her rebellious nature which leads her marriage to Jayant breaking the norms of society. But it could not stand to the touchstone of time. Sometimes she curses herself for her miseries. "Always what he wants what he would like. What would please him. And I can't blame him. It's not he who has pressurized me into this. It's the way I want it to be.... Have I become fluid, with no shape, no form of my own?" (49).

Indu does not admit her failure in selection of her life partner and drags herself in the strained married life. Her passionate love for Jayant confuses her all the time "as if there is something shameful in total commitment" (143). Her conflict is resolved only after meeting Naren to whom she confesses as a woman: "I felt hedged in, limited by my sex. I resented my womanhood because it closed so many doors to me" (79).

Even in her professional life she is expected to curtail her freedom and submit to the demands of her editor. In other words she submits herself to the society. She is so much compelled by the circumstances that she cannot resign from the post. Jayant advises her to compromise: "What can one person do against the whole system! No point making a spectacle of yourself with futile gestures. We need the money, don't we? Don't forget, we have a long way to go" (17).

It is quite obvious that Indu is not happy with Jayant even though she dare not leave him. What she longs for is completeness within herself which she finds not so easy to achieve:

> This is my real sorrow. That I can never be complete in myself. Until I had met Jayant I had not known it...that there was somewhere outside me, a part me without which I remained incomplete. Then I met Jayant. And lost the ability to be alone. (31)

When Indu returns her parental home after an interval of ten years on the summons of Akka, it comes as a revelation to Indu. It is the occasion when she really comes to know Akka, Atya and others in the family. If her sexual encounter with Naren reveals her passionate self to her, the reentering of the ancestral home makes clear to her as nothing else does, what is wrong with her marriage. Naren who was so natural to her and the easy compatibility that develops between the two, makes her to take the most daring step of surrendering herself to him not once but twice in the novel. She indulges in the act with much wild abandon and cherishes it later without any guilt consciousness.

With the passage of time, she comes to realize the lacking in her relationship with Jayant. She, who had sworn proudly that she would never pretend, pretended before Jayant, her husband by not revealing to him her whole self but revealing only that he wanted to see. In the act of pretendness, she had wronged both herself and Jayant. She realized that there was nothing shameful in her need for Jayant. It did not degrade her from a normal human being. She did not deter from the chosen path. Akka had left a big legacy for her but she spent the money for Mini's wedding and found a better way of spending the money. At last, Indu achieved what she had been aiming for personal freedom and completeness and integrity within herself. Her decision not to reveal to Jayant about Naren proves this: "That had nothing to do with the two of us and our own life together" (187). Indu's quest for selfhood is now fulfilled. She realizes the roots and affirms her individuality: "There were other things I had to tell him. That I was resigning my job. That I would at last do the kind of writing I had always dreamt of doing" (187).

As Indu, in *Roots and Shadows*, belongs to a tradition bound family; so Saru in *The Dark Holds No Terrors* belongs to a tradition bound family which leaves scars on her psyche. Sharing the similar backdrop as that of Indu, Saru has no love lost for her family, especially her mother. Since she bears the stigma of discrimination in the family only on the sexual basis, she develops a severe hatred towards her mother. The words of discrimination uttered by her mother made a permanent imprint on the tender mind of child Saru. She remembers: "He's different. He's a boy" (45). These words establish the tradition-bound Indian mother against whom Saru has to rebel all her life. Her anger makes her revolt against her mother: "If you are a woman, I don't want to be one" (63). Much against the family sentiment, she seeks the medical profession. The second incident of revolt is observed when she marries Manu breaking all the social taboos of caste. Defiance seems to be the second nature to Saru: "She defies her mother to become a doctor, defies her caste to marry outside, and defies social conventions by using Boozie to advance her career" (Kumar 1983: 821). Saru realizes that her marriage to Manu instead of the expected freedom led her once again into unwanted bondage.

Saru's success as a doctor brings a strain in her marital life and disintegeration in her relationship with Manu. She affirms: "He had been the young man and I his bride. Now I was the lady doctor and he was my husband" (42). Saru's success brings insecurity in Manu and Saru recognizes the fact: "Now I know that it was there it began...this terrible thing that has destroyed our marriage" (42). Though Saru's success as a doctor is intolerable for Manu, yet he does not ask her to give it up. He cannot do without the material comforts made available by Saru. He tries to soothe his male ego by asserting himself over Saru physically. This transformation from a doting husband into a sadist invokes terror in the heart of Saru. Saru comes to detest the word love: "Love...how she scorned the word now" (72). Despite her hatred of Manu's sexual sadism Saru refuses to take any action and loathes to admit failure. Like Indu of *Roots and Shadows*, Saru also refrains from announcing it to the world that her marriage has been a failure. She admits: "I have been clinging to the tennous shadow of a marriage whose substance has long since disintegrated because I have been afraid of proving my mother right" (200). She admits: "I had come away from my parents in a fever of excitement after the last battle. The die was cast, the decisions taken, my boats burnt. There could be no turning back. There would be no turning back. Then, this ridiculous anti-climax" (37). Saru came back to her father's home only to experience her mother's total rejection to herself: "Daughter? I don't have any daughter. I had a son and he died. Now I am childless" (196). Nevertheless, she is racked by a terrible feeling of guilt:

> There can never be any forgiveness. Never any atonement. My brother died because I heedlessly turned my back on him. My mother died alone because I deserted her. My husband is a failure because I destroyed his manhood. (217)

It seems Saru marries Manu defiantly in order to get away from the mother who accused her of having killed her brother. But, unfortunately this support turns out to be nothing but a mirage. She comes back to her parental home in a frustrated mood. Even the parental home does not provide the expected refuge. Instead of feeling overjoyed at being back home she feels suffocation. She even fails to relate to her father: "As she drank her tea... too sweet and strong...he sat gingerly on the edge of his chair, like an unwilling host entertaining an unwelcome guest. And that, I suppose is what, I really am. What gave me the idea that I could come back? (18). Feeling like a "homeless refuge" Saru "knelt down in front of her suitcase which, like a homeless refugee, still lay desolately in the hall...which is my room? I have none..." (32).

In the due course of time Saru realizes that neither Manu nor her father can be her refuge. She has to seek her own refuge and find her true self. This journey into herself reveals to her that she has to be at peace with herself before achieving anything: She decides "not to pretend anymore, not to struggle —it brought nothing but solace" (198). Integrity is the key to wholeness and she realizes:

> The guilty sister, the undutiful daughter, the undutiful wife...all persons spiked with guilt. Yes, she was all of them, she could not deny that now. She had to accept these selves to become whole again. But if she was all of them, they were not all of her. She was all these and so much more. (220)

Learning to trust oneself is the first step towards self-actualization and Saru is able to achieve this. Her earlier doubts as to retaining her professional integrity as a doctor evaporate in air as she tends to Sunita's illness. She tells her father: "And, oh yes, Baba, if Manu comes, tell him to wait. I'll be back as soon as I can" (221).

With this self-realization occurs the tacit understanding that any meaningful relationship is interdependent. In fact, Shashi Deshpande has successfully tried to portray in her fictions to present an image of modern young women struggling to synthesize both their professional and private lives. Maria Miles has expressed the same idea:

> The career woman (today) has not only to face the opposition of her surroundings and to struggle against many objective obstacles, but she is often divided in herself because she often subscribes to the Indian idea of womanhood. Her problems arise, firstly, from the contradictions between this image and the demand of a new social situation and then from the discrepancy between new aspirations and lack of opportunity. (1980: 130)

This is the self-same situation which the protagonists of *Roots and Shadows* and *The Dark Holds No Terrors* have to face. Both Indu and Saru have similar predicament in life. Both hate the suppression faced at home, have their respective parental homes, got married to the man of their choice in a gesture of rebellion, find marriage to be an entrapment rather than haven, try to take refuge in their ancestral homes. Finally, they engage themselves in self-exploitation, realize "their own truths" and assert their individuality.

In order to achieve their freedom, both Indu and Saru seek marriage as an alternative to the bondage created at their parental homes. They reset the role of a daughter and look forward to their new roles in life with hope; but it proves to be an illusion. Indu's marital relationship with Jayant and Saru's with Manu is not quite dissatisfactory. The financial and professional success leads to discord and disharmony in both the cases. They experience sexual disappointment and humiliation. Both entered into extra-marital relationship which also proved to be equally dissatisfactory. Indu's sexual encounter with Naren provides new insights into her own self which proves to be as meaningless as that of Saru's in the end. Saru's affair with Boozie fails to provide any sexual fulfilment either. Both Indu and Saru find love to be more physical than anything else. Saru declares: "Love...how she scorned the word now. There was no such thing between man and woman. There was only a need which both fought against, futilely...turning into the thing they called love" (72). Indu is equally scornful of love. She says: "Love is a big fraud, a hoax, that's what it is...it's false" (157). They are not endowed with any guilty feelings about their extra-marital affairs. They seem to take it in their stride and even feel proud about it.

Thus, we can conclude that both Indu and Saru think marriage hampers their individuality and see it more as a "trap" rather than a "bond". Despite their disillusionment with marriage and all that it entails, they are able to preserve their identity, realizing their own personal and private limitations. Thus, they become sign and signature of new women of today who claim to be equal to their male counterparts in all spheres of life. Secondly, they love freedom and autonomy and make personal decision of their fate for which they themselves are fully responsible. Yet, the heroines have been able to come out from the traditional, socio-cultural and familial structure which make them independent and emancipated for which they fight as true feminists.

Feminism in *That Long Silence* and *The Binding Vine*

4

Since the dawn of independence in India, many changes in social, political, literary and economic milieu have taken place. The most important and noteworthy change in Indian English fiction is the emergence of a new interest in the plight of Indian women in a rapidly changing social milieu. Many novelists have made attempts to analyse the predicaments of women from various angles. Though the problems of women have been drawing the attention of all major Indian Writers in English, these problems have formed the bulk and core of the creative output of Indian women novelists writing in English. The contribution of women writers to the variety and validity of the Indo-Anglian novel is appreciable. The women writers' fictions provide searching insight and ample deal of human understanding. The potential of human achievement can be realized through their writings. Without assessing the work done by these writers, no one can gather the implications on Indo-English fiction.

The feminist struggle for liberation can also be looked upon within the framework of freedom crisis. Woman, born to be free as man, finds herself constrained and curbed by the patriarchal society, not only in India but in most parts of the world. This is due to the primarily patriarchal culture of the world. Woman has been treated as the subordinate sex and has to conform to male standards. Feminist writers of the Western countries identify a search and a rebellion in the pattern of women's lives, a rebellion against the patriarchal core of society, and this is transmuted into artistic expression. The assertion of woman's right to freedom is present at least in thinking and has a reasonable bearing on society. On the other hand, in India, works of feminine plan for freedom have only been isolated and lonely cries in the wilderness, mute and desperate calls to reconstruct the groove of society. In a book-review, T.N. Dhar observes:

> Deshpande, however, gives a specific dimension to Jaya's identity-crisis, because her awareness of herself had remained buried under the overpowering weight of custom and tradition which rule our lives in India. (1990: 7)

The woman has been the silent sufferer from the time immemorial. She as silent sufferer, forever waiting for creative and emotional release in the opening out of the womb in case of the ordinary, or the flowering of artistic expression in the case of the 'different' woman, seems to be a role pattern in the fiction of Indian women writers. The agony of waiting offers the tension and the complication while the suffering offers the fictional material. The resolution comes forth in different forms. In Kamala Markandaya, for example, resolution always comes as reconciliation with society while for Anita Desai it is submission to a more or less malignant fate. In the fiction of Shashi Deshpande, there is triumph after the long silence. There is a battle and there is pain. But, in the long run comes victory. Adele King, in a book-review, opines:

> In spite of its ambiguous ending, Deshpande's novel seems less pessimistic than many contemporary women's novels. Perhaps this is because of the allusion to Jaya's family, a series of aunts and uncles who represent an order within which she may begin to function. Jaya, not burdened with romantic questions about whether she loves her husband, is able to see her relationship to him in realistic terms. This view of family and society is the major way in which the Indian experience of being a woman differs from the western one. (1988: 727)

Shashi Deshpande's *That Long Silence* (1988), acclaimed masterpiece of feminist writing in Indo-Angalian fiction, is an expression of the silence of the modern Indian woman. Many women writers have tried their hands at expressing the long silence which had turned woman into non-entities, but they could only provide the psychological depths to their characters. They presented either the unreal sentimental romances or succumbed to the temptation of mouthing feminist ideology. But Shashi Deshpande's success lies in her representation of real life experience. This novel of hers highlights the image of the middle class woman sandwiched between tradition and modernity. Anjali Yardi, in a review of *That Long Silence* has opined thus:

> *That Long Silence* is Deshpande's fifth novel; its level of craftsmanship is as high as its commitment to literary values is strong. Although the story is filtered through the consciousness of the first person narrator Jaya, the other characters have a flesh-and-blood individuality. Jaya, for example, quite distinct from her friend Mukta on the one hand and her cousin Kusum on the other, as these two are from one another. (1990: 20)

It depicts the inner conflict of Jaya, the protagonist, and her quest for the self or identity. Deshpande herself says:

> And then I wrote *That Long Silence* almost entirely a woman's novel nevertheless, a book about the silencing of one-half of humanity. A lifetime of introspection went into this novel, the one closest to me personally; the thinking and ideas in this are closest to my own. (Jain 2000: 210)

The novel opens with Jaya and her husband Mohan moving back into the old Dadar flat in Bombay from their cosy and palatial house. Mohan is accused of corrupt practices at office and an inquiry against him is set up. The children have gone out for a holiday with their family friends. He expects Jaya to go into hiding with him; but she refuses to honour his wish. Since Jaya is alone in the small old Dadar flat, she gets ample time for self-introspection. This is why she becomes an introvert and goes into deep contemplation of her past and her childhood. If there had been no such crisis in their life, she would never have given a thought on herself or her individuality. Adele King opines: "Jaya finds her normal routine so disrupted that for the first time she can look at her life and attempt to decide who she really is" (King 1988: 77).

She manages successfully to suppress her feeling for seventeen years of her married life because she thought it more important to be a good wife than being a good writer. In her zeal to play the role of a loyal wife and caring mother, she has suppressed her desire which lead her to self-actualization and fulfillment. She suppresses not only her writing career but also her association with her neighbour, Kamat. Her career as a successful writer is jeopardized right in the early years of her marriage. A short story of hers bags the prize and also gets published in a magazine. She is on the threshold of getting recognition as a creative writer of some merit, when Mohan expresses his displeasure at a particular story written by her. The story is about a man who cannot reach out to his wife except through her body. Mohan suspects if the man portrayed in the story is not he himself, and is apprehensive lest people should take him for the man in the story. She thinks, "Looking at his stricken face, I had been convinced I had done him wrong. And I had stopped writing after that" (144). But the writer keeps herself writing. She begins to write under a pseudonym, which doesn't help, and her stories are rejected one after another. Her neighbour, Kamat, analyses the reason behind the successive rejections and tells her that her stories lack strong emotions as she has suppressed her anger and frustration. But she cannot express her anger or feelings lest it should damage her relation with Mohan. She had learnt to control her anger, as Mohan considers this trait in a woman as "unwomanly" (83). She tells Kamat: "Because no woman can be angry. Have you ever heard of an angry young woman?" (147). At this Kamat warns her against indulging in self-pity as it would only prove destructive to her. He admonishes her: "I'm warning you—beware of this 'women are the victims' theory of yours. It will drag you down into a soft squishy bog of self-pity. Take yourself seriously, woman. Don't skull behind a false name" (148). Later she begins to write light humorous pieces on the travails of a middle class housewife in a column entitled "Seeta". She not only gets encouraging response from the readers but also a nod of approval from Mohan. Jaya says:

> And for me, she had been the means through which I had shut the door, firmly, on all those women who had invaded my being, screaming for attention; women I had known I could not write about, because they might—it was just possible—resemble Mohan's mother, or aunt, or my mother or aunt. (149)

Therefore, she had merely been glossing over the reality or truth, and smothering her inner conscience to avoid endangering her marriage. She denies in her writings the reflections of her individuality or self to play the role model of a typical Indian middle-class woman. Kamat, her neighbour, is competent enough to understand her literary capability and criticises her for writing such stuff: "You know something I never can imagine you writing this" (149). Adele King rightly remarks: "In Jaya's stories they lived happily ever after although she knows the falsity of the view of life" (1990: 166).

Her association with Kamat, a widower living above her flat, lends another dimension to Jaya's personality. She is drawn towards him as he treats her as his equal and offers constructive criticism to Jaya on her writings. He even receives her mail at his address to help her to avoid any confrontation with her husband as he disapproves of her writings. He focuses his attention on her, as he is lonely. Unlike other men he does not have aversion to cooking and such other domestic chores meant to be performed by women exclusively. She feels so much at ease in his company that her womanly inhibitions wither and she opens up her problems to him. He warns her against wallowing in self-pity and asks her to pursue her literary career by giving expression to her real inner-self. Being inspired by his valuable advice, she kept on writing which may be termed as a silent but effective tool of revolt against the patriarchal society giving a new dimension to the Indian feminism. Arati Biswal's views expressed in a article are noteworthy:

> She rejects the image of Mohan and herself as "a pair of bullocks yoked together". Her awareness of an unjust

> system that coerces a woman to play second fiddle: to accept the position as an inferior being brings in her a sense of outrage that ruefully reminds her of rigid rules of Sanskrit drama that forced women to speak Prakrit, while reserving the classical Sanskrit for the superior male characters. Jaya refuses to accept such distinction. She refuses to concede to Mohan the authority he wielded over her earlier. (1997: 43)

There are so many reasons which hinder the fulfilment of her individuality. In her zeal to play out the role of a loyal wife and caring mother, she smothers her real self. Like other women she has been indoctrinated right from her childhood. She does not protest the change of her name from Jaya to Suhasini at her marriage just to keep Mohan happy. Half-heartedly; but her inner consciousness never accepted it. In her article "Feminism *vis-à-vis* Women's Dignity: A Study of Shashi Deshpande's *That Long Silence*," T. Asoka Rani remarks:

> The fact that Jaya was rechristened as Suhasini by her husband on their wedding day confuses Jaya in her search for identity. The pseudonym, under which she operates as a writer further complicates the issue. Jaya stands for revolt whereas Suhasini symbolises submission. Jaya rejects the name Suhasini and it is significant as a manifestation of her protest against such customs. But her sense of identity is never certain. She is torn between being Jaya, herself and Suhasini, the good wife; between building a self as a writer and a self as a wife and mother. (1996: 20)

Her dress and her appearance are the proofs of her submission to Mohan's livings, replicating an absorbed family woman. She has systematically suppressed her free will as she has been taught "the importance and necessity of stable marriage and family—family as security, as a source of emotional strength" (Uma 1989: 4). But the same is denied to her. The crisis at Mohan's office begins to affect the affairs at home. She realizes that Mohan has lost interest in her. At the Dadar flat she has time enough to think over her relations with Mohan, and also to analyze and recognize her suppressed "self". Her emotional crisis comes to such a juncture that she is afraid lest something should happen to Mohan. She cannot imagine a life without Mohan:

> The thought of living without him had twisted my insides. His death had seemed to me the final catastrophe. The very idea of his dying had made me feel so bereft that tears had flowed effortlessly down my cheeks. If he had been a little late coming home, I had been sure he was dead. By the time he returned, I had, in my imagination, shaped my life to a desolate widowhood. (1996: 97)

This type of fear is born in her mind due to her split psyche. She is the representative of the urban, middle-class woman who is educated and has the exposure to liberal western concepts. Her upbringing demands the suppression of the self so that the marriage can survive. As she finds herself unable to free herself from the traditional code of conduct and her pent-up feelings make her neurotic. The advices of her aunts keep ringing in her ears, and this becomes the cause of her undoing. For instance, Vanita *Mami* advises her just before her marriage: "Remember Jaya, a husband is like a sheltering tree. Keep the tree alive and flourishing, even if you have to water it with deceit and lies." She further says: "If your husband has a mistress or two, ignore it; take up a hobby instead—cats, may be, or your sister's children" (31). Although Jaya does not take Vanita *Mami's* counsel seriously but for her part, she does not prove herself different from her. When the occasion to choose between her family and husband arises, she chooses the former.

Vanita *Mami* represents other facets of the traditionally suppressed woman. After her marriage her life was ruled by her mother-in-law. As a daughter-in-law her role has remained, at best, a passive one and she is allowed not to participate in decision-making. Jaya recalls:

> Since the day she got married she, like the rest of Ai's family, was dominated and ruled by that ghoul, her mother-in-law, my other-*ajji*. Even Vanita *Mami's* saris were chosen for her by the old woman. Later, there was Ai, who went back to her old home after Appa's death; there still is Ai. (45)

The adoption of Kusum was the only protest she could register successfully. For her, the husband is a sheltering tree, and marriage the only destiny for a woman. The image of Saptagiri Aji also reinforces the traditional concept of docile wives and silent women. She is surprised and indignant at Jaya's behaviour towards her husband, "Look at you—for everything a question, for everything a retort. What husband can be comfortable with that?" (27).

Women are the victims for generations of conditioning in which a woman is unchangeably slotted. The husband is traditionally given the role of mentor and guide. To serve one's husband is to serve God! Feminine incapability is exaggerated to increase the authority of the husband. Simon de Beauvoir says: "Marriage incites man to a capricious imperialism" (Beauvoir 1997: 483). Among human beings the temptation to dominate is universally irresistible and the traditional marriage provides this opportunity to men. In orthodox Indian marriages, it is enough for the husband to be approved and admired, he wants immediate unquestioned obedience to his commands. Simon de Beauvoir reflects the opinion:

> All the resentments accumulated during his childhood and his later life, those accumulated daily among other men whose existence means that he is browbeaten and injured—all this is purged from him at home as he lets loose his authority upon his wife. He enacts violence, power, unyielding resolution; he issues commands in tones of severity; he shouts and pounds the table: this farce is a daily reality for his wife. He is so firm in his rights that the slightest sign of independence on her part seems to him a rebellion; he would fain stop her breathing without his permission. (Beauvoir 1997: 483-84)

One can come across such a situation while studying the marital relationship between Jaya and Mohan. When the times are smooth, the relation between the two moves smoothly. Unlike her mythical counterpart Sita and Gandhari, she remains stuck to her husband and children, but when the crisis in life begins she is not willing to go into hiding with her husband.

She is ashamed of the incident and Mohan defends himself by saying, "It was for you and the children that I did this. I wanted you to have a good life, I wanted the children to have all those things I never had" (9). Mohan's trouble is the creation of his own wrong doings, but he expects her to share this crisis unconditionally. Indra Bhatt observes that Mohan wants to "use his wife as buffer, an opiate to soften the impact of the forces he has set into motion against himself" (Bhatt 1991: 157). Jaya feels herself totally lost as she is taken for granted by Mohan. She realizes that her own feelings and emotions don't mean anything to him. Her realization that she is a non-entity in his eyes hurts her. For women across the world in general and Indian women in particular, there is no easy escape-route available. They have to carry on, unwillingly, the slavery imposed by marriage. It is noteworthy to quote Beauvoir here:

> The chains of marriage are heavy, and the wife must somehow accommodate herself to a situation from which she cannot escape. Some, full of importance, become tyrannical and shrewish matrons; some become complaisant, masochistic victim and slave of their families. (1997: 494)

The novelist has, thus, voiced the agony of modern Indian women who are at cross-road unable to decide the right path of their emancipation. They have to rely upon themselves. They cannot break the institution of marriage which provides them productivity, motherhood and protection. They should struggle against the old fashioned patriarchal mind set-up and seek more freedom within the pious wedlock. The radical type of feminism cannot flourish on the Indian soil. In an earlier incident when her parental uncle Ramu *Kaka* shows her the family tree wherein even boys of the family find mention but her name is missing. When she asked her uncle regarding her name missing, he replied: "How can you be here? You don't belong to this family! You're married, you're now part of Mohan's family. You have no place here" (143). Jaya is also shocked to find no mention of her mother, her aunts and even *Ajji* who kept the family together. She is full of anger and desperation over such gross gender discrimination.

Many women forums of post-independent India realized what Jaya, the mouthpiece of the novelist, had in her mind. Credit goes to the Indian literary feminist movements which brought daughters as partners in their parental property. Though they have got equal status in the parental home by law, yet much more is required to eradicate this social evil. The Indian women have opted their own way to get rid of this discrimination. Certainly, the victimized won't treat their own girl children differently, which will be a tool to achieve the desired goal of feminism. The novelist seems very realistic in the sense that she suggests marriages are not based on love but convenience. Jaya is content to play the role of a caring wife as long as the economic and social conditions are fine. She happily plays out the role model of Gandhari:

> If Gandhari, who bandaged her eyes to become blind like her husband, could be called an ideal wife, I was an ideal wife too. I bandaged my eyes tightly. I didn't want to know anything. It was enough for me that we moved to Bombay, that we could send Rahul and Rati to good schools, and that I could have things we needed...decent clothes, a fridge, a gas connection, travelling first class. (61-62)

Unlike Sita, she does not express her willingness to accompany her husband into exile. Mohan's heydays were over, and their marriage runs into rough weather. But she cannot be said to be wholly responsible, as Mohan, too, has his own share of responsibility. He wants to use Jaya as a cushion in this crisis. But she has changed herself much after her marriage. Her aunt's and her father's advices—never to hurt Mohan—have made her bear things without opposition. Soon after marriage a quarrel between the two had led to Mohan's lapsing into silence altogether. She had a guilty conscience and begins to use silence stratagem to avoid any confrontation. The bubble of this long silence gets so bloated that this unexpected crisis burst it. She had been lulled into silence till Mohan was a "sheltering tree". With his safe job and career, her home and children were safe. But the sudden incident against him makes her feel insecure. It is a tragedy that she herself needs somebody to console her that at last everything will be all right. Mohan accuses Jaya and says: "Do you think I haven't seen how changed you are since we came here, since I told about my situation" (12). At this Jaya begins to laugh hysterically, and cannot help it. She herself doesn't know the cause. Mohan is so enraged that he leaves the house in a huff as if he would never return. She is left all alone and at this juncture she gets the news that Rahul has disappeared while holidaying. She feels totally shattered and lost, as there is nobody at hand to help her. She is in a traumatic state for many days, but finally everything is all right. Rahul comes back and she also gets a telegram from Mohan that "All is well". Now she has come to terms with herself. During this period she articulates her long silence—her innermost thoughts, her fears, her doubts and all that she had suppressed during her seventeen years of marriage. While penning down her experiences, she undergoes a sort of catharsis. She has decided not to be passive and silent. She says:

> Well, I've achieved this. I'm not afraid any more. The panic has gone. I'm Mohan's wife, I had thought, and cut off the bits of me that had refused to be Mohan's wife. Now I know that kind of a fragmentation is not possible. (191)

Deshpande has very sensitively presented in *That Long Silence* the aspect of feminine life before the readers. It depicts how a woman's existence is confined within domesticity and how all forms of oppression perpetuated on her are convincingly rationalized generating a closed-mind syndrome. The figures of Mohan's mother and sister can be quoted as examples. In Jaya's narrative, the silent wait of Mohan's mother takes on diabolic features, "the woman crouching in front of the dying fire, sitting blank and motionless, the huddled bundles of sleeping children on the floor, the utter silence, the loud knock at the door..." (35). Mohan's mother had to wait for her husband late at nights, cooking the rice again and keeping it hot as 'he' wanted it fresh, hot and from an untouched vessel, declining to eat what he called, "your children's disgusting leavings" (35). The wife's long vigil and patient wait becomes futile when angry at not having fresh chutney to eat, he picked up the heavy brass plate, throws it at the wall and leaves the house. Silently, picking up the plate she cleans the wall and the floor of the spattered food and sends her son next door to borrow some chillies. Patiently and silently she prepares fresh chutney, lights the fire, cooks the meal again and sits down to wait. When her children, who had woken up by the clanging sound of the plate, finally drift off to sleep again, "She was still sitting there in front of the fire, silent, motionless" (36). What hurts a reader is not only the cruelty of a husband, but also the insensibility of a son, which displays the continued discrimination against women. Her son Mohan, who has been a witness to this incident, never condemns his father. He eulogizes his mother, the 'Virtuous woman' instead, "...she was tough, woman in those days were tough" (36).

Kusum, Jaya's mad cousin, is another victim of gross gender discrimination. She is a deserted wife. Jaya keeps her at home despite the objection from her mother and brothers. After she recovered a little, her brother takes her away home. But she commits suicide a day before her husband is supposed to take her home. Jaya's help-maid, Jeeja, has her own story of oppression. Her husband is also a drunkard who frequently beats her. She does not protest when her husband takes up another woman because she thinks that she has failed him by not bearing a child to him and so he had every right to remarry. She willingly brings up their son after her husband and his mistress are dead.

The chains of traditional marriages are too heavy to break. In the absence of any escape route, wives often seek consolation in obsession, masochism or mental slavery leading to physical decay, disease and death. The continuity of women's suppression, an unacknowledged martyrdom, becomes a part of a housewife's existence. She is expected to subordinate her own needs to those of her family. She is supposed to bear exploitation and suffering with willing fortitude. "The orthodox Indian view interprets any resistance to its andocentric codes as being the influence of western decadence. We continue to cling to forms of female oppression, exalting and glorifying them with practiced rhetoric" (Nabar 1995: 176). The continued exaltation of self-effacing norms creates an environment which pressurizes a woman to accept or at least not to resist them.

Often silence is the only option to women in such situations. They suffer and die without uttering a single word in protest. Mohan's sister Vimala dies in silent agony without getting help from her in-laws, reliving her mother's fate. Her mother's photograph reminded Jaya of "floury hands dealing out a macabre punishment to her face" (38). Jaya can sense red bruises showing through the white clown's mask. Vimala wanted and claimed to be different from her mother, but their suffering binds them together in a common fate. Jaya realizes it when she remarks, "Yet I can see something in common between them, something that links the destinies of the two...the silence in which they died" (39). Whenever marriage becomes strained in the European milieu, divorce or separation is used as the escape route, but the thought of divorce or separation rarely comes to the mind of Indian women belonging to lower strata as well as the middle class. Mrs. Parvati Bhatnagar, in an article opines:

> The lower strata women, consider nothing wrong or shameful in a husband beating his wife. In fact, it is his privilege since he is the symbol of social prestige for her. For a middle class woman, husband is like a shading tree providing a barrier between her and other men. The status of a woman separated from her husband is dubious in Indian society. To have failed in marriage is considered to be woman's worst failure. (2001: 5)

A major problem which the feminist studies and fiction face in terms of thematic clarity lies in the impossibility of a comprehensive representation of feminine problems within the Indian framework. Most of such work centres on the upper middle class urban society. It is considered that with better exposure of education and vocational opportunities the middle-class woman is learning to be more vocal and assertive about her rights. Enhanced economic prosperity and nuclear family pattern have liberated her from the clutches of the cruel family bondage, and she is free to manage her household as she wills. It is perceived that owing to these reasons the role of tradition in perpetuating the bondage of women is gradually diminished. Such studies often ignore the plight of the rural/underprivileged women on the assumption that such women have always worked. This generalization ignores the socio-cultural realities. *That Long Silence* underlines the fact that the drudgery and work do not liberate such women, it only reminds them of their economic and class oppression. Work does not constitute a choice in their life.

Mukta is a widow caring for her old mother and teenage daughter Neelima. She is economically independent, firm and competent in her handling of strange situations, yet unable to overcome the superstitions. However, she wants her daughter to be free of them. She does not riddle Neelima with innumerous fasts of Hartalika and other days. Her desolate life has not sapped away her compassion towards others. She recognizes Jaya's and Kamat's loneliness and sympathizes with it. She comes across a woman who has decided to stoically circumvent social complexities in order to live. Jaya, too, has decided to live her life as it is given to her. Jaya is angry at her silence, as it puts a gloss of placidity behind her silence. She has accepted ill treatment at the hands of her husband, as she could not have a child. Yet she endures it with a patience and with visions of better future for her grandchildren. Nayana, too, views life with a dispassionate objectivity. She wants to have a son, not because she expects any help from him in her old age, but because she does not want her son to be discriminated by society. She knows that a boy shall at least have some effortless individuality, which is denied to a girl, "Why give birth to a girl, *behnji*, who'll only suffer because of men all her life?... No, no, *behnji*,—better to have a son" (28).

This novel portrays the sufferings and deprivations of feminine life by presenting certain characters as stereotyped representatives of traditional womanhood. The novel also presents a critique of the myths which are perpetuated and practised in the context of femininity. But the strength of the novel lies in its bold analysis of the realities about the Indian womanhood. The novel assertively exhibits the thesis that women should have an assertive individuality which includes the capability to take decisions about their life and carry them out with a sense of responsibility. Their emotional-intellectual-economic liberation does not negate the possibility of nourishing and enjoying various relationships which the society and their biological nature have imposed upon them. Nivedita Maitra's remarks in this context are quite relevant. She says:

> Jaya realizes the futility of remaining silent and decides to break the silence. She overcomes the fear of losing Mohan and thus losing the only vocation in life. She regains her identity and establishes herself as a writer, overthrowing the initial fear of annoying Mohan by writing what she had always wanted to write and not what the society wanted to read. (2003: 50)

Within the societal roles of wife/mother/friend/companion she can be herself, by erasing her conditioning and freeing her from her inhibitions. The haunting riddle of the ultimate purpose of a woman's life within the family can be solved when she learns to assess her worth as an individual and shun to be guided by pre-fixed norms about it. Jaya realizes that in order to attain self-hood, a woman must transcend silence, negation and self-alienation. A woman's relation with her family must burgeon within the totality of her life as a woman, only then it can lead to a harmonious fulfillment. Jaya realizes that a holistic yet silent approach towards life is necessary:

> We don't change overnight. It's possible that we may not change even over long periods of time. But we can always hope. Without that, life would be impossible. And if there is anything to know now it is this: life has always to be made possible. (193)

Her decision to cease to be a passive partner and overcome the turbulence in her relationship with Mohan leads her to an uninhibited self-identification. Thus, Shashi Deshpande has woven the tragic tales of Jaya's relations and her acquaintance into the texture of the novel, and so the novel inevitably takes on a feminist character. The novel is about gross gender discrimination and inequality prevalent in society, and yet the novelist is opposed to being branded a feminist writer. She may not conform to the conventional concept of feminism, but she does have her own feminist ideas. In an interview with Malini Nair, Deshpande says:

> The women in my books are people who came to realize what it is to be a woman in the process of their own lives and the situations they face not through books and theories. I think feminism is an entirely personalized perception. It is when you start questioning preconceived notion about your roles. (1989: 5)

In her novel she does not present man as completely bad and woman as completely good. She is realistic in the sense that her stories are very close to life. She is not writing about Jaya only but also about Mohan, as Jaya says: "I am writing of us" (1). In the novel, Deshpande does not put the blame of their marital crisis squarely on Mohan's shoulders but also on Jaya's. C. Anna Latha Devi has rightly remarked:

> The relationship between spouses thrives only when it is partnership between them. Once the superiority inferiority equation enters into it, the rift sets in. Fear and apprehension replace trust and confidence obstructing the path to genuine understanding between them. The psychological block between them leads to lack of communication and there is plaintive silence. (2004: 157)

The novelist suggests that the women should accept their own responsibility for their victimization, instead of putting the blame on others. Jaya mostly blames herself for her suffering. Thus, *That Long Silence* is a serious effort towards "maintaining a credible balance between the sexes" (Deshpande 1985: 7). It is often debated whether or not *That Long Silence* is a feminist novel. Deshpande is against the labelling of her novels as feminist. She says:

> Any woman who writes fiction shows the world as it looks to her protagonist; if the protagonist is a woman, she shows the world as it looks to a woman—to apply the tag of feminist is one way, I have realized, of dismissing the serious concerns of the novel by labelling them, by calling the work propagandist. (Deshpande 1985: 7)

She is aware of the fact that breaking off the bonds of family would result in loneliness and discrimination of the larger social set-up, Jaya looks for happiness and self-fulfillment within the family itself. In a book-review, Jehanara Wasi has expressed her views:

> Deshpande may or may not be a formal feminist, but her novel is both actual feminine writing and potential feminist writing. It is patently the work of a woman on the life of a woman in India. It is also an attempt flashback to psychoanalyse the woman, till she reaches the self-knowledge necessary to enable her to answer the question the novel enunciates. (1991: 116)

She asks for her individuality to be valued equally along with that of man. As long as one half of the humanity are denied decent and dignified lives, it will be a far cry to hope for a better world. But, Jaya, confident of her individuality and hopeful of a change in Mohan's attitude, moves beyond the cultural stereotypes with the firm conviction that 'life has always to be made possible'. Mrs. Parvati Bhatnagar's views regarding women emancipation and identity crisis as mentioned in the novel is noteworthy:

> The message which the writer finally conveys is that a woman's emancipation lies neither in suffering quietly like a fatalist nor in repudiating all claims of the family and society like a rebel she must draw upon her inner strength, which her education and knowledge has given her and bring about a reconciliation between tradition and modernity without losing her own identity. (2001: 6)

Such an optimistic ending of the novel, *That Long Silence*, shows that the day is not far off when men and women will be considered equal and supplement to each other.

II
THE BINDING VINE

Shashi Deshpande strikes a note of realism and optimism in her portrayal of the Indian middle class educated women. Her gift to contemporary women has been to write novels which show women engaged in complex and difficult social and psychological problem of defining an authentic self. But unlike the women protagonists of Anita Desai's novels who in quest of self-hood lose their ability to live in community and maintain human relationships, limiting themselves to individual freedom which damages their ultimate understanding of life, Shashi Deshpande's women characters seek their selfhood within the orbit of family and relationships. Her novels explore important problem of our time without offering a facile recipe for their solution. The women in her novels are neither demi-goddesses nor strong-minded super-heroines. They are normal educated middle-class women who are independent to some extent but vulnerable at the same time because of an inalienable bond of tradition. In a book-review of *The Binding Vine, Nilufer E. Bharucha* is very much notable:

> Deshpande narrates her story in alternating voices and interwoven with her tales are the poems of a long-dead woman. This intertexuality offers another dimension to her narrative. As ever, Deshpande's low-key and often searingly honest writing is worth a careful reading. (1995: 72)

Deshpande's novel *The Binding Vine* (1992) touches a chord in every woman as she responds to it with a recognition of her own doubts, complexes, fears, desires and suffering being mirrored in the narration of Urmila, the protagonist. In presenting women's point of view Deshpande is mainly interested in the clash of tradition and modernity, as reflected in the generation gap and conflict between women. Her young heroines rebel against the traditional way of life, its rituals, ceremonies and patriarchal values. Women like Indu, Jaya, Sarita and Sumi perceive the structuring of men and women in gendered roles, restructuring their human potentiality and fullness. There is in the efforts of these characters a struggle to transcend these restrictive and moulded roles. They rebel, reject and seek freedom from the traditional norms and way of life by escaping into marriage. But Deshpande's novels present women pause at some point in their adult roles as wife and mother, and take a long, careful look into the formation period of childhood and adolescence. Interconnecting these two phases—youth and adulthood, provides a new insight into their lives as women within a particular society. It is undeniably true that the roots of feminism are implanted in the western soil, but its branches are spread across the world. The Indian social environment provided very favourable situation for its florence. Feminism in Indian English literature got sustenance from various native sources such as Indian freedom movement, independence, and spread of education, employment opportunities and legislations for women's rights. It never proved the replica of the western feminism because any genre of literature remains socio-cultural specific. This is why the Indian feminism has its own flavour and taste. As Sarbjit Sandhu points out, "Shashi Deshpande's protagonist are not very brave.... Heroines, but women struggling to find their own voice" (1991: 51).

Evangeline Shanti Roy has also expressed the same view in her article "Shashi Deshpande's *The Binding Vine*: A Quest for the Anchor of Life"

> The Deshpande protagonist is never a radical militant feminist who wants to overthrow all social, moral and sexual taboos in order to become a free woman, but a woman who feels the need to go beyond socially and culturally determined roles to carve a space for herself within the typical Indian situation, to discover who she is and retain her selfhood without sacrificing family ties and age-old values Deshpande attempts to redefine human relationships, especially man-woman relationships in the context of the changing Indian society and thus identify the values which endure. (2001: 75-76)

The Binding Vine depicts the plight of Urmi, the protagonist, who is an educated middle-class woman grieving over the death of her one-year-old daughter Anu. She is so sensitive that, in the long run, she shares the sufferings and sorrows of other people also. If she had not undergone such a personal loss, perhaps she would not have had any concern with others. Thus her narrative comprises three tales—one about herself and the other two about Shakuntala, a rape-victim's mother, and Urmi's mother-in-law, Mira, a victim of marital rape. The novel begins with Urmi grieving over her dead infant daughter. She is unable to forget her because her memories haunt Urmi. She fights with the memories but also realizes that forgetting is betrayal, "I must reject these memories, I have to conquer them. This is one battle I have to win if I am to go on living. And yet my victory will carry with it the taint of betrayal. To forget is to betray (21). She also realizes her responsibility to her living son Kartika who needs her love and watches her anxiously. It is true that she does not take every death of her kith and kin in this way. When her father died she could bear the shock easily. She says: "Papa is only a memory, a gentle memory" (27). But Anu is different. When Inni wants to have a framed photograph of Anu in the wall, she reacts bitterly: "I don't need a picture to remember her, I can remember every bit of her, every moment of her life. How can you imagine I need a picture...?" (68).

When her friend Lalita asks how many kids she has, she replies, "Only one, a son," but soon she realizes that she has done injustice to Anu. She gets filled with a sense of guilt as if she was betraying Anu: "How could I, Oh God, how could I? That was betrayal, treachery, how could I deny my Anu...only one son...how could I?" (106). S. Indira rightly remarks: "She clings to her pain and allows her memories of Anu, every small incident to flood her with longing and a great sense of loss" (1995: 22). Obsessed with the memories of her daughter she comes across a photograph of her mother-in-law Mira which is introduced as "Kishore's mother, Kartika's grandmother" (42). She sees a group photograph of Mira and from the formality of the picture she conjectures that it was taken to mark "an occasion—Mira's wedding perhaps—a parting of ways for a group of friends, the end of a chapter" (43). The trunk from which she gets the photograph contains many books and diaries of Mira. The poems of Mira are written in Kannada and the diaries are written in English. Inquisitive to know more about her she asks *Akka* about her. *Akka* tells her that her brother saw Mira at a wedding and fell in love with her. Since then he had "single-minded pursuit of an object: Marrying Mira" (47). He was suggested as a good match for Mira and in this way the marriage was arranged. She died while giving birth to Kishore.

Urmi came to know the difference in handing over of Mira's property to her. When *Akka* hands over little bits of Mira's jewellery, she says, "They are Kishore's mother's...I kept them for his wife." But when she hands over the book and diaries of Mira, she says, "Take this, it's Mira's." "She did not mention Kishore at all, as if she was now directly linking me with Mira" (48). This shows that a woman loses her identity after her marriage. She is seen either as a wife or mother who in a way erases her real self and imposes another alien self on her. The difference made by *Akka* symbolizes that the poems and diaries are self-actualizing, whose identities are not dependent on men. "Urmi, the novel's narrator, mourning the death of a young daughter, is haunted by the poems of her dead mother-in-law, and by the destiny of a rape-victim in a hospital ward" (Hussein 1993: 25).

In an aggrieved state she happens to meet Shakuntala, mother of a rape-victim, Kalpana. She meets her in the hospital where her sister-in-law, Vanna works. Kalpana is lying unconscious and her mother thinks that she has met with a car accident. Dr. Bhaskar, the doctor-in-charge, on examination reports that Kalpana has been brutally raped. Her mother Shakuntala's reaction is that of a typical Indian mother bred in an oppressive male-dominated society. She tells Vanaa: "It's not true, you people are trying to blacken my daughter's name" (58). Listening the conversation between Vanna and Dr. Bhaskar she cries in agony and fear. She says: "No, no, no. Tell him, Tai, it's not true, don't tell anyone. I'll never be able to hold up my head again, who'll marry the girl, we're decent people. Doctor", she turns to him, "don't tell the police" (58). Most Indian mothers would react in a similar way as they are concerned about their daughter's marriage. The novelist has very clearly presented Shakuntala's agony, anger, helplessness and fear. The character has been presented so realistically that it leaves a sense of introspection in the readers. Shakuntala is in a traumatic state and is sobbing. Urmi escorts her home and from there starts her association with her. She pays regular visits to Shakutai's place to inquire after Kalpana's state. It is during these regular visits that Urmi comes to know about Kalpana from Shakutai. She swings between two extremes; sometimes she is all praise for Kalpana and sometimes puts all the blame on her. Kalpana's character is full of paradoxes. She says:

> She is very smart, that's how she got the job in the shop. Kalpana even learnt how to speak English. People in our *chawl* used to laugh at her, but she didn't care. When she wants something, she goes after it, nothing can stop her. She's stubborn, you can't imagine how stubborn she is. (92)

She further says that Kalpana is secretive in nature as she did not tell her mother even about her pay. Shakuntala also laments for having given birth to a pretty child like Kalpana. Her heart is full of praise when she talks about her daughter's physical appearance. She says:

> She's very pretty, my Kalpana...she's not like me at all. When she was born, she was so delicate and fair, just like a doll. I wondered how a woman like me could have a daughter like that. (93)

It is undeniably true that she loves her daughter very much but the roots of her love start to shake when she puts all the blame on her shoulders, as she bursts out:

> Cover yourself decently, I kept telling her, men are like animals. But she went her way. You should have seen her walking out, head in the air, caring for nobody. It's all her fault, Urmila, all her fault. (147)

Although Shakutai puts all the blame on Kalpana, Urmi finds it difficult to reason out with her that Kalpana is not responsible in any way for the brutal rape: "It's not her fault, no, not her fault at all" (147). She fails to convince Shakutai and is enraged at the fact that this would lead to the rapist's getting away scot-free. Here we find her reactions born of the values deeply rooted in her by the age-old patriarchal social set-up. She was not born with these values; rather they were embedded into her by the patriarchal norms. Strict codes of conduct have been framed for a girl's speech and conduct so that she can't invite men's attention. A girl must observe the social norms regarding how she speaks, dress and carry herself in society. A girl is supposed to speak less and if possible the least as her words may send wrong signals to men. Similarly her dress should be decent, i.e.

the contours of her body should remain hidden. A girl is always asked to behave herself in society and she is not allowed to interact much with men. Any deviation from these norms invites the wrath of the family-members as it invites danger of her modesty getting outraged.

Shakuntala does not want this incident to be informed to the police. She knows that if she lodges a complaint to the police, she herself and her daughter would be ready to face a greater injustice and humiliation. A victim of rape is loser on two counts. First, she is looked down upon as a *kulta* (a characterless woman) which leaves her in a much miserable plight. As soon as such cases come in the knowledge of the society, it becomes a Herculean task to find a suitable match for marriage. Indian women has to bear a lot of injustices silently meted out by the monstrous male-dominated society. Focusing upon the lot of the rape victims Laeeq Futehally, in a book-review, points out:

> Rape is the most disastrous result of being a woman. There are dozens of other injustices and hardships which surround and penetrate a woman's life; and all these together build up a situation in which rape in accepted as a risk which women are fated to face. (1993: 89)

Deshpande further explains the conduct of police investigation in such cases. It is the duty of the police to encourage the rape-victims to complain against the guilty persons so that they can be punished by the courts of law. But surprisingly the police officer registers the case as a mere accident to the great shock of Dr. Bhaskar, the doctor-in-charge. He bursts out in anger, and tells Urmi:

> You should see the marks of his fingers on her arms where he had held her down. And there were huge contusions on her thighs—he must have pinned her down with his knees. And her lips bitten and chewed. (88)

The investigating police officer knows the fact that it is a rape case, but he has his own escaping logic. His logic also approves the strict patriarchal norms of the society. He forgets that ladies are also the equal citizens of the country. His insensible intentions are obvious in his conversation with Dr. Bhaskar. He tells Dr. Bhaskar: "She's going to die anyway, so what difference does it make whether, on paper, she dies the victim of an accident or a rape?" (88). He further adds "her name would be smeared" (88). Shakuntala also thinks in the same direction. She knows that it will ruin not only her family's prestige but also undermine the marriage prospects of her daughters. She is worried not only for the marriage of Kalpana but also for Sandhya, the second daughter. Credit goes to the society governed by Manu's laws which depicts a woman as a being full of "carnal passions, love for ornaments, impure desires, wrath, dishonesty, malice and bad conduct" (Arora 1991: 11). This is the reason Kalpana, the representative of rape-victims, is held responsible herself for such a heinous crime.

Shakuntala has her own tragic past. She was deserted by her husband for another woman, and she was left all alone to look after herself and her children. Dr. Bhaskar is shocked to think how women like her who themselves had no peace and happiness in marriage could think of marrying away their daughters. Urmi tells Dr. Bhaskar that marriage provides security to women. She makes an apt remark as in the patriarchal social set-up; an unmarried woman is socially vulnerable. Y.S. Sunita Reddy observes: "It is indeed, an irony that to avoid brutalization of one kind, women willingly submit themselves to a brutality of another kind in the institution of marriage" (Reddy 2001: 95).

Urmi wants justice to be done to Kalpana by getting the culprit punished by the court of laws. She is the lonely crusader in her struggle against the brutal behaviour of the so-called civilized man dominated society. Despite disapproval of Vanna and Urmi's mother she brings the matter to the press. She gets success in getting the case reopened and with this the identity of the rapist is revealed who is none but Prabhakar, Shakutai's sister's husband. Sulu is so much ashamed of her husband's behaviour that she immolates herself leaving behind the grief-stricken Shakutai.

Shakutai herself is a saga of tragic life. Soon after her marriage she was left alone by her husband in her father's home.

Her husband left for Bombay on the pretext of earning a livelihood. Even after spending six months in Bombay, he did not return from there. She crossed the line of patience and joined her husband in Bombay. She was surprised to realize that her husband was lazy and worthless. She gave birth to three children and decided to work for the maintenance of her children. Despite such a sacrifice her husband deserted her and the children in order to get physical attachment with another woman. She tells Urmi, "That's been the greatest misfortune of my life, Urmila, marrying that man" (110). Since her husband has deserted her, she is to blame not only for husband's desertion of her but also for anything that goes wrong in the family, for example Kalpana's rape. The Indian society seems so insensible that her forbearance of her personal tragedy in marriage and the privations she undergoes in the aftermath are thrown to the winds. She bitterly tells Urmi: "What you can expect, they say, of a girl whose mother has left her husband?" (147). Her putting up with such a husband and fending for herself and her children are of no avail in an oppressive patriarchal social set-up. Evangeline Shanti Roy points out, "She seeks to explore the myth of man's superiority and the myth of woman being always dependent and thus ushers in the winds of change at least in sensitive readers" (2001: 81).

Shakuntala's sister, Sulu, has her own tragic life. She is affectionate and helpful in nature. She helps her as much as possible and even takes upon responsibility of bringing up Kalpana, but that was not to be. Sulu's husband Prabhakar had lusted after her, and Sulu under pressure from her husband had proposed to Shakutai Kalpana's marriage to Prabhakar. Kalpana is infuriated at Sulu and ridicules her. Sulu had been so much suppressed after her marriage that she made such a proposal. Shakutai praises Sulu for her affection, helpfulness and good nature. Shakutai tells Urmi:

> After marriage she changed. She was frightened, always frightened. What if he doesn't like this, what if he wants that, what if he is angry with me, what if he throws me out...? Nobody should live like that, Urmila, so full of fears. (195)

The novelist suggests here how sometimes a marriage makes a woman extremely meek and submissive. Sulu's suicide, the tragic finale of Kalpana's tragedy clearing the mystery of her rape, is another revelation that unsettles both Shakutai and Urmila. It is Sulu's husband Prabhakar who raped Kalpana, as all along he wanted her to be his mistress and could not bear her getting married and getting away from him permanently. After realizing the terrible truth, Sulu killed herself. Like a typical lady, she considered her barrenness responsible for her husband's heinous crime committed on Kalpana.

After all the shocking revelations, traumatic tragedies and hysterical denial of life, one finds Shakutai getting on with her chores calmly and resolutely. However burdensome our ties are, however painful our experiences are, one can never opt out. The main urge is always to survive, to get on with the business of living, even if it comprise a daily routine that cares of a hundred trifling matters, bringing an order and rhythm to it. Realizing this Mira says, "Just as the utter futility of living overwhelms me, I am terrified by the thoughts of dying, of ceasing to be" (203).

Yet another saga of misery, submission and sorrow is that of Urmi's late mother-in-law Mira. The novelist here ventures into a completely untouched subject of marital rape in Indian Writing in English. She has touched upon the subject in her earlier novel *The Dark Holds No Terrors,* wherein the protagonist Sarita undergoes the traumatic experience of the nightly sexual assaults by her frustrated husband as she is a successful doctor and he is an underpaid lecturer. In *The Binding Vine*, Mira has aversion to physical intimacy with her husband but she has to put up with his obsession forever. She gives voice to her inner-self in her poems "in the solitude of an unhappy marriage, who died giving birth to her son at twenty-two" (48). It so happens that after many years of her marriage, Urmi receives an old trunk full of books and a few other things from Mira's husband's stepmother, referred to as *Akka*. Among these books Urmi finds Mira's diary which is "not a daily account of her routine life, but a communion with herself" (51). When *Akka* hands over Mira's jewellery to Urmi, she says, "They're

Kishore's mother's" but while giving books and diaries to her, she says, "Take this, it's Mira's" (48). It shows that a woman loses her identity after her marriage. She is seen either as a wife or mother which in a way erases her real self and imposes another alien self on her. The difference made by *Akka* symbolises that the poems and diaries are "self-actualizing, whose identities are not dependent on men" (Martin 1994-95: 10).

Urmi goes through the poems in Mira's diaries and gets a glimpse of her troublesome married life. She comes to know from *Akka* how Kishore's father had pursued and married Mira, a college student. The poems and entries in the diary are sufficient enough to prove the forced sexual activity. Mira had to undergo in an incompatible marriage. The extent of her molestation in marriage can be measured from the following lines:

> But tell me, friend, did Laxmi too twist brocade tassels round her fingers and tremble, fearing the coming of the dark-clouded, engulfing night? (66)

One of the entries in the diary reveals her aversion to sexual activity with her husband. She writes:

> And so it begins. 'Please,' he says, 'Please, I love you'. And over and over again until he has done, 'I love you.' Love! How I hate the word. If this is love it is a terrible thing. I have learnt to say 'no' at last, but it makes no difference, no difference at all. What is it he wants from me? I look at myself in the mirror and wonder, what is there in me? (67)

Such passages embody the psychological fears and physical sufferings of Mira. Urmi wants to share this suffering with Vanna, her childhood friend and now her sister-in-law but she can't, because "I cannot speak of Mira, of Mira's writing, to her. That is another pocket of silence between us. One can never see one's parent as a sexual being; her or she is merely a cardboard figure labeled 'parent'" (83). Urmi remembers the poem behind which lies the man "who tried to possess another human being against her will" (83).

Don't tread paths barred to you
Obey, never utter a 'no';
Submit and your life will be
A paradise, she said and blessed me. (83)

Urmi decodes Mira's loneliness from the fact that the latter rarely mentions her family in her poems. This loneliness was a part of her being. When she came to her in-law's house, she was christened Nirmala—the first estrangement from her identity, her known self. One of her poems is written in reaction to this horrible incident:

A glittering ring gliding on the rice
carefully traced a mane 'Nirmala'.
Who is this? None but I,
My name hence, bestowed upon me.
Nirmala, they call, I stand statue-still,
Do you build new without erasing the old?
A tablet of rice, a pencil of gold
can they make me Nirmala? I am Mira. (101)

But this strong assertion remains a private experience; it never becomes public in her lifetime.

Urmi feels the burden of the dead on her. She had taken several things of the dead-Bai Ajji's silver pins, her saris, and Mira's bangles—but none of these meant much to her. Contrasted with things, Mira's poetry is "like a message being tapped on the wall by the prisoner in the next cell" (115). Urmi visualizes the moments when and where Mira could have written the poems. Certainly, she did not possess a room of her own. Urmi says: "I can see her stealthily, soundlessly getting out of bed, sitting down on the floor by the window perhaps, forgetting everything while she wrote" (127). Mira's diary also reveals her meeting with the rising poet Venu who had later become a grand old man of Indian literature. When Mira gives him some of her poems to read, he said, "Why do you need to write poetry. It is enough for a young woman like you to give birth to children. That is your poetry. Leave the poetry to us men" (127). This is also a kind of brutality because "even to force your will upon another is to be brutal" (133). This reflects the agony of a creative woman in an andocentric world. This is subordination by domestication. The same kind of anguish is reflected by Kamala Das in her poem "An Introduction":

> Dress in sarees, be girl
> Be wife, they said. Be embroiderer, be cook
> Be a quarreler with servants. Fit in.
> Oh Belong, cried the categorizers. (Das 1984: 17)

This is a scheme of depriving woman of imagination and the power of communication. It would not be out to place to see what Cora Kalpan says in this context:

> To be a woman a poet presents many women poets with such a profound split between their social, sexual identity, (their human identity) and their artistic practice that the split becomes the insistent subject, sometimes overt, often hidden or displaced, of much woman's poetry. (1986: 70)

This silent effort of Mira to use language as a means to her redemption may be treated as "a demand for access to and parity within the law and myth-making groups in society" (Kalpan 1986: 71). She uses her pen as a weapon to save herself from abuse, anonymity and mutilation in the prison house of her husband.

It is ironical that Urmi reads Mira's poems as a hunter to find out the real self of Mira. Every time while reading the poems she is filled with the excitement of a hunter. But soon this relationship changes. "It is Mira who is now taking me by the hand and leading me...where? I don't know, I have no idea what lies at the end of this remarkable journey, but on the way I have seen" (135). The centrality of Mira in the fictional world of *The Binding Vine* is further confirmed by the borrowing of the title of the novel from one of the poems of Mira which is about the womb-piercing joy of her pregnancy, the binding vine of love. The poems of Mira haunt Urmi so much that she decides to resurrect her by publishing them. But when Vanna comes to know about this plan, she is enraged. She feels that Urmi is a traitor who will destroy the honour of the family by publishing the poems. "It's as if the knowledge of what her father did, of what he was, has threatened something, disturbed the inner rhythm of her being, so that there is a sense of disharmony about her" (181). In fact, male-oriented societies nourish women in such a way that they start looking at the world and interpreting it from male point of view.

Urmi is surprised to see Shakutai, whose husband has already deserted her for some other younger women, worried about the marriage of Kalpana who is, in the words of the doctor, "neither dead nor alive" (86). But she soon realizes that women like Kalpana's mother find security in marriage. At least they are "safe from other men" (88). Marriage in the life of such women acts as *purdah* or view which serves a "provision of symbolic shelter" (Papanek and Minault 1982: 7). Since mother Shakutai is afraid of the boys of the Chawl, she bitterly remarks that they behave "like dogs panting after bitches" (148). She had even thought of marrying Kalpana to Sulu's husband Prabhakar who was "mad" after her. Kalpana out rightly rejected the offer and ridiculed Sulu. When she decided to marry a boy of her own choice she was raped by Prabhakar. Adele King's views on one of the possible reasons behind rape are remarkable:

> Perhaps the worst problem in the culture, however, in the insistence on virginal purity for young girls, so that even the victim of a rape is blamed and becomes a modern figure for Sita in the *Ramayana*. The non-Indian reader is perhaps surprised both by the submissions of many of the women...and by the strength of the modern generation who refuse to be treated as victims. (1994: 430)

Sulu's suicide symbolizes the anguish of the weakened soul of the typical traditional Indian women. Depicting the plight of Indian women, Mulk Raj Anand's remarks are noteworthy:

> No women in our world is beyond the threat of rape, because of the suppressed energies of the male, though the taboos of patriarchy, which deny sex before marriage and make male young—young into wanton animals who assault any possible victim, when possessed by lust. (Anand 1988: 109)

Thus, the major characters of the novel symbolize the miserable and hopeless lot of innumerable Indian women who suffer silently and their voice remains smothered. The message Shashi Deshpande gives is that the invasion of a woman's body even in marriage can sometimes be as traumatic as rape. A similarity can be seen in this novel and "Intrusion" a short story by Shashi Deshpande. It's a story about a honeymooning couple wherein the husband forces his unprepared wife into the sexual act, which was equivalent to rape. The story is sensitive in the sense that the insensitive husband takes no cognizance of his wife's sense of humiliation. Focusing upon the suffocating situation for the women in the Indian society as presented in Shashi Deshpande's novel *The Binding Vine*. Dr. Taisha Abraham remarks:

> The most consistent move in the novel is one of unravelling in order to restate the "binding-Vine" of patriarchy. Deshpande uses interesting techniques to foreground there women as helpless victims.... In a novel based on "silencing" of Indian women by patriarchal/cultural norms, brought out, for example, by the Police Officer who records Kalpana's rape case as an accident, saying: "for all you know she may be a professional," Deshpande's own position as a writer seems interesting.... Deshpande has broken silence and written several novels. (1994: 72)

In case of Harish and Vanna also we see Vanna's submission just to keep the marriage intact. She longs for a son and the same is denied to her by her husband. After the birth of a second baby-girl she expresses her desire to Harish for a son. Harish consoles her by saying that she should not be one of those women who crave for sons. He also asks her as to why she thinks for sure that the next child would be a son. Despite all these arguments she is ready to take a chance. Urmi gets terribly irritated at her constant refrain "Harish says". She tells her "Assert yourself. You don't have to crawl before him, do you?" (80). She is also critical of her going out to work and also doing domestic chores all by herself and thus spoiling him and in the process denying love and care to her children. This leads to her daughter, Mandira, to grow with her own notions of the role of a woman as a mother and wife. She thinks that the duty of a woman is to first look after her home and children. She expresses her displeasure at her mother's leaving her and her sister in the care of an *ayah*. She even tells Urmi: "You know Urmi auntie, when I grow up, I'm never going to leave my children to go to work" (72). Her notions are in no way different from the traditional role of a woman.

Shashi Deshpande attempts at satirizing pseudo-feminists like Priti, who are over-enthusiastic about fighting for equal rights for women, but harbour displaced notions about women's freedom. In a case filed by a husband against his wife for restitution of conjugal rights, the court had ruled that the husband couldn't force the wife into physical relationship against her will. Priti is extremely excited whereas Urmi remains sober. Priti says: "Isn't it radical, absolutely earthshaking in this country I mean? Can you imagine the consequences?" (37). But Urmi thinks that one judgment by a single judge, which can be appealed against will make no difference to the entire womankind. She has a practical approach towards their problems and she knows that all such victims cannot go to courts. Thus, by making a dig at pseudo-feminist like Priti, she puts forth her own brand of feminism. But Adele King has a different view for the liberal kind of feminism indirectly advocated by Shashi Deshpande:

> Deshpande treats her characters with quiet irony and presents question for which there is no clear answer. Is it better to have disturbed the poor family by publicizing the rape in the newspapers to obtain an official apology from police for their botched investigation, when this publicity leads to a feeling of shame and the death of an innocent woman? Is Urmi justified in publishing her mother-in-law's poems when their description of her husband's father will bring him pain? Perhaps the acceptance of her narrative is the furthest removed from the experience of modern western readers. (1994: 430)

Thus, Shashi Deshpande has presented Urmila as a chaste wife whose sympathy for the less fortunate women is sparked off by her daughter's death. In spite of her longings and frustrations,

Urmila is not a radical feminist but one who, as Basavaraj Naiker opines: "Having entered a *Chakravyuha* from which there is no escape, they want to make the best of their given life by hardening themselves to face the harsh realities of life" (2001: 126). Besides it Deshpande has taken a bold step forward by exploiting the working women's needs of the head, heart and the anatomy. Urmila has all the bitter experiences of being a woman, her subordinate position in the patriarchal society, injustices, etc.; but unlike militant feminists she does not despise the motherhood which is the essential quality and highest bliss in the life of a woman. In her mind the difficult process of child bearing, nurturing and the shock of loss, through the death of the child leaves deep impression on the whole personality of women. Mira's awareness of the new life taking shape within her relates her to the world. In one of her poems she mentions:

> "But how escape this cord this binding vine?
> Fear lies coiled within this womb-piercing Joy." (136)

Santosh Gupta's remarks are quite relevant here:

> Urmi begins to feel that motherhood can change a woman irrevertibly and create its own deep bonds that can make other relations seem secondary. She begins to value women's experiences as mother and the responsibility of women towards each other. (1999: 99)

The foregoing analysis establishes the notion that Shashi Deshpande is an Indian feminist writer who does not go to the extremes because she knows that the "walls of anguish or thunder of curves or growls of anger do not by themselves turn into great literature" (Kripalani 1968: 109). It is significant that in the creative female world of Deshpande all men are not villains. The husband of the protagonist Urmi is good to her and she is fully satisfied with him. But she realizes the responsibility to her own caste—*The Stri Jati*—and struggles to bring its truth before the society. This embodies the depth of the dimensions of personality of Deshpande's heroine. The earlier protagonists of Deshpande seek their own way of salvation. Thus, Saru in *The Dark Holds No Terrors* fights to bring the husband-wife relationship on equal level where there should be no discrimination. Indu, in *Roots and Shadows*, is worried about her interactions with the varied personalities in her large family and her resolution to overcome her own personal crisis. Jaya in *That Long Silence* copes with her own suffering, silence and surrender and wins her freedom as an individual. Contrasted with all these is Urmi who is concerned with the redemption of her own caste. The effort of Urmi to publish Mira's poems aims at discovering the strangled voice articulating woman's silent discourse, deciphering the coded language and liberating the imagination of women from interior to exterior. This may be taken to mean that Deshpande converts a muted woman into a talking woman and provides the cause, will, strength and means to articulate the silence of women.

Urmi's effort to publicize the gruesome reality of Kalpana's life is an effort to oppose a "culture in which such feminist dreams have been replaced by fundamental patriarchy that divides women into rigid categories based on function" (Walker 1990: 69). Though not free from the dangers of being treated as a propaganda literature, *The Binding Vine* occupies a significant place in the Indian feminist fiction. It succeeds in deconstructing the interior colonialism of which women have been victims. By its abundant use of poetry, which is an integral part of the novel, *The Binding Vine* deserves to be treated as *Campu Kavya*, a creative literature which uses both prose and poetry. It can be said to be a new development in Indian English fiction. Lakshmi Holmstrom, in a book reviews, expresses almost the same feeling about the novel and the novelist:

> .... Her novels are fiction, about fiction, and particularly about women's fiction. This novel foregrounds ethical and political question about the exhumation of Mira's poems and publishing them; of publishing Kalpana's story, of politicizing the personal. Urmila's decision to speak out comes at the end of a period of self-examination and learning, and it is contrasted with the sensationalist and stridently opportunistic 'feminism' of Priti. (1993: 53)

It is said that literature is the mirror of society and a storehouse of information on the cultural and sociological aspects of its people. "The role of the writer is to feel the pulse of the society in consonance with its culture" (Jaiswal 1976: 14). Feminists argue that literature has all along been turned to the point of view of the male element. Woman is often "marginalised", "repressed" or "silenced" in literary works. An idealised image of woman is presented in literature concealing the bitter reality of her position in patriarchal society. Bringing about the difference in male and female experience and its expression in literature, Virgina Woolf says:

> There is the obvious and enormous difference of experience in the first place; but the essential difference lies in the fact; not that men describe battles and women the birth of children, but that each sex describes itself. (Woolf 1965: 26)

She also desired that she should write and be read only as a woman and not as a 'surrogate' for men. The women writers, therefore, have to write constructively to provide role models for the oppressed women. By reinterpreting old myths and questioning the validity of tradition and customs that circumscribe women in narrow slots, Indian women novelists have to continue challenging the operating codes of morality which subordinate women in the social structure.

Shashi Deshpande, comparatively a recent entrant into the literary scene, portrays the new Indian women and her dilemma in her novels. She concerns herself with the plight of the modern Indian women trying to understand herself and to preserve her identity as wife, mother and above all, as a human being. In her novel *That Long Silence*, it comes to the notice of the readers that Jaya, the protagonist, is rechristened as Suhasini by her husband on their wedding day. It confuses Jaya in her search for an identity. The pseudonym under which she operates as a writer further complicates the issue. Jaya stands for revolt whereas Suhasini symbolizes submission. Jaya rejects the name Suhasini and it is significant as a manifestation of her protest against such customs. But her sense of identity is never certain. She is torn between being Jaya, herself and Suhasini, the good wife; between building a self as a writer and a self as a wife and mother. Through the process of reliving the past in her mind, Jaya gets the guidance for her future. She decides to break her long seventeen years of silence and gives up being a passive and silent partner to Mohan. She decides to assert herself as an individual and also as a woman, wife or mother. Though she chooses to remain in the family, a change has been wrought in her situation. She has come out of the confining slots allotted to her by the patriarchal society. Earlier, Jaya had denied certain parts of herself that did not fit into the straitjacket of 'wifehood'. Now she asserts:

> I am not afraid anymore. The panic has gone. I'm Mohan's wife, I had thought, and cut off the bits of me that had refused to be Mohan's wife. Now I know that kind of a fragmentation is not possible. The child, hands in pockets, has been with me through the years. She is with me still. (Deshpande 1989: 191)

Some Indian women writers, being inspired by the feminist movements in the west, made a total switch over to the outside, seeking freedom from everything even their own culture. Deshpande's protagonists find freedom not in the western sense but in conformity with the society they live in with drifting away from one's culture. Jaya's decision is not a meek surrender to circumstances, but a sensible compromise between the mutually conflicting ideals of conformity and non-conformity. Deshpande doesn't accept the theory that 'women are victims'. The 'dependency syndrome' in women is responsible for their victimization and she desires that women need to offer resistance and emerge as strong-willed individuals to face life, to share responsibilities, and not to escape from it. The novelist appears to be aware of the fact that breaking off the bonds of family would result in loneliness and disintegration of the larger social set-up, Jaya looks for happiness and self-fulfillment within the family itself. She asks for her individuality to be valued equally along with that of man. As long as one half of the humanity are denied decent and dignified lives, it will be a far cry to hope for a better world. But, Jaya, confident of her individuality and hopeful of a change in Mohan's attitude, moves beyond the cultural stereotypes with the firm conviction that 'life has always to be made possible'. Such an optimistic ending of the novel, *That Long Silence*, shows that the day is not far off when men and women will be treated equally. We can hope for the world in which there shall be no sex discrimination, women will live dignified as the equal partner of the human race.

The theme of *The Binding Vine* is not constructed of feminity, but its deconstruction. The psychological approaches that Urmi achieves are through the psychoanalytic approaches to gender rather than sociological ones. Deshpande takes the feminine point of view, and emphasizes the suffering and alienation which women as daughters and mothers endure. But the psychological transformation that Urmi achieves is more through an awareness and a realization of the multiple and contrary identities which a woman possesses. Urmi, herself, had to bind together her conflicting identities of 'neglected' daughter, 'abandoned' wife, and 'grieving' mother.

Once Urmi was asked by her brother, Amrut, 'Do women want to be dominated?' Urmi's answer was that no human being wants to be dominated. Love is the most felt need. Urmi further tells him, "From the moment of our birth, we struggle to find something with which we can anchor ourselves to this strange world we find ourselves in. Only when we love do we find this anchor (137). But love makes one vulnerable. So we put on 'armour' and in the process of survival, we do terrible things. The main urge was always to survive. The answer to 'What shall I do?' in the face of life's interminable problems is silence. Sages and philosophers had tried to find an answer. But 'detachment', love, brotherhood, non-violence—they are just words. They mean nothing to our living. Dharma, Dharma, Dharma, the *Mahabharata* endlessly, tirelessly repeats, yet at the end, the poet cries out in despair, "I raise my arms and I shout, but no one listens" (202).

Though the utter futility of living overwhelms one, one is also terrified by the thought of dying, of ceasing to be. Mira had realized this. It is the 'binding vine' of love, with its cruelty and its selflessness, that binds together the conflicting multiple identities of one's self. Mira had found peace at the thought of the child within her. Shakutai discovered that she had to go on with the routine task of life for Kalpana and her other children, or stop living. Urmi's 'armour' falls away at her mother's belated confession that she loved her. An integrated consciousness may be an illusion for ordinary mortals—but the 'spring of life' is refilled and nurtured through the redemptive powers of love. Love is compassion, and tolerance in dealing with the ordinary occurrence of everyday life. One can never opt out of this '*chakravyuha*' of human existence. Love is the only factor that prevents us from falling apart. And this Urmi understands through a recollection of those instances that had embodied tenderness and affection. Through the lives of Mira and Shakutai, Urmi realizes that the identities she possesses transcend gender division. It is an individual that her search for happiness begins. Life is to live and all human beings, both man and woman, live in an amicable and harmonious society without breaking the sociocultural fabric of the society. The only need is to realize in 'live and let me live'. Laeeq Futehally rightly points out:

> Ms. Deshpande in a fine writer and *The Binding Vine* is a very good read. It is an interesting story, and you want to know what happened next. That it has a message is not to denigrate it—quite the contrary. We find that in the space of a short novel, she has managed to say everything that could be said about the position of women in India. And, while granting that it is a piece of fiction we can not help exclaiming in the worth of an old song "It's true, it's true!". (1993: 91)

After all the shocking revelations, traumatic tragedies and hysterical denial of life, one finds Shakutai getting with her chores calmly and resolutely. However burdensome our ties are, however painful our experiences are, one can never opt out. The main urge is always to survive, to get on with the business of living, even if it comprises a daily routine that takes care of a hundred trifling matters, bringing an order and rhythm to it. Realizing this, Mira says, "Just as the utter futility of living overwhelms me, I am terrified by the thought of dying, of ceasing to be" (203). Considering the fates of Mira, Kalpana, Shakutai and Sulu, Urmila regains her courage. Accepting the freedom and advantages of her life as a gift, she decides to be content with her life, hoping that Kishore will remove her armour one day and she would reach him. Anu is gone but she still has Kartik. With a new understanding of life and relationship, Urmila realizes that with all the betrayals and cruelty, life is worth living as there are flashes of love, concern, understanding and reconciliation that brighten it. The bonds thus help us to continue with life, the greatest gift of God.

In *That Long Silence,* the quest for an authentic selfhood on the part of the protagonist finds an artistic expression through her rebellion against the patriarchal core of society. The novelist explores her public and private realms of experience her creative urge and artistic zeal free her from cramped domestic and societal roles. She resolves to assert her individuality by breaking the long silence, by putting down on paper all that she had suppressed in her seventeen years' silence. *The Binding Vine* is a novel with a difference. Urmi, the protagonist, draws the attention of the society towards the agony of the raped victim and is determined to get Meera's poems published. Sarita, Jaya and Indu are fighting only their own battles, but Urmila is a different woman. *The Binding Vine* is a welcome change from the previous novels. The hope for Indian women lies in fact that in spite of meek acceptance of the situation, we have self-sacrifying women like Urmila. Thus, we come to the conclusion after studying the two novels *That Long Silence* and *The Binding Vine* that the novelist has tried to find out the right solution for the women community that is mutual understanding, love, sympathy, compassion. She does not advise the Indian women to revolt against their counterparts like the militant feminists. She stresses the need to find out the solution within the periphery of marriage, within the Indian social setup of the family bonds.

Feminism in *A Matter of Time* and *Small Remedies* 5

Shashi Deshpande is an ever shining star in the sky of novel writing in Indian English. She has been successful in holding her position high as a feminist writer by articulating the anguish, agony and conflict of the modern educated Indian women, caught between tradition and modernity, struggle for self-expression and individuality. She deals with the inner world of the Indian women in her novels. She portrays her heroines in a very realistic manner. Basically, she writes about the plight of women and their failures in the fast changing socio-economic context of India. She writes about the conflict between tradition and modernity in relation to women of the middle-class society. The story revolves around the women's desires, efforts and failures in the traditional Indian society. She is a typical Indian feminist writer. She makes it clear that hers is not the strident and militant kind of feminism which holds the man as her counterpart in the western countries. Her description of women's world is authentic and credible. She seems to have taken cudgel to voice the injustice meted out to the middle-class women in her novels. It would not be an exaggeration to mention that human relationship is the main concern of hers.

Shashi Deshpande's novels present a social world of many complex relationships. Many men and women live together and journey across life in their different age groups, classes and gendered roles. Doubt, anxiety and often a feeling of void of values push characters in her novels to intense self-examination. The women are particularly caught in the process of redefining and discovering their own roles, position and relationships within their given social world. In the extended families that

Shashi Deshpande presents, two or three generations live together. She presents the modern Indian womanhood in the novels. Her own struggle as a writer to focus on women's issues, problems and experience is equally symptomatic of the resistance to feminist expression that prevails in India in the middle of twentieth century. She tries to maintain distance for herself from women's lives and point of view through the use of male narrative voice. As a woman writer, her dilemma was either to give voice to women's concern and be branded as a 'woman writer', removed from the mainstream of literary scene, or to deny her feminity and write like a man either with the male name or male narrative voice. The dilemma has been faced by her thoughts and her concern with women's lives. The live experiences and viewpoint of women represent after all "one half of humanity". Her empathic claim that she is a feminist came gradually to her as her main literary concern. It became an acceptance for womanhood as a positive thing, not as a lack. The concerns of women are primarily with the family and the community. Deshpande has looked into women's changing perspectives and their search for bonding within families as a mode of strength.

Deshpande uses this point of view to present social reality as it is experienced by women. To present the world of mothers, daughters and wives is also to present indirectly the fathers, sons and husbands, the relation between men and women, and between women themselves. In presenting women's point of view Deshpande is mainly interested in the clash of tradition and modernity, as reflected in the generation gap and conflict between women. Her young heroines rebel against the traditional way of life and patriarchal values. Jaya, Sarita and Sumi perceive the structuring of men and women in gendered roles, restricting their human potentiality and fullness. They struggle to transcend the restrictive roles. They rebel, reject and seek freedom from the traditional norms and way of life. Shashi Deshpande's portrayal of women of different generations presents the divided world of women in the traditional and modern ways of life. Her female protagonists are from the middle-class. Besides her class identity, she cannot betray her gender identity. She says, as writing is born out of personal experience, the fact that I am a woman is bound to surface. Besides, only a woman could write my books—they are written from inside, as it were.

A MATTER OF TIME

Shashi Deshpande's fifth novel *A Matter of Time* was published by Penguin Books, India in 1996. Her novels mainly explore a woman's psyche. Her earlier novels *Roots and Shadows*, *The Dark Holds No Terrors*, *That Long Silence* and *The Binding Vine* deal with feminist issues. The present novel *A Matter of Time* (1996), too, deals with the same subject. Yet a woman's inner life is not the only concern of this novel. Here the inner life of woman emotionally isolated from her family is reflected and refracted in the embryonic women represented by her daughters. Deshpande does believe that she is a feminist and her concerns are universal. She writes about silent, sobbing women, mothers, grandmothers, aunts, sisters, grand-aunts, daughters and whole lot of women community. Her writing is gender specific. Feminism is at the core of her novels. She deals with a woman's psyche and the way she is made to feel an inferior being, an unwanted child, an unnecessary burden on the family for instance, Kalyani is in *A Matter of Time*. In her book-review, Usha Bande aptly observes:

> There are three generations of women with their impregnable silence and suffocating life, but it is the impatient new generation ready to fight it tooth and nail that provides a whiff of cool breeze. How successful will this new woman be in getting justice is, in fact, a matter of time. (1997: 42)

A Matter of Time deals with the human predicament of three women representing three generations of the same family. Shashi Deshpande, for the first time, has made a man the protagonist of the novel, but it doesn't mean that she has focused entirely on the man. Like her other novels, she has given ample expression to the women's pain, suffering and endurance in marriage. The novel moves around an urban, middle-class family of Gopal and Sumi with their three daughters—Aru, Charu and

Seema. It begins with Gopal entering home and telling Sumi that he is leaving home for good. Sumi gets perplexed and finds herself unable to react verbally. She narrates all the incidents next morning to her daughters about it, "almost exactly repeating Gopal's words, leaving out nothing" (9). In a review of *A Matter of Time*, Latha Anantharaman opines:

> Here the inner life of a woman emotionally isolated from her family is reflected and refracted in the embryonic women represented by daughters. Sumi returns to her parents' home with her three daughters after her husband walks out on her. (1997: 76)

Sumi is shocked with Gopal's action and lapses into complete silence, trying simultaneously to feel things normal for her daughters. But they feel restless as "Sumi, despite her façade of normality, has a quality about her—a kind of blankness—that makes them uneasy" (10-11). This crisis not only leads to an intense introspection by the women characters in the first person narrative but also by the male protagonist Gopal. In a review of *A Matter of Time,* Meenakshi Mukherjee says:

> Enigmas are concealed in the interstices of silence and nothing is fully explained. The broad circumstances of the estrangement of Kalyani and Shripati are gradually revealed but the possible causes are left unsifted, hinting at something unspeakable.... Deshpande's ability to leave things unsaid invests the novels with rich inconclusiveness of life. (1997: 30)

Although the debate on her identity as a feminist writer still rages, Deshpande shows she has the wisdom to sympathetically dive deep into male protagonist's psyche.

A Matter of Time revolves around the absence of the principal character Gopal. He has left his home forever leaving behind his wife Sumi and three daughters. After Gopal's desertion, Shripati, Sumi's father brings them to "Big House" —their parental home. His absence from the family has created a unique tension for Sumi, Aru, Charu, Seema and other characters. Each of them tries to find out the reason behind his desertion. For Sumi's mother, Kalyani, it's not only a great tragedy, but also a matter of shame and disgrace. She cries out: 'No, no, my God, not again', she begins to cry, sounding so much like an animal in pain" (12). Sumi's grief, anger and humiliations are so deep that she remains calm and composed outwardly but she is very restless inwardly. She becomes an enigma for her parents, sister and cousins: "She accepts Goda's dumb sympathy, Devaki's fierce loyalty and Ramesh's stupefied bewilderment, as if they are all the same to her" (20). They fail to deal with her apparent stoicism. Sumi's daughters seem to have taken up the threads of their life in the "Big House", but she remains totally lost and confused even in her childhood home. She confesses that Gopal's desertion has left such a void that she cannot find her bearings and there are no one to advise her which way she should go. The incident had made a telling effect on her body and soul: "With Gopal's going, it was as if the swift-flowing stream of her being had grown thick and viscous—her movements, her thoughts, her very pulse and heartbeats seemed to have slowed down" (28). Meenakshi Mukherjee presents her views on the desertion of Gopal thus:

> This motivation might have been metaphysical or existential, like Gautam Buddha's, but its repercussion on the family are starkly material. Gopal tries hard to articulate his position but cannot satisfy anyone—least of all his militant daughter. (1997: 30)

Her daughters feel hurt by her apparent stoicism, as they want to share their mother's loss and sorrow. Devaki or Devi even cries to her and tell her, "And may be I'm crying because you don't" (107). At this Sumi expresses her sense of great humiliation and loss: "What do I say, Devi? That my husband has left me and I don't know why and may be he doesn't really know, either? And that I'm angry and humiliated and confused...?" (107).

Gopal's desertion leaves behind a wave of shock not only for the family members but also for the readers. There are some unsolved questions, i.e., why did he marry Sumi? Generally it is seen that arranged marriages, sometimes, become hellish resulting in divorce, desertion, suicide, etc. because the couples are tied up in wedlock without knowing each other's likings and dislikings. But that case of Gopal and Sumi is different. Theirs was a love-marriage. Gopal himself is puzzled and asks himself "Why did I marry Sumi? Because I met her—it's as simple as that" (65-66). Thus, the marriage is devoid of initial romance, but is the inevitable outcome of a matter-of-fact relationship. The contract was easy and its breach even easier. But their marriage cannot be said to be incompatible as their first physical consummation is fulfilling and gratifying to both. Gopal recounts the union later: "And I knew then that it was for this, this losing yourself in another human being, that men give up their dreams of freedom" (223). Deshpande does not assign any tenable reason for Gopal's desertion and readers remain in the dark.

Kalyani is very much worried about her daughter, Sumi, whose husband has deserted her. In Sumi's life there is a vacuum owing to Gopal's abandonment. Sumi tries to find out clues to his probable motives in his past acts and utterances. Once Gopal had explained that *Sa-hriday* in the sense of oneness is an impossible concept. He accepts the traditional view of marriage where God unites the two hearts. He also believes that the husband and wife are two halves of one thing. But he realizes that he was not successful in the idealistic expectations of his marriage. He could not feel himself a *Sa-hriday* with Sumi in an unexpected condition. Gopal's absence leaves her in a state of vast emptiness. She feels, "I can't find my bearings, there are no makers any more to show me which way I should go" (36). Yet it is from the depth of her despair that she tries to transform her emptiness into meaning in order to redefine her identity. She does not remain a passive mother, but an active agent. We cannot forget that Sumi, like her mother, is a suffering, oppressed and wronged woman. Yet she doesn't question the man, her oppressor.

One possible reason for Gopal's decision to quit home may be his sense of alienation and loneliness born of his abnormal childhood. He is unable to come to terms with the fact that he was born of a union of his father and his father's brother's wife. A conflict rages in his adolescent mind for the reason that led to his marriage. Later in his life, he happens to read *Hamlet* and found some similarities between his own and Hamlet's predicament:

> It was when I read *Hamlet*, fortunately much later, that the most terrible version of my parents' story entered my mind.... In this story my father became a man succumbing to his passion for his brother's wife, the woman complaint, a pregnancy and a child to come and then, after the husband's convenient death (no, I couldn't, I just couldn't make my father poison his brother) a marriage of convenience. (43)

When his father was alive, he was unable to relate himself to his father as he considered him as his mother's guilty partner. Later their death leaves a great void in his life. He gets completely shattered at the realization that his sister Sudha and he himself did not share the same father. He later reflects: "That was a betrayal that cut away at the foundations of my life" (52). Thus, we see that Gopal has been nurturing a sense of alienation and loneliness since his childhood. He reflects: "All human ties are only a masquerade. Someday, sometime, the pretence fails us and we have to face the truth" (52). The above lines are sufficient enough to prove his pessimistic approach of life. Perhaps it is the realization that had compelled him to walk out on his family. But, it is just a riddle for the readers as the novelist does not mention any obvious reason till the end of the story. However, Gopal's desertion had another aspect on the boldness of Sumi. This hardship made Sumi able to face the obstacles of life and challenges. Keerti Ramchandra, in a book-review of *A Matter of Time*, says:

> Gopal's departure comes as a mixed blessing for Sumi as well. All this while she had been content to be a wife and mother, subordinating herself to her husband and daughter. Her interpretation of Draupadi's choice of disguise as Sairandhri, reveal a sharp mind but one that had deliberately shut itself off. (1997: 20)

There are several factors responsible for disintegration of marriage, viz. Western education, lack of choice for the bride and groom, differences in the socio-cultural backgrounds, etc. Keerti Ramchandra's views are noteworthy here:

> Relationship breakdown because there is an inherent reticence in most people, especially those who come from the same background as the Pandit family governed by a strict code of conduct, a sharp awareness of duties and obligations, the characters in the novel constantly, walk the tightrope of living upto expectations. (1997: 20)

Gopal's desertion may have another reason. Sumi thinks that he may have taken *Sanyas*—a way of life as a stoic person, but as per the code of *Sanyas* he must wear saffron clothes, keep a bowl in his hands to keep whatever is given in charity by the people. He could have been seen begging from door to door, he should have become the follower of any religious cult. But Sumi fails to find any characteristic of a stoic person. She reflects her views:

> I have begun to think that what Gopal has really done is to take Sanyas. I'm surprised none of you have thought of that. But look what's happened—it's not he who's going around with the begging bowl, it's I who am doing that. (123)

It seems the novelist wants to convey a message to the readers that even in the event of a man's desertion for stoic purpose is also a kind of injustice to the woman. It is just escaping from the joint responsibility of rearing the children, providing them proper education and getting them married. If a married man runs away from his home in search of God, salvation, etc., it is of no use for the woman he has married. Thus, we come to this conclusion that the Indian women have been facing this type of social injustice for centuries.

> Aru has a thousand and one questions—why is her grandmother Kalyani so oppressively silent and fear ridden? Why isn't there any communication between her grandparents? Why has their father left them? (Bande 1997: 42)

Sumi's daughter Aru is rebellious by nature. She raises a voice of revolt against her father. She meets Gopal, her father expecting no sympathy for herself or her mother from him. She wants to unravel the strange behaviour of her father. She asks

Gopal "Why did you marry? Why did you have children?" (65). Her searching question makes Gopal re-examine his motives in fleeing from the family. Aru is disappointed to see the tragedy of her grandmother and mother. Out of frustration she declares "I'm never going to get married" (76). She holds strong views on patriarchy and how women, in general, get victimized as a result of unwise actions of men. She is critical of Gopal. She does not want to see Gopal going scot-free.

> The only character to grip the readers' imagination is Aru. She tries all her strength, will-power and heroine efforts to set things right. Probably, the novelist looks with hope at the new generation to penetrate the silence and make women speak up for themselves. (Bande 1997: 42)

Aru meets a feminist, Surekha, a lawyer by profession. However, the activist lawyer does not find it a case of the usual marital discord. The novelist has also reflected the injustice meted out to women in matters of property ownership. Sumi is shocked to know that her maternal grandfather's property, which should have been inherited by Kalyani, is bequeathed to her father: "Why did they not give it to her? She finds herself looking into conundrum of justice, a well so deep, dark and unfathomable, that she draws back" (196). Bande Usha in her book-review points out thus:

> There is woman's lib material as Aru meets a feminist, Sulakshana, a lawyer by profession, an activist by conviction. Then, some light on the cause of women's education; and then a whole narrative devoted to silent, brooding women, unhappy, yet lively, clinging to their past, yet living in the present. (1997: 42)

Kalyani had every right to the ownership of the property, but the same is denied to her. Further, Aru is surprised to know that women find no mention in the family tree, although they went through thick and thin while discharging their respective duties to the family. Aru is again surprised when her lawyer-friend, Surekha, whom she meets to sue her father for maintenance, tells her: "Do you know that Manu doesn't mention any duty to maintain a daughter? The duty is only towards a wife, parents and sons" (204). The utmost desire to get a son, is to be witnessed in Kalyani-Manorama relationship as she gives birth to two baby-girls. She wins favour of her mother when she gives birth to a baby-boy though a mentally retarded one. But that favour is short-lived as she loses her only son in confusion at a railway station. Deshpande's quote from the *Brahad-Aranyaka Upanishad* (1.5.17) sums up the Indian psyche:

> Whatever wrong has been done by him, his son frees him from it all; therefore he is called a son. By his son a father stands firm in this world. (91)

The novelist doesn't leave out the issue of female sexuality. Surpanakha, the mythical Ravana's sister, becomes a symbol of female sexuality. Sumi recalls her mother's statement that she was as ugly as Surpanakha. Since then she has been thinking of Surpanakha and the unpleasant incident in which her nose is cut off when she flaunts her love to Rama and Lakshmana. She reflects:

> Female sexuality; we're ashamed of owning it, we can't speak of it, not even to our own selves. But Surpanakha was not, she spoke of her desires, she flaunted them. And, therefore, were the men, unusual to such women, frightened? Did they feel threatened by her? I think so. Surpanakha, neither ugly nor hideous, but a woman charged with sexuality, not frightened of displaying it. (191)

Unlike the earlier novels, Deshpande gives voice to the man's point of view. Gopal's thoughts and feelings are laid bare before us. Motherhood has been given too prominent a place in literature and society that a father's feelings go unnoticed. Gopal's sense of alienation and loneliness since his father's unholy marriage remain so even after his marriage. Earlier, too, he felt himself like an outsider and even after marriage the feeling doesn't leave him:

> I saw it when Sumi put the baby to her breast. For I knew, when I looked at them, that they belonged as I never did. Even when Sumi was impatient, when she showed a flash of temper as she often did for being deprived of her sleep,

> they were together in that magic circle. Woman and child. And I was outside. A man is always an outsider. (68)

The mother son bond is so deep-rooted in a man's psyche that it is nearly impossible to extricate oneself from it. When Shankar expresses his inability to protect his wife from his mother's sharp tongue saying, "She gave me birth, she brought me up, she looked after me..." (216). Gopal reflects: "That's a debt we can never repay, it's a burden we can never lay down" (216).

The novelist ends the novel on a tragic note. The reunion of Gopal and Sumi is an unusual one. When he comes back his home, she neither cries to him nor does she ask him for any explanation. Everything is normal as Sumi enters the room and finds him having lunch and reading poems. As soon as the lunch is over, she finds him in a happy mood, laughing and talking to the others and her daughters, but for herself she realizes that "We can never be together again" (88). She says:

> All these days I have been thinking of him as if he has been suspended in space, is nothingness, since he left us. But he has gone on living, his life has moved on, it will go on without me. So has mine. Our lives have diverged, they now move separately. (85)

Thus, she seems to have come to terms with her present situation with a new-born understanding to move ahead in her life without any bitterness for the man who had been the cause of her humiliation and suffering. Siddhartha Sharma rightly observes:

> Now she is a new woman with a new understanding and consciousness all set to begin her life anew and confidently as a teacher and creative writer. But this was not to be. Sumi and her father, Shripati, meet their tragic end in a road accident. This gives a philosophical dimension to the novel. (2005: 63)

Deshpande has flashed light on the cause of women's education and liberation. The modern education has helped the women to strive for liberation—liberation from the old age male dominance and the so-called militant way of struggle as prescribed by the western feminists. The whole novel is devoted to silent, brooding women, unhappy, yet lively, clinging to their past, yet living in the present. The male characters do not play any active role in the story. On the other hand, Gopal and Shripati—the two male characters have been presented as the root cause of all the sufferings. The novelist tries to exonerate the male by bringing in some strong, loving and responsible figures. But they come and go, flitting like shadows. The real balance is tilted by Gopal and Shripati. Gopal's exit reminds us of Anita Desai's protagonist in her story *Surface Texture* and Nirode in *Voices in the City* and Arun Joshi's *Billy Biswas*.

Shashi Deshpande's writing is primarily concerned with the women's sufferings. Most of her writings come out of her own intense and long suppressed feelings about what it is to be a woman in our society. It comes out of the experience of the difficulty of playing different roles. Her writing comes out of her consciousness of the conflict between her idea of herself as a human being and the idea that society has of her as a woman. As a woman writer she deals with gender-related experiences. It comes out of a concern for the human predicament. Thus, Deshpande has ventured out of the cordon she had confined herself to and articulates the agony, pain, doubts and fears of her protagonists—male and female alike. She does not fight for justice to women at man's cost, but presents their respective limitations as spouse. In an interview, she tells Vanamala that she desires to reach a stage where "I can write about human beings and not about men and women" (Deshpande 1987). And she has proved several times that she remains unsurpassed as a writer of middle-class lives. Shama Futehally aptly observes: "Those who have read and reread Deshpande over the years are united in describing her as a 'middle-class' writer" (Futehally 1997: 111).

SMALL REMEDIES

Shashi Deshpande's latest novel *Small Remedies* (2000) is described as "a complex and hard hitting novel of extra-ordinary emotional range" by critics. The novel reaffirms Deshpande as one of India's best writers of fictions. *The Hindustan Times* hailed Deshpande's art of storytelling with these words "an extremely talented storyteller with an uncommon way with words". Her novels like *The Dark Holds No Terrors, Roots and Shadows, That Long Silence, The Binding Vine* and *Small Remedies* present a realistic plight of a middle-class woman torn between two roles—traditional and modern, between inner duties and outer duties, between family and profession. Her female characters like Sarita, Jaya, Indu, Urmila and Madhu are ordinary middle-class women down to earth and face the crisis of life silently and internally. The women of Anita Desai and Nayantara Sahgal belong to a slightly upper stratum of society, whereas Shashi Deshpande portrays the average middle-class woman with her deeply felt but never so well expressed experience of life's little ironies.

Shashi Deshpande analyses the characters in the light of social-cultural modes and values that have given Indian women their image and role in society while probing the Indian women's identity and quest from space and selfhood. The issues and themes in the novel arise from the situation of women who are standing at the cross roads of the transitional society changing to traditional from modern. Rashmi Gaur, in her article "Suffering and desire in Shashi Deshpande in *Small Remedies* opines:

> A closer scrutiny of her work convinces one that her women struggle to obtain selfhood by dissolving their permission, by including strength to survive with dignity and by analyzing their problems rationally. Her women refuse to surrender before anxieties, indoctrination, social conditioning and resultant oppression. But they never stoop to the level of neurotic protest. (2002: 33-34)

It seems Deshpande has honed her skills to perfection in this novel. Her protagonist is still the urban, middle aged and educated woman, but her canvas has broadened to encompass a cross section of people who belong to different communities, professions and a level of society. In a book-review of *Small Remedies*, Lakshmi Holmstrom has rightly remarked:

> Deshpande is, I think, one of our finest writers of English. It is always a pleasure just to read her work. Her style is

> elegant, and at the same time it is substantial, weighty in the best sense. If it doesn't have the inventiveness and playfulness of some of the newer and younger writers, it is still full of surprises, the surprise of exactitude. (2000: 4-5)

Small Remedies covers three generations of Indian women, and the three central women characters. It embodies the transformations that have taken place in women's lives over the last hundred years. It reflects the illustration of the Kierkegaardian Axiom. "Life must be lived forward, but it can only be understood backward." Ritu Memon in her book-review "Pentimento," says thus:

> This juxtaposition, this backward glances, this excavation of the past is the key to Madhu's realization of self, and Deshpande's use of it in fiction in the clearest example of the Feminist project of recovery at its most enabling, and sobering. (2000: 25)

Madhu has now accepted the simple truth that it is not necessary to know all the answers to the questions that life throws up. "That what we call truth has nothing to do with the truth that emerges through words" (255). Chandra Holm, in an Article, says:

> That truth comes home to Madhu not abruptly but slowly as she witnesses the lives around her. One such instance is an Upanayan Ceremony she witness in the Bhavanipur Temple, a ceremony that is marked with muted pain and grief. The death of the father had not meant that the Upanayan could not take place. Life had to go on. (2000: 158)

The novel *Small Remedies* is divided into four different texts (a) Savitri Bai's text (b) Leela's text (c) Meenakshi's text (d) Madhu's text. The texts of Savitri, Leela and Meenakshi form the background of the novel and Madhu's text forms the foreground of the novel. The novel begins with the description of Bhavanipur, a small village where Madhu, the narrator of the novel, comes to write the biography of Savitribai Indorekar, doyenne of Gwalior Gharana. Madhu has been commissioned to write Savitribai's biography wherein she was to be presented as a heroine. Surprisingly she refuses to present her as such since the latter had been a victim of gender discrimination prevalent in our patriarchal social set up. Just to impose the current concept of heroism on an old lady seemed not only impractical but out of place to Madhu. But she presents her as a young woman who had led a sheltered life not only as a child in her parental home but also as a daughter-in-law in an affluent Brahmin family. It is her daring independent nature that makes her seek her own identity and elope with a Muslim *tabla* player to live in a strange town. Although born in a tradition-bound orthodox Brahmin family, she makes a name for herself as a great classical singer. Madhu records how Savitribai felt hurt when her grandmother asked her to stop singing immediately during her performance at a family gathering. Madhu recalls: "In Neemgaon she was 'the singer woman' and there was something derogatory about the words, yes, I can see that now, about the way they said them" (29). Madhu recalls her as a frail woman and brings her to life by portraying vividly the minute details of her physique. She recalls her in the following words:

> I remember Savitribai as a small sized woman. Even from my child's perspective she had seemed petite. Age and illness have so shrunk her that she's a doll-sized woman now.... The skin is fine and delicate, even if it is crinkled like tissue paper. Her arms are slim and firm, but the hands, with their branching of veins, seem incongruously large for those delicate arms. (14)

Savitribai further narrates the story of her childhood to Madhu though she is a girl-child she is treated as a "precious jewel". Usually in those days girls were considered as a burden on the family. But Savitribai is fortunate enough to be born with a silver spoon in her mouth. She affirms:

> I was my parents' first child, a very pampered child. My father was the eldest of three brothers, so I was the first grandchild in the family. There were the daughters' children, of course, but they didn't count. They were not really our family. Everyone made a great fuss of me, not

> only my parents and grandparents but my uncles, my aunts—all of them. By the time I was two, I had almost my own weight in gold ornaments. (27)

As a child she is influenced by her mother's songs. She says:

> It was my mother who showed me the beauty of music. She had a sweet voice. She sang the sort of songs women sang then, *aarti* songs, ritual songs, stotras. When she sang the Ramraksha, it become something quite different from what it was when the women just recited it; the music transformed it altogether. I loved listening to her when she sang it. I even picked up a few verses on my own. (27)

Right from her childhood, Savitribai is a girl of independent nature. She seems more influenced by her mother than her father. She challenges the notion that father is the head of the family and he (father) has the sole authority to decide the daughter's life. As a young woman she marries to a Brahmin called Sadashivrao from Pune and becomes the mother of a daughter called Meenakshi which forms the third text of the novel.

Savitribai's love for music forces her to listen to music secretly. Once her father-in-law observed her activities and realized her genuine passion for music and encouraged her to learn music. The lesson of music starts in a dark dirty corner of a home. The women in family started gossiping. She does not care for these things and develops a good relationship with Gulamsaab—a *tabla* player during her course of learning and one day she elopes with him. Breaking all the barriers of caste, religion and marriage codes, she started to live with him. How can a married Hindu wife, a mother of a girl-child stay with a Muslim without marriage when women were dictated and ruled by men? She is rebellious by nature and challenges the code of Manu. She proves that 'her life is her own'. She is competent enough to take decision in her own life. From the very beginning of her childhood she had understood the gross discrimination meted out to women in the society where there was one law for men and another for women. She remembers how men could lead a life of their own likings with impunity, while women were criticised and looked down upon if they showed any deviation from the roles assigned to them by the society. In a society "where each family had its place marked out for it according to religion, caste, money, family background, etc." (138), Savitribai's father with his unconventional ways stood out from society. He was a widower, bringing up a daughter on his own with a male servant at home. He was unconventional in the sense that he would observe no ritual or religious rites and would openly indulge in a drink or two every evening. Nevertheless, all his unorthodox behaviours never invited any censure or disapproval from society. On the other hand, as soon as it came to Savitribai, it was a different story: "Being a man he could get away with much. He could live the way he wanted, without open censure or disapproval" (139). People are shocked and disapprove of Savitribai's action as soon as she elopes with a *tabla* player to some other town. In the course of time she begets a child from him.

Even Savitribai's father-in-law was not a man of high moral character because he had a mistress. He could get away with his way of life without any censure or disapproval from society. The mistress was a well-known *Thumari* singer. He used to visit her regularly and the people around knew this. It was just an open secret and women gossiped about it. Credit goes to the patriarchal society which never raised any furore over it. A man choosing a wife from his own class and a mistress from another was not highly objectionable. It would not be wrong to say that such type of practice for a handful people of the so-called aristocrat class was a matter of status symbol. Since her father-in-law himself was involved in this practice, he never discouraged or blamed her but she had to undergo great mental torture as she was treated like an untouchable among women. Savitribai tried to enjoy a little more freedom than sanctioned to women was a great cause for contempt and jealousy to other women, and they started to make sarcastic remarks on her when she came back from her music classes. Only a little deviation from the social norms lays her open to much contempt and ridicule, and also to be treated like an outcast by her own kind. The tortuous experience she undergoes is revealed in the following lines:

> For Bai to develop a relationship with another man, a tabla player, a Muslim—this must have been not only unimaginable, but the height of criminality. Did anyone blame the father-in-law for this? As the head of the family...to indulge in his love of music, even to have a singer as mistress, was all right. But for a daughter-in-law to be learning music, and that seriously, as if she was going to be a professional! Surely there was outrage, surely there was anger in the family. Rules could be modified for the daughters, sometimes they were, purely out of affection, but daughter-in-law carry the weight of the honour of the family, its reputation, its *izzat.* (220)

The same tortuous experience of Savitribai gets reflection in the following lines:

> To be set apart from your own kind, not to be able to conform, to flout the rules laid down, is to lay yourself open to cruelty. Animals know this, they do it more openly, their cruelty towards the deviant is never concealed. But the subtle cruelty of persistent hostility leaves deeper wounds. There's always the temptation to succumb, to be back to the normal path and be accepted. To resist the temptation speaks of great courage. (220-21)

It was a matter of gossip that the Director of a radio-station who had helped Savitribai in getting contracts with the radio was her lover. He was a regular visitor to her place. In course of time a daughter is born to her from him. Madhu recalls how children would tease the girl by calling the Station Director her *mama*, a euphemism for mother's lover. While narrating her life story to Madhu, Savitribai did not accept the fact she had any lover, but it was an open secret in the small township of Neemgaon that the Station Director was her lover because he had done so many favours to her in the capacity of being a Station Director, and had been visiting her quite frequently. In a patriarchal set up of society Savitribai was an immoral woman because she had left her husband's home. Like her father and father-in-law, she had also led a most unorthodox life but had also paid a high price for it as a woman. Madhu aptly remarks:

> They, unlike the men in the same families, were outside the circle of respectable society, their futures marked out for them, the ordinary life of ordinary women denied to them because of their birth. Nature is blind. It distributes qualities uncaring of social class, caste, gender. Bai was, in a sense, born into the wrong class. But so to perhaps, were many of the women who were born into professional families. If they had the freedom (was it freedom?) to artists, they were denied the right to live the life most women do, the life Bai herself opted out of. (221)

Savitribai has led a most unconventional life. She is ashamed of her youthful indiscretions as while relating her life-story to Madhu. She concealed her inmate relationship with Ghulam Saab and also the fact that she had a daughter from him. It shows Savitribai's anxiety over her past's reckless action, which she considers a blemish on her character and responsibility. She keeps herself aloof from her illegal daughter Munni, lest it should tarnish her image. But this dissociation of hers from her daughter is too much for Madhu as she herself is a devoted and loving mother, grieving over her son's death. Madhu cannot digest the fact that Savitribai has kept herself dissociated with her daughter born out of wedlock and has kept it as a topmost secret. She gave Munni her name 'Indorkar' which she had adopted as her very own identity as singer and which comprises neither her maiden name nor her married one; all this smacks of her possessiveness as she claims her as exclusively her own child, neither her husband's nor her lover's. In her quest for identity she has become very selfish and possessive, for she gives the child her own identity for her own sake, but disowns her when it comes to sacrificing her hard-earned name for her only child. She loves the child till her own emotional needs get fulfilled but when it comes to Munni's own identity and happiness; she selfishly keeps her out of her life, recoiling under the guise of respectability and a good name. Madhu wonders as to why a woman who had the courage to walk out on her marriage and family, feared to make public the fact that she had born a child out of wedlock. All these incidents reveal her utter selfishness. It does not prove that she had done something for the betterment for the women folk. She does not show her courage to keep the matter open as it happens in the western culture. It seems she had done some injustice with Munni. Munni had to face the stigma of being labeled as the child born of two partners having illicit relationship. In the west such things are gaining acceptance gradually, though not respectability. But, in the Indian context it is almost impossible. Madhu feels that she could make Savitribai immortal if she made public her most guarded secret.

For the sake of keeping her good name and identity untarnished, Savitribai had to pay high. She sacrificed her married life, her only daughter Munni, and finally her relationship with Ghulam Saab during the last days of her life. "Both Ghulam Saab, her lover and Munni, her daughter, no longer part of her life" (167). She is the lonely traveller in the journey of life. One's journey of life becomes less troublesome when accompanied by life partner and children. In case of life partner's absence, the journey of life continues with the most important companions—the children. But we see the miserable condition of Savitribai when she disclaims her own child Munni. The love for the child has got its expression in these words:

> The desire for a child, the anguish of childlessness—these have been a part of humankind since ancient times. Both the *Ramayana* and the *Mahabharata* begin with tormented desire for children. From the beginning, the child has been the single most important factor of human life. And why not? A child is a beginning, a renewal, a continuation, an assertion of immortality. (168)

But after a long struggle she succeeds in creating her own space, her own individual identity as an artist amidst the male-dominated society. Her teacher insists her to be original—a creator of her own life. Her teacher says: "That Todi was mine. You can never get that. You have to create your own; it will come through your life, your experiences, your joys and sorrows" (133).

Savitribai is a true disciple of her guru. She followed his advice both in her life and music. She refuses to do any new experiment with classical music. This is the saga of struggle. She suffers, struggles, sacrifices every thing in life but gets success in paving the way for every Indian woman. Madhu asserts:

> In this story I see the artist, the woman in search of her genius, of her destiny. But the artist was born of the woman. First there was the woman and then the artist. Is it possible to cut the umbilical cord, to serve the connection between the two? Did Bai manage to do this? (133)

Madhu, the wife of Dr. Som and mother of a child Aditya treats the life of Savitribai as an ideal for herself. When she comes back to Bhavanipur, she faces an emotional crisis after the death of her son Aditya. Ira Pande, in a book-review of *Small Remedies,* says:

> Madhu has tortured herself with the knowledge that she could have been on the bus that killed her son, that her husband and she had failed as parents to protect. (2000: 22)

Finally she comes to realize that no one is safe or protected forever. It is true that she works for the women's upliftment which brands her as a Feminist, yet she has the kindness of a mother as is expected from a lady. It is a surprising fact that her childhood was deprived of mother's love and affection. Her lonely childhood and stay with her aunts' family which was rather intolerant make her exceptionally sensitive. Rashmi Gaur says: "The initial trauma subsides when she marries Som and has a son. Madhu has grown up without her mother, brought up by her father and Babu, a man-servant. She never really bothered about not having a mother figure" (2002: 34). She herself has not any great sense of respect for mothers. She mentions mothers as "drab creatures, forever working, scolding their children" (182) and it does not create any sense of deprivation in her. But the time she begets a son, the world of hers changes. Her life, as that of a traditional woman, is complete with her son, "What can you give my Lord, I who have everything?" (229).

> The emotional bond, the trust between she and her husband has gone.

Som, an intelligent man guided by the society, questions Madhu's chastity, her serenity. He asks:

> 'Tell me the truth,' Som says over and over again. He dismisses the truth of our life together, of our love, our friendship, our life as parents of a beloved son. What he wants is something separate and distinct from these things, something which really is, though he refuses to recognize this, a minute part of a whole. To him, that part is the whole. (255)

Madhu, being innocent of the cruel male psychology, discloses to him a secret that she had slept with a man when she was fifteen. The man with whom she spent one night was none but one of her father's friends. Certainly she was not mentally matured that time. That selfish and greedy man took the chance of having sexual relation with her in guise of consoling her when her father died. She affirms:

> It's one of my father's friends, but not one of the 'kakas'. This man is different. A taciturn man who lives alone in a single room, he's a rare visitor. I don't know him as well as I do my father's other friends, but I know he's a welcome visitor, that my father likes him, he admires him. He is a painter, he did a picture of me as a child which still hangs in my father's bedroom. [...] he stops speaking, he begins to pat my back, the pats too hard, hurting, the hands of man unused to doing this kind of thing. [...] Now this man is holding me close, tight, I can smell his body, his clothes with their distinctive smell—of turpentine? [...] His body seems to be the one centre in my disintegrating world, the one solid thing I can hold on to in the maelstrom whirling about me. I want more—I want to feel his skin on mine, to feel his breath on my face. Do I know this? Do I admit this to myself? Is there still an innocence in my feelings, my responses? (266-68)

It is true that the man who was of her father's age did not apply any force in making the physical relation with her, but he came to console her and embraced her, pat her on the back and after remaining in contact for sometime she got intoxicated because it was the first time any man's body came so close. She says:

> His hands, his touch, his breath—I am conscious of these things, I feel intoxicated, a little heady with them, so that I stop thinking. There is a moment of strangeness, of fear, when I realize he is fumbling at my clothes, at his own, but at the contact of bare skin, the fear is immediately overlaid by a sense of shock, like plunging into cold water. There's the joy of feeling the cool water against my bare skin, its ripple teasing my body, caressing my skin. Pleasure runs swiftly along my nerves, through my body. I am conscious of my body, of the rich sap within it, rushing to meet and mingle with him. [...] making me aware of the pleasure, the pleasure that reaches the climax despite the pain, the agonizing pain, when my body accepts him, when it mingles with his. (268)

Madhu expects her husband to be a friend to understand and share the truth of her life. But that innocent Madhu did not know that the disclosure would bring a lot of trouble in her marital life. Som, her husband, is unable to come to terms with her act. The relationship between the two begins to disintegrate. Madhu fails to comprehend Som as she is unaware of the typical male psychology. In our society where a woman is treated like yet another commodity to be possessed and exclusively consumed for the owner's gratification, a woman becomes the husband's private property. A woman is not to indulge in such acts with others before or after marriage, and is required to serve her husband with single-minded devotion and loyalty. Even if the husband is lecherous, she is not to question him. The society has a sex-centered morality. Y.S. Sunita Reddy has aptly remarked: "Our society has been so conditioned as to categorize women as immoral on the slightest deviation on their part from the normal course of behaviour" (Reddy 2001: 132).

Thus, we see that Madhu is victimized twice. First of all, she suffers a lot due to the double standard of the male-dominated society; secondly she suffers due to her innocence. Had she not disclosed her pre-marital sex relation with Chandru, her married life would not have faced troubles. Here Som represents the typical male psychology. As soon as he learnt the lone pre-marital sex relation of his wife, he felt disturbed. "For Madhu it was never real, it was always like dream, not a part of life. However for Som, it is a shattering revelation. He is shocked, disbelieving and grieved..." (R.J. Singh 2005: 21).

The novelist tries to draw the attention of the society towards the double standard adopted by the man. It is a well-known fact that Som, the husband of Madhu, had a full-fledged relation with a married woman before his marriage with Madhu. She says: "Purity, Chastity and intact hymen—these are the things Som is thinking of; these are the truth that matter" (262). It is note-worthy here that pre-marital sex can lead to disintegration of marriage; but this rule is applicable only on the women.

Madhu expected her husband to be a friend to understand and share the truth of her life; but it was not to be. The statement of Chandru is very much relevant: "Men and women can never be friends. Men can be brothers, fathers, lovers, husbands, but never friends" (254). After the revelation of the premarital relation, Madhu and Som become strangers to each other. Madhu remarks: "We are like two travellers embarked on a terrible journey, rocketing at a dangerous speed, on the verge of going out of control, yet unable to help ourselves" (258). Madhu, the honest and innocent lady, is put on trial because she is a woman. Although Som pretends to be normal in his behaviour, yet he stops to have any conjugal relation with her. Ranjini Jyothi Singh remarks:

> Slowly Som becomes possessed of the thought that she is not completely his own. Unable to accept the idea that his wife is not the woman as he imagined before the marriage, he reacts violently. (2005: 22)

In course of time, she finds the torture at climax when Som brings up the names of all those persons who could have been her lovers. This incident filled her heart with hatred against the male psyche. She did not reply anything to him. But she feels that silence "Makes thing worse, it's a bigger barrier between us than my words had been" (256). If we go back to the days of the *Ramayana*, women were subjugated to the flame test to prove their chastity. Sita, the wife of Ram, was also innocent and helpless at the time of her kidnapping by Ravana, the king of Lanka. When Ram got her free, she had also to undergo flame test to prove her chastity. It is also a black-spot on the forehead of the men. Sita herself was not guilty; rather it was the security lapses of Ram. In the long run, she was abandoned by Ram. It was a kind of tyranny meted out to the women of then society. It prevails even in the postmodern age where woman have to face the ordeal of fire to prove her chastity. Madhu is completely heartbroken. She decides to live alone in the big world but it is also impossible for a woman to live alone and peacefully. One day, Som breaks the wall of silence. He writes a letter to Madhu: "Come home. We need to be together at this time" (323).

What Savitribai rejects Madhu accepts. Madhu like Saru, Jaya, Indu and Urmila accepts the reality of life. Though emotionally free from Adit's death she accepts to spend life with Som after a lot of pain. The novel ends with a question—Can woman live as an individual in an Indian society? The destiny of an average Indian woman is the destiny of Madhu. Savitribai is an exceptional character. The second character Leela is also an ideal. Her role resembles to Savitribai's role. She is a passionate believer in the communist ideology. She breaks away from her family to seek the fulfilment in public life. The first and the second texts of the novel resemble to each other for they are the stories of successful women one in art and the other in politics. The third and the fourth texts of the novel resemble to each other for both the characters have no other alternative except the acceptance of life. The two characters Savitribai and Leela have paved their paths themselves. In a book-review of *Small Remedies,* James Gerein says:

> Leela and Savitribai represent prototypical Indian feminists, generations ahead of their time and successful in their chosen careers, both of whom sacrifice more than they should have had to in order to achieve what they want. (2000: 804)

They reject the centuries old tradition, social custom and their family to achieve higher goals. Through the character of

Savitribai, Shashi Deshpande wants to convey the message to be your own light. *Small Remedies* is a novel which clearly indicates the development of the novelist's philosophy of life. The epigraphs of the books can be looked at to understand her philosophical thoughts and to trace their development. If the epigraph quoted from *The Dhammapada* "You are your own refuge; there is no other refuge. This refuge is hard to achieve" (7) of her first novel *The Dark Holds No Terrors* indicates that only support Saru can find is within herself, the epigraph quoted from *The Rig Veda* "Father of the earth, protect us. Father of the sky, protect us; Father of the great and shining water protect us,—To which God shall we offer our worship? *Small Remedies* points at the futility of searching for a God to whom we can offer our homage. It tells us that there is no such homage that can protect us, that there is really no protection from life's disasters. All that we can hope are remedies, and for these we do not have to look beyond the little acts of kindness that people around us extend to us.

The Indian women novelists, particularly of the 1980s onwards have articulated woman's aspiration, her professional endeavours, her newly established relationship with man and the changed perceptions of motherhood. Feminist writers like Shashi Deshpande, Anita Desai, Arundhati Roy, Manju Kapoor, Namita Gokhale, Shobhaa De and others have presented different types of resistance to the patriarchal norms. These novelists have thematized the expediency of self-representation, protested against the limitations of women's lives and emphasized on resistance. The man-dominated society treats most of resistant practices such as cross-dressing, adulterous love, economic independence, women's sexuality as transgression. But Rajeshwari Sunder Rajan has a different opinion: "With change in social perception these and a number of other practices no longer remain transgressions" (1993: 71-72). These practices are becoming the accepted modes of living and thinking.

The two novels *A Matter of Time* (1996) and *Small Remedies* (2000) can be treated as resistant texts which transcend the mundane and ultimately reconcile with the harsh realities of life. Deshpande raises a problem, questions it, fights it and then works towards acceptance and reconciliation. Having gone through her novels, one comes to realize that there is no easy solution to life's existential problem and the choices before us are not unlimited. The best course would be to undergo the trials and "make life possible," as Shashi Deshpande's Jaya realizes in *That Long Silence*. Sufferings elevate an individual and redeem the novels from becoming grim sagas of troubled life. A minute observation at the endings of these two novels can bring some fruitful results in this connection. At the end of *Small Remedies*, the protagonist, Madhu, reconciles with life with an epiphanic observation: "How could I have ever longed for amnesia? Memory, capricious and unreliable though it is, ultimately carries its own truth within it. As long as there is memory, there is always the possibility of retrieval, as long as there is memory, the loss is never total" (324). The ending is compelling and before putting down the novel, the reader does not help the temptation of going back to the beginning and ask, "What is it all about?" Likewise, the ending of *A Matter of Time* upholds dignity and strength in life. Watching his mother-in-law, Kalyani and his daughter Aru bidding him farewell, Gopal contemplates:

> If it is indeed true that we are bound to our destinies, that there is no point struggling against them, even then this remains—that we do not submit passively or cravenly, but with dignity and strength. Surely, this, to some extent, frees us from our bonds? (246)

Thus, we observe that Deshpande gives emotional direction and effort to her works and achieves a formal wholeness.

It is necessary to place the works and their authors in the socio-cultural perceptive to be able to understand the issues she raises, defies, and draws attention to, the freedom she visualizes and the acceptance she suggests. Shashi Deshpande was born in a Brahmin family and grew up in Dharwad and Bombay. She knows both Marathi and Kannada languages. She is also familiar with the two cultures. Though her novels are written in English, yet they do not reflect the English socio-cultural environment. They reflect the urban middle-class environment. *A Matter of Time* and *Small Remedies* have the historical and cultural ethos of Maharashtra and Karnataka. In *A Matter of Time* the rhetoric builds around the history of family that shifts to Karnataka with Peshwa Madhavrao's entourage. In *Small Remedies*, the cultural ethos is of the orthodox Brahmin community of the late nineteenth and early twentieth century Pune. Since the main action of both the novels takes place in later half of the twentieth century, there is convincing intermingling of the past and the present, which provides an important point to interrogate the received hegemonic structure.

If a reader contends that Shashi Deshpande concerns herself in these novels with female resistance would be to put the novels in a slot, to look them from a very narrow viewpoint. The novelist is too subtle an artist to deal with the surfaces. *A Matter of Time* resists patriarchy through presenting the three female characters in disadvantageous circumstances. Even though there are the more irritating questions of metaphysical, mythological and historical dimensions. The novelist draws the reader's attention to these problems and the text takes up the fight. Similarly, in *Small Remedies*, Savitribai Indorekar's rebellious act to break away from her family for her love of music is not an isolated, whimsical, individual decision. It transcends personal borders and becomes a part of the key social and political agendas undertaken by the late nineteenth century women such as Pandita Ramabai, Anandibai Joshi, Kashibai Kanitkar, Tarabai Shinde and others who had the courage to stand up against the oppressive social regime. The protagonist-biographer Madhu exercises her choices, rejects her husband's essentialist approach and reconstructs her 'self'. By accepting the challenge to write the biography she exerts her artistic and intellectual capacities. Writing itself is an act of empowerment and inversely, where there is power there is resistance. These female characters try to live on their own terms, resisting its vagaries with stony silences, balanced self-assertion, and immersion in the arts. Thus, we can conclude that after pain and suffering, they gain inner vision and the strength to reconcile.

A Matter of Time opens with a graphic but somewhat saddening description of the 'Big House' named "Vishwas" with roots deep into the historical past, where the future drama is set to be enacted. This is the house where Sumi returns with her three daughters after Gopal's desertion. Their stay helps to unravel the history of the house and its three generations of master and mistress. The Big House stands as a potent symbol of patriarchy. It was built "by a man not just for himself, but also for his sons and son's sons" (3). Ironically, the house "built to endure" and built for the male heirs, witnesses the uncanny decree of the inscrutable when two female inheritors—Kalyani and Aru—stand at the threshold, bidding farewell to the last of the males, Gopal.

The novel *A Matter of Time* is divided in three parts and each has an epigraph from the Upanishads. The part-I begins with a line from the *Brhad-Aranyaka Upanishad* (II.4.1), "'Maitreyi,' said Yagnavalkya, 'Verily I am about to go forth from this state (of householder)," (1). Through the incident of Gopal-Sumi, the author works out an entire patriarchal structure which has generated the value-system. A man can shed his responsibilities, but can a woman? Gopal provides an answer which also reflects the patriarchal thinking that a woman does not have existential problems as she is fulfilled through childbirth. He says: "For a woman, from the moment she is pregnant, there is an overriding reason for living, a justification for life that is loudly and emphatically true. A man has to search for it, always and forever" (68). Gopal's desertion is an indication that he cannot cope with the household responsibilities; Shripati deserts his wife to punish her for her carelessness towards her little son who wandered away to be lost in the crowd. Shripati should have counted on his two daughters, Premi and Sumi.

The craving for son hovers over the narrative, unobtrusively. The epigraph to Part-II, "The Family" begins with a line from the *Brhad-Aranyaka Upanishad* (I.5.17) "Whatever wrong has been done by him, his son frees him from it all; therefore he is called a son. By his son a father stands firm in this world" (91). The family becomes complete when a son is born; a woman feels fulfilled being the mother of a male child. Kalyani has been the sufferer for being born a girl while her mother expected a son. There is another darker aspect: her birth makes her mother insecure because she is afraid that Vithalrao may marry another woman for sons. Even Sumi, the modern Indian lady, is not free from the socio-cultural construct. When Gopal deserted, a thought flashes across her mind—could it be that Gopal despairs because they have no son? Though Sumi understands Gopal's motives and the nature of his crisis, yet the fact that the anxiety and doubt should cross her consciousness is in itself a forceful indictment of social preferences. Part-III, "The River" shows the flow of time. The epigraph is an extract from the *Katho-Upanishad* (I.1.25) where Yama asks Nachiketa not to probe the mystery of death: "Whatever desires are hard to attain in this world of mortals, ask for all those desires at thy will. O Nachiketa, (pray) ask not about death" (181). Interestingly, this part is populated with female achievements—Sumi recognizes her individuality and becomes more self-assertive; Kalyani gets back her identity; grandfather learns to interact with his granddaughters, and Aru celebrates her eighteenth birthday; in this part again, death claims two lives; the formidable patriarch and his self-supporting daughter (Sumi) depart together on their final journey. Here, the epigraph highlights Nachiketa's questioning, not Savitri's who had an equally strong argument with Yama. Is it the male-orientation of the culture the author is hinting at?

The novel does more than just narrating a tear-soaked tale of suffering and endurance. First of all, it subtly shows the difference between the values ascribed to stereotypical male and female traits in which man's needs take precedence over women's needs. Secondly, it depicts many faces of female resistance that make survival possible. Both Shripati and Gopal leave the domestic sphere because they cannot cope with life's commitments. Gopal has an unexplained existential drive and he leaves everything behind, including a happy family, in his quest for the self. Shripati looks himself against all communication because of frustration, anger and despair. For him, nursing his suffering self is far more significant than caring for his wife. He forgets or rather does not wish to recognize that the grief of having lost a son is not his alone; it is Kalyani's as well. Thus by running away from the field, the two men try to escape from their duty and responsibility towards their families.

Sumi accepts Gopal's decision placidly not because she lacks the courage to counter him but because she knows the futility of remonstration. Arguably, her protest would not have availed much; we realize this when we encounter Gopal's tight-lipped response to all those who reached him in their efforts to bring him back. Sumi was aware of his resolve since long and she knows the impossibility of reclaiming him, "I just want to get on with my life.... Let him go, Aru, just let him go" (61). A sincere look at her refusal to react to Gopal shows not a passive acceptance of man's supremacy but a contestation, a critique of tradition. The novelist corroborates this point when in an interview she asserts, "Sumi's acceptance is not passive, she blacks out the unpleasantness. She has a good opinion of herself; she is more concerned with getting on with life. She does not want pity; she would rather do anything for pride. She distances even her husband" (Ramarao 1998: 256). Her way of resistance is balanced and motivated towards reclaiming her identity. She becomes economically independent, immerses herself in gardening, writes and directs plays and thus discovers herself. Significantly, her next play is supposed to uphold woman's sexuality through the story of Surpanakha. Getting a better job, she decides to accept it. She meets Gopal several times during the year and there is no rancour in her, no acrimonious debates follow. They meet, exchange news; she tells him of her new ventures and about the daughters. She speaks freely of life and leaves Gopal wondering at her vivacity. "There is a spark to Sumi", Gopal thinks and as she confronts the past with admirable self-control, Gopal longs to possess her. It is the triumph of Sumi's restrained resistance that her *Sanyasi* husband should crave for her once again.

Kalyani's strategy of defiance is far more formidable in its impenetrable silence. She is the victim of the power game and she has endured the anguish of rejection. First, Manorama, her mother, rejected her mentally for being born a girl-child; in addition, Kalyani somehow failed her mother on every count—

she was neither beautiful nor intelligent and not even healthy and she had adopted the strategy of resisting her mother's dominance by her stoic silence. Her silence is like a rock, as Surekha, the feminist lawyer, finds later; it is "so dense and hard that Surekha's words bounce back at her" (211). Manorama devices a plan to keep the property in the family; she almost forces Shripati (her brother) to marry Kalyani. Both Kalyani and Shripati bear the burden of this decision, both remain unhappy. After Shripati ceases all communication with her, Kalyani does not react with show of emotions. It is Shripati who is confined to an accursed loneliness, not Kalyani. However, Kalyani is not unaffected. She, too, is under the heap of untold sufferings. We can read the suffering self of the one who knows the pain of desertion, who has experienced the anguish of rejection. She pleads: "Gopal, don't do this, don't let it happen to my daughter, what happened to me" (46). But by and large, she maintains a stoic silence. Silence can be a powerful tool of resistance when it practises a lack of participation in the social power relations.

Though the three women are victims of patriarchal dominance, they reclaim her lost situation by angry protests; Sumi regains her identity when her merit as an individual is recognized; and Kalyani feels empowered when Shripati's will, referring to her as Vithalrao and Manorama's daughter and not as her wife, is read out to her. She does not feel the sting of having been robbed of her marital status. "On the contrary, it is as if the words have given her something more than the house, restored something she had lost; they seem, in fact, to have strengthened her" (245).

In *Small Remedies*, the author explores the role silence plays in preserving the self from total loss. The novel is multi-dimensional with death at its foreground, music at its background and the complexities of existence as its thematic basis. Structured as a biography within a biography, it is "a profound piece of writing about love and loss, grief and hope, rebellion and sacrifice, and above all about the promethean will to resist, endure and survive" (Bande 2001: 27-28). Savitribai Indorekar, the doyen of Hindustani music of the Gwalior gharana, recounts what she wants to reveal. The scar of having been rejected by her own child and the agony of rejecting that child is safely hidden behind her rigid refusal to speak of Munni, her daughter. Madhu makes efforts to probe the depths to understand the suffering woman but the aged singer determinedly avoids it. One of the reviews of the novel reads the story as author's persistent efforts to rouse the reader's sympathy for a bereaved mother, and observes that "the great venture of trying to record and interpret the life and art of the great musician is marginalized" (Kaul 2000: 7) because of this distraction.

The novel begins with a simple exposition: "This is Som's story. Or rather, Joe's story as related to us by Som." In fact, it is the story of all those who realize the "imperfectability" and yet "move forward to self-knowledge and acceptance of a 'flawed' self, past mistakes and future failures" (Jain 2003: 280). Joe and Leela, Lata and Hari, Tony and Rekha, Madhu and her father, Som and their son Adit, Savitribai, Gulam Saab, and Munni are all caught in the web of life. All have their different talisman as small remedies that make the big disasters bearable, those small, unhappy moments of life—"moments of laughter, affection, love, joy and support" (Holms 2000: 5). Disasters cannot be warded off as the epigraph extracted from the *Rig Veda* to the novel *Small Remedies* indicates in the beginning:

> Father of the earth,
> Protect us;
> Father of the sky,
> Protect us;
> Father of the great and shining waters,
> Protect us,
> —To which God shall we offer our worship? (1)

This prayer from the Rig-Veda speaks of the human dilemma. The small remedies that are external to us; "the Ganeshas in the niches, The decorated threshold, the mango leaf *torans*, the Oms, the Swastikas, the charms and amulets—all to keep disaster at bay, to stave off the nemesis of a jealous god" (81) are but desperate remedies. Human beings have to find their own strength to stand firm and that strength lies within. It is that strength that sustains Savitribai, Madhu and Leela through grief and pain, anguish and agony.

Music is at the core of the story and so is creative writing. Bai forgets herself in music and Madhu makes efforts to draw her pain in writing. Art is beyond caste, class or religion; Savitribai comes from an orthodox Brahmin family; Gulam Saab and Hasina are Muslims. At the altar of music, they have one faith—their music. It is politics that creates problems, not art; and Deshpande raises the fangs of politics. The communal violence that stirred up as political revenge after Babri Masjid's demolition claims Savitribai's daughter Minni alias Shailaja Joshi and so also Madhu's son, Adit. Later in the novel, Madhu experiences violence when some fundamentalists assault her for supporting the concert. The pain of both the bereaved mothers is unimaginable but while one maintains a stony silence, the other lays the blame on the male ego that traumatized the boy and sent him away. It is also significant to know why Madhu blames her husband. Years after their marriage, when Adit is almost 17, Madhu tells Som of her first sexual experience. Som is obsessed by the revelation, which for him is adultery. He would be at rest only if she condemned it as rape and professed innocence. Madhu stands firm, refusing to surrender to his condescending attitude, his angry outburst and allegations of infidelity. Shashi Deshpande questions the adequacy of the accepted social norms, conceptual construction of 'woman' in terms of recognizable images, models and makers; she critiques the politics of control and socio-cultural determinants against women that require complete erasure.

Both Bai and Leela had dreams and both learnt how to realize those dreams despite social barriers. It is significant that Hasina should sing Akka Mahadevi's bhajan "I saw a dream, I saw a dream" at the concert before Bai is lost in coma and Madhu discovers her inner strength to remember Adit without hurt. It is befitting tribute to Leela and Bai—women who dared to dream and brought those dreams into reality, howsoever harsh. Deshpande does not resist women dreaming, but she resists the structure that does not allow them to dream. Her protagonists may not be brave heroines, as some may assert but they are women struggling to find their own way and own voice.

The feminist theory which distinguishes between biological sex and socially constructed gender is evident in the novels *The Binding Vine* and *Small Remedies*. The distinction between biological sex and socially constructed gender is foregrounded to give different examples of the construction of femininity. It appears in these novels that the theme is not the construction of femininity, but its deconstruction. The psychological transformation that Urmi and Madhu achieve is through the psychoanalytic approaches to gender rather than sociological ones. Deshpande takes the feminine point of view, and emphasizes the suffering and alienation which women as daughters and mothers endure. The psychological transformation of these protagonists is due to awareness and realization of the multiple and contrary identities which women possess.

Though the utter futility of living overwhelms a person, one is also terrified by the thought of living, of ceasing to be. In *The Binding Vine,* Mira had realized it. It is the 'binding vine' of love, with its cruelty and its selflessness, that binds together the conflicting multiple identities of one's self. Mira had found peace at the thought of the child within her. Shakutai realized her duty and decided to go on with the routine tasks of life for Kalpana and her other children. Urmi's 'armour' falls away at her mother's belated confession that she loved her. Madhu, the protagonist of *Small Remedies*, being motherless never felt the lack of mother's love as a child. But she finds Savitribai neglecting her daughter, Munni. She does not express any sympathy for this act. On the contrary, she on her part is a very caring mother, conscious of every need of her son, Aditya. Unlike militant feminists, she does not hate motherhood. And integrated consciousness may be an illusion for militant type of feminists, but the 'spring of life' is refilled and nurtured through the redemptive powers of love. Love and tolerance are the basic needs in the everyday life. One can never opt out of this 'Chakravyuha' of human life. Love is the only factor that prevents us from falling apart. Urmi understands through a recollection of those instances that had embodied tenderness and affection. Thus, we see that the protagonists of these two novels come to terms of life. They realized that new-women should struggle for their rights equal to male counterparts in a very cautious way. They cannot achieve goals overnight as it is difficult to cast off the age-old traditions and customs. The feminine qualities of motherhood, sisterhood, love, compassion, etc. are no barriers in their paths to emancipation. They should get proper education, and develop tolerance. Deshpande, through these protagonists, conveys the message of a new type of feminism that is different from that of European feminists. She advises them to be self-reliant in order to achieve the goals without disrupting the social as well as the moral values.

Conclusion

6

A minute study of Shashi Deshpande's novels reveals her deep concern for the miserable conditions of the Indian women. The Indian women feel smothered and fettered in a male-dominated and tradition bound society. She portrays her woman characters in the light of their hopes, fears, aspirations and frustrations who are very much conscious of their strength and limitations, but find themselves helpless by the opposition and pressure from a society dominated by the patriarchal mind-set. She highlights their plights and the subsequent degradation particularly in the Indian society.

Deshpande's women protagonists are victims of the prevalent gross gender discrimination, first as daughters and later as wives. They are conscious of the social, political and economic inequalities and injustice meted out to them. They start struggle against the oppressive and unequal nature of the social norms and rules which suppress their capability and existence. Fettered to their roles in the family, they question the subordinate status destined to them by the society. Although she has a small volume of writing to her credit, her works have drawn great critical attention and acclaim for her sensitive and realistic representation of the Indian middle-class women. Her sincere concern for women and their lot is strongly voiced in all her novels. Initially, she had in her mind people from real life in India to write about, but as she proceeded, spontaneously and involuntarily women become the focus of her writings. Once in an interview with Vanàmala Viswanatha, Shashi Deshpande made it clear: "It all starts with people. For example, *The Dark Holds No Terrors* came to me when I saw a couple" (Vanamala 1987: 8).

Among other novelists experimenting consciously with the Indian writing in English, Shashi Deshpande has a unique place. She is an Indian, thus her writings reflect the Indian social background. She often uses Marathi words which are sufficient enough to present the customs and traditions prevalent in Maharashtra and Karnataka. Some words such as Kaka, Kaki, Atya, Dada, etc. are essentially Marathi and Hindi words and might be difficult for the readers who don't know this language. But Shashi Deshpande is more conscious for literary qualities of her creative works than for language. It is noteworthy about her language which is transparent. She is an Indian to the core of heart and writes especially for the Indian readers. In an interview with Vanamala Vishwanath, Shashi Deshpande affirms:

> If you try to make everything easy for everyone then, you end up belonging nowhere. So, I have left it at that—characters in their locales, without providing glosses for the western readers [...]. Also literature can be appreciated even without understanding every word of it—one can still respond to the core of it. (1987: 11)

Deshpande is gifted with inborn literary talent of mind which got matured with her experiences in life. It is undeniably true that she graduated in economics and law but these subjects don't have much impact upon her literary career. Though she is the daughter of Sriranga, the famous Kannada dramatist, the Bernard Shaw of Kannada theatre, yet she never got any guidance from him in field of novel writing. Deshpande affirmed in an interview with Vanamala Viswanathan:

> If I should criticize him, I should say he was somewhat detached from us...never guided us. May be if he had directed us at an early age, I could have done better. He never did that. (1987: 9)

It is obvious that Deshpande does not want to write for publicity, but to present the society as she observes it. She is not bothered about name and fame; this is the reason in spite of the fact that she had been writing for quite a long period, she was still unknown. She earned name and fame only when her novel *That Long Silence* was published by the Virago Feminist Press, London:

> It is meaningless that people know me as a person and not know what I've written. I feel publicity is not good thing for a writer. It detracts from your work. You become more interested in yourself as a person than as a writer. I'd rather be known for my books than for myself. (1989: 10)

Many Indian women writers have got their education in foreign countries which kept them apart from the traditional Indian women. The traditional Indian women suffer, submit and adjust themselves to the circumstances. Some other women novelists like Anita Desai, Nayantara Sahgal, Ruth Prawer Jhabvala have portrayed in their novels this aspect of women's life without having the first hand experience of it. Shashi Deshpande has projected this aspect of Indian women with more sensibility and instructive understanding as she belongs to this category, in the sense that, unlike other women writers, she is born and brought up on the Indian soil, got her education in India and wrote about India. The projection of the women world in her novels is more authentic credible and realistic. She knows what Indian women feel. She does not want to be categorized with other writers of Indian writing in English, she has a unique place among the novelists writing in English. She declares that she is just like any other regional writer but her medium of writing happens to be English because it is the only language she knows well. In an interview with Vanamala Vishwanath, Shashi Deshpande says:

> I'm isolated—I'm not part of any movement and not conscious of readers to impress. To get wider recognition here and abroad, you have to be in the university and places like that with the right contacts. I'm an ordinary woman who writes sitting at home. None of these things are within my reach. This has, I believe, done good. It has given me great freedom. I'm happy with this anonymity. Once you get publicity conscious, your writing becomes affected. I'm truly happy with this freedom. (1987: 11)

Deshpande has not tried to make her woman characters stronger than they are in real life. Rather she has exposed their passivity, anxiety and confusion. Promilla Kapoor remarks:

> The educated women demand more sexual freedom and independence but are very sure about what they should do with the same, which leads them to a bitter confusion, anxiety and tension. Their psychology is still wedded to tradition. They have started recognizing the need for change, but at the same time they continue to cling to the old values as they have been brought up with them. (1973: 268-69)

The same picture of women has been drawn in Shashi Deshpande's novels: "My characters take their own ways. I've heard people saying we should have strong woman characters. But my writing has to do with women as they are" (Vishwanath 1987: 12). It is true that Shashi Deshpande has not deliberately made women the centre of focus in all her novels. As a matter of fact, she wanted to portray the whole society in her writings; but somehow, as the characters took shape, the women characters turned out to be the protagonists. Most probably, Deshpande herself being a woman felt more for the women characters could understand the mundane reality, the complex structure of man-woman relationship better. She believes that everyone should live within the relationships. She says:

> It's needed. It's necessary for women to live within relationship. But if the rules are rigidly laid that as a wife or mother you do this or no further, than one becomes unhappy. This is what I have tried to convey in my writing. What I don't agree with is the idealization of motherhood —the false and sentimental notes that accompany it. (Vishwanath 1987: 13)

In an interview with Gita Vishwanath she expressed her views on feminism and man-woman relationship as follows:

> When I write, I don't write as a feminist. I keep saying this over and over again.... I do not write as a feminist novelist. But my ideology is going to permeate my writing; and my feelings, thoughts and ideas about women are very

> important parts of my ideology.... I mean human relationship, not just women but what human beings in general are like, what the loneliness of a human being is like—these are equally important parts of my writing and when I am called a feminist writer, these are missed out and this is what I really object to. (2005: 228)

Deshpande does not want any kind of propaganda. Her main concern is the human beings. She affirms: "I want to reach a stage where I can write about human beings and not about women or man" (Vishwanath 1987: 14).

The main themes that have found expression in Shashi Deshpande's novels are: inner conflict and search for identity, parents children relationship, and concept of marriage and sex. Above all, the theme of silence rooted in the complex relationship between man and woman holds a great fascination for Shashi Deshpande. She deals with the inner working of the female psyche.

Roots and Shadows depicts the life history of Indu, a middle-class young girl, brought up in an orthodox Brahmin family headed by Akka, the mother surrogate. The novel begins with the heroine's return to her ancestral home. The parental home initiates her into an understanding of the meaning of human life. Here she discovers what her roots are—as an independent woman and a writer; and what her shadows are—a daughter, a mother and a commercial writer. She rebels against Akka, her conventional world, her rigid values and marries Jayant. Ironically, she realizes the futility of her decision. In order to attain freedom, she seeks marriage as an alternative to the bondage inevitable in the parental family. She looks forward to the roles of a wife with the hope that casting herself in a role which will help her in winning her freedom. Her baffled longing to achieve a complete personhood is clearly suggested: "This is my real sorrow. That I can never be complete in myself. Until I had met Jayant, I had not known it.... Then I met Jayant. And lost the ability to be alone" (31).

In a traditional society, marriage is the promised end; but in feminist fiction it becomes the enclosure which restricts the movement towards a perception of herself as an independent human being and not forced by the circumstances or the social prescriptions. Unlike western militant feminist, she does not denounce marriage as a barrier in the path of women emancipation. In an interview with Gita Vishwanath, Deshpande says: "This is why marriage interests me.... But yet, marriage is important for me and so is the family these are the two relationships one is generally concerned with (2005: 229). Indu arrives at a realistic understanding of love as a physical instinct: "Love that is a word I don't really understand. It seems to me an overworked word." She realizes: "The sexual instinct...that's true. The maternal instinct...that's true too. Self-interest, self-love...they're the basic truths" (158).

Indu happens to experience disillusionment in sex and suffers a silent sexual humiliation. She does not feel any guilt in her extra-marital relationship with Naren and decides not to tell Jayant about it: "That had nothing to do with the two of us and our life together" (187). This decision shows her boldness and practical approach of life. The novel gains its feminist momentum in this assertion of Indu; of her autonomy and her awareness that she exists as a person. She has the knowledge of self-respect. She has learnt how to free herself of guilt, shame and humiliation. She takes firm decisions: "That I would at last do the kind of writing I had always dreamt of doing. That I would not, could not enrich myself with Akka's money. That I would, on the other hand, pay for Mini's wedding" (187). She has learnt to see not only her life full of possibilities for growth and grace but the very meaning of life itself. "I felt as if I was watching life itself...endless, limitless, formless and full of grace" (184).

Indu has a better realization of detachment and non-involvement in her life. To great extent credit goes to Naren who made her realize these values of life. Naren's detachment made it possible for her to remain unaffected by anything. He could never be anybody's husband or beloved. Her rejection of him afterwards had left him completely untouched, whereas she knew she could shatter Jayant completely with her rejection, which made Jayant so precious to her. It is remarkable here that she did not want detachment and non-involvement. It was only for the dead, not for the living. She realized that this was nothing shameful in her need for Jayant. It did not make her less of a human being. She knew that her love was not a restricting bond but a uniting bond. It would enable her to lose herself in Jayant, which alone would create harmony in their life. She felt that she must reveal to him her whole self with all her weakness as well as strength and all her virtues and vices. That alone would make perfect understanding possible and give them a better chance for happiness. All of a sudden, her vision became clear and she knew what she must do. She had been looking upon Akka only as an inconsiderate and interfering old woman, but she knew her better later on. She realized that Akka had been a pillar of strength which had enabled her to act according to her beliefs. She knew she must rise up to Akka's expectations. If she had not chosen Indu, only a great grand niece as her heir because she believed Indu was capable of showing the same indomitable courage and strength and fulfill her obligations and responsibilities, setting aside all other thoughts. Any freedom she desired she must seek within the peripheries of her obligations and responsibilities.

For Indu the old house was like a trap. She had to come out of it. She must sell it even if she had to sell it to Shankarappa who wanted to demolish it and have a big hotel built on the site. But it was a very painful decision to take. Four generations of the family had spent their life in the house. Every corner of the house could tell its own story about the persons who had lived in it. She was overcome by the sense of desolation and bereavement. But she reminded herself that she must not allow soft feelings to come in the way of doing what she thought was the right thing to do. Shankarappa was kind enough to wait till Mini's wedding. Indu also took the same decision. Besides it, she decided to pay for Mini's wedding for which she had criticized Kaka with the spirit of a crusader. She realized that she had no right to judge others. She not only paid for the wedding, but also attended it and enjoyed it. She was mused to see a happy sense of participation despite the earlier animosities and conflicts.

In her personal life also she decided not to take the coward's way. What kind of home could she build on dishonesty and pretence? She would go back to Jayant and see if that home could stand the scorching touch of honesty. She also decided to resign her job and devote herself to the kind of writing she had always dreamt of. In this way we see that in the end she achieved the freedom. She did not let anyone, neither Kaka nor Atya, nor Jayant come into the way of doing what she believed was the right thing to do. She had conquered her fears and achieved harmony in life.

Thus, Shashi Deshpande makes her heroine choose security through reconciliation. The ethos in the novel is neither of victory nor of defeat but of harmony and understanding between two opposing ideals and conflicting selves. This is quite true reflection of the basic Indian attitude. Indu's predicament is also the representative of the larger predicament of Women in contemporary India where the new socio-economic forces have shaken old cultural modes. The break-up of the joint family, the nucleus of Indian cultural life is the immediate and visible symbol of this imminent change.

The way an intelligent and sensitive lady like Indu who was so very choosy in her affections is made by the writer to resolve her doubts and uncertainties is very alarming. She had to commit adultery to come to terms with her married life. Indu's casual attitude to what she had done is quite shocking. Indu's uncompromising and paradoxical feminine self that frantically longed for self-expression finally finds its roots in the home and with her husband. She has confronted her real self and she knows her roots. She need not be ashamed of her body and sexual needs. She is capable of taking decisions not only for herself but for others too, and life does not come to an end with individuals whether it is Indu or Jayant. She lives to see life with the possibilities of growth. She succeeds in discovering the meaning of life in her journey to individualization.

The Dark Holds No Terrors should not be considered a feminist novel only on the basis of the female centrality in it. Any definition of feminism framed would be highly arbitrary as the very concept differs from man to man. If woman's consciousness of her predicament, her wanting to be recognized as a person rather than as a woman, her wanting to have an independent social image would be considered out stepping the limits, the novel has definite feminists' limitations. This novel is certainly a feminist novel in the Indian context. Saru, the protagonist, is aware of the discrimination done with her right from her childhood. The framework of the novel provides good acoustics for women's voice and establishes that women should also have choices in her life. But Shashi Deshpande does not glorify women's sufferings. Though she creates a sufficient amount of sympathy for her protagonist, it is not on the grounds of her being a female sufferer. She maintains commendable objectivity and avoids generalization and partial views.

Shashi Deshpande is certainly aware of the women's plight in the male-dominated society especially when the woman is not economically independent. The novelist has mentioned a woman who being ill-treated by her in-laws commits suicide by drowning in a well. There is another reference of a woman who is tied to peg by the in-laws in the cattle shed. Saru detests the merciless judgement of her mother who casually dismisses the topic saying, "she perhaps deserved it". The focus here is not on men's cruelty to woman but woman's cruelty to woman.

Saru, the protagonist is not ready to accept the mute role practised by the wives. The wife of one of Manu's friends accepts total effacement of her very presence and position by remaining a silent, unobtrusive "nameless waiter in a hotel" till the end of their dinner, unintroduced to her friends. The lady remains a shadow whereas Saru would like to be the substance itself casting a shadow "if I cast no shadow, I do not exist" (144). Saru has an utter sense of contempt for Sunita who is happy to change her name to "Gitanjali" just to please her husband. The change of name however is not a willing annihilation of her personality for the sake of her husband but a putting on of the romantic mask of being a contended wife.

The society presented in *The Dark Holds No Terrors* is certainly going through a transition period where at least economically independent women could have choices in life.

Saru has a deep sense of respect for the dignified, self-reliant, teacher friend Nalu, who despises all compromises and remains single to lead a meaningful life of convictions. Even among men there is Padmakar Rao who complains that his wife cannot relate to him on equal terms but waits on him, does not call him by name and could talk of only middle class concerns like economizing the family budget even though she does not need to. Saru's vehement advocacy of women's subordinate position, while rehearsing her speech for the women's college and her inability to render the same speech there is, makes her to show a strong reaction against the traditional stand and her inability to adhere to that way of life. She accepts it as the way of bliss in the traditional sense of the term but she would take the road less travelled. Despite the agony it causes, the difficulties she has to steer through, there could be no turning back.

In the article "The Dilemma of a Woman Writer", Shashi Deshpande affirms: "A woman who writes of women's experiences often brings in some aspects of those experiences that have angered her, roused her strong feelings. I don't see why this has to be labelled feminist fiction" (1985: 33). *The Dark Holds No Terrors* is certainly a protest novel especially in the Indian context in the sense that it reacts against the traditional concept that "everything in a girl's life, it seemed, was shaped to that single purpose of pleasing a male" (163). The protagonist has sufficient reasons to protest as her husband basks in her glory by day and takes vengeance on her at night. There are some references from Betty Friedan and Virginia Woolf's idea of a woman's right to "a room of her own". Whether it is gratuitously referred to or introduced with a purpose, the strength of Shashi Deshpande's novel is that she has not let it get trapped in the framework of clichés borrowed from the women's Liberation Movement in the West.

The Dark Holds No Terrors is not confined to the limitation of feminist problems. Putting Saru, the central figure of the novel, Shashi Deshpande probes the universally relevant issues of human relationships, man's tragic aloneness, etc. Even Saru, who sees the ultimate human reality in the human body and its process of decay, sees aloneness a painful but inescapable human condition. She realizes that the suffering of multitudes does not mitigate one's own suffering in any way and she is doomed to sit and watch happiness recede from her all by herself. It is the realization that helps her to understand the mother's last words: "that's what all of us have to face at the end. That we are alone. We have to be alone" (194).

The feeling of homelessness is indicative of inner disintegration. Saru, sometimes, sees herself as two separate halves, "a two-in-one woman", a confident professional in the white coat by day and "a trapped animal" by night. At other times, it is mere dichotomy, it is total disintegration. Shashi Deshpande uses effective images like the woman possessed by Devi and the ventriloquist's dummy to show the rift and distance between the activator in her and the actions carried out by her. There is a constant fear in her that even as a doctor she was just a "well trained animal...capable of making the right noises, the right gestures automatically" (23) and that some day the activator would fail and people would perceive "the white coat containing nothing". The profession, however, is a "Vital Crutch" without which she could not hold herself up together.

Though the novel deals with an uncertain situation, Shashi Deshpande makes use of effective concrete images to drive home the reality and gravity of the problem. When Saru goes back to her father's house after several years to revive the relationship in need of a confidant, the door opens "with reluctance of disuse". The barrenness of the yard where "not even weeds grow" suggests the impossibility of human relationships. The sole hollyhocks are indicative of the sole relationship of the father with Madhav. Later when they grow a garden, it points to the growing relationship and productive independence. The doodling of Saru with "One circle entwined in another" apart from suggesting the intricacy of the problem shows that it is a self-created situation. The images of thickly populated trees with no gap in between, "the frightening confinement" and "the brooding darkness" bring the message of no escape.

The Dark Holds No Terrors presents the inner drama of Saru that has a lot to do with the past. Hence, narration is introspective sliding across the past and present through effective "quick cuts". Occasionally, Deshpande sidetracks a bit of philosophizing on human life, grief, happiness, pain, man's aloneness, etc. and these digressions make the novel a bit too wordy. She never leaves anything unsaid to evoke rich suggestions. Some elements like son's importance in the family, girls getting importance only during haldi-kumkums, a woman possessed by Devi, find an appropriate mention in the novel which deals with woman's status and the dichotomy within her personality. They do not in any way seem forced upon the canvas. But while using some of the mythical details like Pathar Panchali, Dhruva's becoming the North star or mother's listening to Duryodhana's story, Shashi Deshpande reveals an eagerness to point out their respective relevance in the novel for fear of their getting lost on the readers. The strength of the novel is that in spite of close involvement of the author with the subject, she is able to step out of the woman she is and to present a fair picture of life. She gifts her protagonist with a double vision and Saru is as critical of herself as of others. All along, it is the woman's point of view that is presented but there is hardly any trace of sentimentalizing or over-dramatizing of woman's issues. While offering sufficient sympathy for the protagonist, the novelist never takes side. This is a remarkable achievement for a writer who belongs to the suppressed sex and it is noteworthy that she has dedicated the novel to her husband.

The Dark Holds No Terrors effectively brings out the psychological problem of a career woman, never before seriously and artistically discussed in Indian English fiction. If one does not consider the novel as a feminist one, this would just be discounting the serious concern of the novel. The novelist is justifiably puzzled at such an attitude. Her dilemma is expressed in these words: "When a man writes of the particular problems a man is facing, he is writing male propaganda. Nobody says that. Why is it said only about women writers?" (1985: 33). This novel definitely transcends feminist constraints. Shashi Deshpande does not indulge in clichés worked to death by the women's liberation movement and thus saves the novel from degenerating in a feminist probe and explores the premise of half-lights, provides the outlines and spares as the clinical details.

Shashi Deshpande is such a novelist who very carefully avoids the western feminists' concept of emancipation and presents the Indian version of emancipation where one searches for the whole of her 'identity' and not fragmentations of herself. Despite the swirling restlessness, Saru emerges as a whole woman who is not dependent on anyone outside her. Deshpande cautiously puts aside the western notion of a women's emergence in terms of separation from her life-partner for an existence without any relation to male and society, a life in isolation is no existence. Having suffered the long conflict between the cultures of the colonized and colonizer, the Indian woman, Saru, establishes herself neither as a totally liberated woman, the typical western nor as an orthodox Indian, the submissive female.

The only goal of feminism must not be the achievement of individual identity and female autonomy. The women should maintain a balanced relation between the basic human values like motherhood and responsibility of the family. There is a need to harmonise the man-woman relationship as equal partners. Women should understand that victory does not lie in the subjugation and destruction of the male, rather in bringing him to see the indispensability of each other's space. The responsibility lies upon women writers like Shashi Deshpande, who use literary device to raise the voice of Indian women, to maintain social harmony and mutual understanding among men and women.

In *That Long Silence* (1988) the feminist struggle for liberation is looked upon within the framework of the freedom crisis. The quest for an authentic selfhood on the part of the protagonist finds an artistic expression through the protagonist's rebellion against the patriarchal core of society. Like a radical feminist, Deshpande uses the term patriarchy in the popular sense of "male domination and then power of relationship by which men dominate women" (Beechey 1979: 66). The novelist explores Jaya's public and private realms of experience. In this novel, we are exposed to the life of the sense as well as the agonized feeling of the narrator-protagonist, Jaya—a housewife and an unsuccessful writer. Her creative urge and artistic zeal free her from the cramped domestic and societal roles. It releases her from emotional upheaval. She resolves to assert her individuality by breaking that long silence, by putting down on paper all that she had suppressed in her seventeen years silence.

That Long Silence projects through the character of Jaya, the plight of the middle class woman and the fact that the basic male psyche has not undergone any fundamental change. Most of the men still join the "motivated campaign to eliminate women who step out of the accepted line of social conformism" (Nabar 1995: 12). The novel records the fact that the changing social dynamics has brought a change in the socio-economic-educational awareness among the women, but they still have to create a niche in various modes also threatens the emancipated future of women. Economically independent women are also driven to feel such constraints.

That Long Silence portrays the sufferings and deprivations of feminine life by presenting certain characters as stereotyped representatives of traditional womanhood. The novel also presents a critique of the myths which are perpetuated and practised in the context of feminity. But the strength of the novel lies in its bold analysis of the realities about the Indian womanhood. The novel assertively exhibits the philosophy that women should have an assertive individuality which includes the capability to take decisions about their life and carry them out with a sense of responsibility. Their emotional-intellectual-economic liberation does not negate the possibility of nurturing and enjoying various relationships which the society and their biological nature have imposed upon them. The haunting riddle of the ultimate purpose of a woman's life within the family can be solved when she learns to assess the worth as an individual and shuns to be guided by pre-fixed norms about it.

Jaya realizes that in order to attain selfhood, a woman must transcend silence, negation and self-alienation. A woman's relation with her family must burgeon within the totality of her life as a woman, only then it can lead to a harmonious fulfillment. Jaya realizes that a holistic yet resilient approach towards life is necessary:

> We don't change overnight. It's possible that we may not change even over long periods of time. But we can always hope. Without that life would be impossible. And if there is anything to know now it is this: life has always to be made possible. (193)

Her decision to be a passive partner and overcome the turbulence in her relationship with Mohan leads her to an uninhabited self-identification. The novel clearly spells out the faith that a woman's desire to succeed like an individual does not negate her desire for love, marriage and domesticity. A balanced and purposeful life is not a utopian fancy for a woman if she liberates herself from the stereotyped conditioning of the society and is not dependent on the male presence to authenticate her thoughts, emotions and deeds at every step. This novel aesthetically communicates the essence of the creed of feminism along with the contemporary realities.

The main purpose of a feminist is primarily concerned with the recognition of women as a being, an autonomous being. They want women to realize herself through self-analysis. Such a quest for one's own identity forms the theme of Shashi Deshpande's novel *That Long Silence.* Jaya, the protagonist, thinks of her past days and tries to analyse her identity. In the very beginning Jaya was rechristened as Suhasini by her husband on their wedding day. This incident confused Jaya in her search for an identity. The pseudonym under which she operates as a writer further complicates the issue. Jaya stands for revolt whereas Suhasini symbolizes submission. Jaya rejects the name and is a kind of protest against such customs. But her sense of identity is never certain. She is torn between being Jaya, herself and Suhasini, the good wife; between building herself as a writer and a self as a wife and mother. Through the process of reliving the past in her mind, Jaya gets the guidance for her future. She decides to break her long seventeen years of silence and gives up being a passive and silent partner to Mohan. She decides to assert herself as an individual and also as a woman, wife or mother. Though she chooses to remain in the family, a change has wrought in her situation. She has come out of the confining slots allotted to her by the patriarchal society. Earlier, Jaya had denied certain parts of herself that did not fit into the straitjacket of 'wifehood'. Now she asserts:

> I'm not afraid any more. The panic has gone. I'm Mohan's wife, I had thought, and cut off the bits of me that had refused to be Mohan's wife. Now I know that kind of a fragmentation is not possible. The child, hands in pockets, has been with me through the years. She is with me still. (191)

Being inspired by the western feminist movement, some Indian women, in their eagerness for freedom, made a total switch over to the other side, seeking freedom from everything, including from their culture. Shashi Deshpande's protagonists find freedom not in the western sense but in conformity with the society they live in without drifting away from one's culture. Jaya's decision is not a meek surrender to circumstances, but a sensible compromise between the mutually conflicting ideals of conformity and non-conformity. Deshpande does not accept the theory that "women are victims". The "dependency syndrome" in women is responsible for their victimization and she desires that women need to offer resistance and emerge as strong-willed individuals to face life, to share responsibilities, and not to escape from it.

Feminism in its early stages visualized an exclusively all female world where men would have only peripheral functions. However, the present day feminist thought, while seeking to destroy male hierarchy, is not against sexual dualism. Feminism is necessarily pro-women but it need not be anti-men. P. Ramamoorthi aptly remarks:

> The attempts to create 'female enclaves' are extremist reactions but the recent trends in feminist literature are an indication that it is possible for a woman to live in the world where man also live. (1991: 38)

Shashi Deshpande also holds a similar view, rejecting a separatist view aware of the fact that breaking off the bonds of family would result in loneliness and disintegration of the larger social set-up. She asks for her individuality to be valued equally with that of man. So long as one half of the humanity is denied decent and dignified lives, it will be a far cry to hope for a better world. But, Jaya, confident of her individuality and hopeful of a change in Mohan's attitude, moves beyond the cultural stereotypes with the firm conviction that 'life has always to be made possible'. Such an optimistic ending of the novel, *That Long Silence*, shows that the day is not far off when men and women will be valued equally and they will be complimentary to one another in a world where there will be no discrimination on the basis of sex and women will live with self-respect and dignity. Another important insight that Shashi Deshpande imparts to us through Jaya is that women should accept their own responsibility for what they are. They have contributed much to their own victimization, instead of putting the blame on everybody. It is only through self-analysis and self-understanding, through vigilance and courage, they can begin to change their lives. They will have to fight their own battle; no body can do anything else for them.

The Binding Vine projects the two main issues of female bonding and resistance to the patriarchal ideology. Urmila, the protagonist seems deeply motivated from the pain of her baby-daughter Anu's death. In suffering, a unique sense of fellowship is forged, not only with the living but also with the mute and the death. Urmila has a deep sense of sympathy for Shakutai and her young daughter Kalpana, who is brutally raped and consequently lying unconscious. She also has the same feeling of sympathy for Mira, her own dead mother-in-law who suffered marital rape. Feminine solidarity or female bonding runs a strong undercurrent in the novel. The novel celebrates women's coming together with other women as friends and companions, and sharers of life rather than as rivals for approval by men. This novel also depicts a story of mothers and daughters where Urmila grieves for the baby daughter who is dead and Shakutai weeps for Kalpana who is dying. There are some other pairs of mothers and daughters like Urmila and her mother Inni, Vanna and her mother Akka, Vanna and her young daughters. In spite of some differences, each of these relationships reinforces the idea of the binding vine.

Urmila writes the story of Mira's life from her poems and diaries and insists that Mira is not a symbol but a person. This is the reason she refuses to typify her. In order to construct a female tradition, she says that we have to know our mothers and grandmothers to know our situation. Sharing of experience and supporting are the essential parts of bonding as seen in Urmila's keen interest in reconstructing Mira's harrowing experience. She accepts: "It is Mira who is taking me by the hand and leading me..." (135). The title of the novel also reflects the predominant theme. *The Binding Vine* presents a female world in which women come together in a feeling of fellowship. Vanna, her mother Akka and Urmila's mother Inni come together in her tragedy. Urmila runs to assist Vanna when her children need care. She stands by Shakutai in hour of grief. Shakutai, Kalpana and Sulu belonging to the working class are further pushed to the periphery and subaltern status as they are deprived of the privileges of class, caste and education enjoyed by Urmila who is able to speak for them and help Kalpana in the end. In her relationship with this woman, Urmila is able to forge the binding vine of womanhood in love and sympathy which functions as a strategy of empowerment.

Another theme that emerges as equally powerful is that of resistance to patriarchal ideology and the narrative locates this resistance in different modes of experience. Like most of the protagonists of Deshpande, Urmila is not dependent upon man for survival and asserts both her economic as well as psychological independence. She raises the voice of protest in the novel which protests against the patriarchal attitude to the issue of rape. Two forms of the gender violence are juxtaposed here in the case of Kalpana and Mira. If Kalpana lying in unconscious state represents the silenced subaltern, in Mira's poems and diaries, writing itself becomes a mode of resistance. Urmila's account of the incident of Kalpana's rape is loaded with ideological undertones. Shakutai's insistence that the police should not be informed as it will lead to Kalpana's disgrace exposure—an exposure of the attitude towards the rape victim and the patriarchal ideology that rape disgraces the victim rather than the culprit. When Shakutai laments it was Kalpana's fault, Urmila subverts the patriarchal logic, exploding: "are you blind? It's not her fault, no, not her fault at all.... The man who did this to her. Don't you see, can't you see he is the wrongdoer" (147-48). The fictional structure finally provides utterance to the subaltern voices of Kalpana and Mira, when the press forces the hospital not to move her out and Urmila makes definite plans to publish Mira's poems.

The feminine consciousness in the novel recognized difference between a 'women's vision' and a 'men's vision'. While watching a Hindi movie, Urmila comments upon the heroine singing a song as she gets ready to meet a lover, smiles at her reflection while she draws a *Kaajal*-lined finger across her eyelids. It seemed too narcissistic, the woman's admiration of herself. Now I realize—this was not a woman looking at her self. It was a man looking at a woman, this was how a man saw a woman. A man's vision (125). Another interesting incident can be traced when Venu, the well known writer advises Mira: "Why do you need to write poetry? It is enough for a young woman like you to give birth to children. That is your poetry. Leave the other poetry to us men" (127). Recognition of the difference works as a mode of resistance.

There is a vine of sympathy which binds Urmila with Shakutai and her unlucky daughter, Kalpana. At the same time she seems bound with same vine of sympathy with her own mother-in-law who is no more now. When she accidentally found the Kannada writings of Mira safely kept in a trunk on the loft, she came across the sad life story of Mira. She is sad to learn that Mira, being a sensitive girl, did not love her husband who could not understand her feelings. Mira's husband possessed her physically, but could not comprehend her psychic and artistic dimension. Thus, Mira was subjected to rape in marriage and being a lady of sensitive nature, had a great hatred for the so-called "love" or sexual act. It was just a marriage of two bodies and never a marriage of two minds and hearts. Consequently, Mira being frustrated with the torturous married life, tried to achieve her true identity by writing beautiful poems. That was the only escape route from the sense of isolation, humiliation and emptiness of life. Urmila, too, is deeply touched by the tender feeling expressed in the poems.

Like Shakutai and Mira, Urmila, too, is not happy with her married life. It is undeniably true that her marriage, unlike Shakutai and Mira, was not arranged and married a man of her choice. She tries her level best to remain like a good housewife and find pleasure in her home, husband and children. But it was not to be. She meets the same fate like a traditional Indian housewife. Her husband, being an officer in the Indian navy, comes home once in a year to spend his time with his wife and children. Urmila wants to live permanently with him at home and fears that she may lose him forever. Urmila surrenders herself to satisfy him through sex; but she finally finds repulsion for that—a quality that she shares with her own mother-in-law. She longs to attain spiritual pleasure, but she does not succeed in this matter. Kishore never tries to understand her spiritual aspects of life. Despite Kishore's long absence from home, she never tries to look at another man for armour. Unlike a modern educated and emancipated wife, she keeps herself always as a chaste wife. This shows her deep love for her husband, her loyalty to her husband. We can come to this conclusion that Urmila is a sensitive woman rather than a radical feminist and can be taken to be the mouth-piece of the novelist. She derives consolation for herself from extending sympathy to similar woman like Shakutai and Mira whose pain is much deeper than hers. In spite of the difficulties and obstacles created by the patriarchal society, these women characters try to canalize their emotion in different ways because they have strong will power for survival. Thus, the novelist Shashi Deshpande gets success in presenting the optimistic vision, beauty and truth of life in the Indian context.

Urmila experiences life and assess herself and her surroundings that brings her out of anxiety. It enables her to cope with the death of her daughter and become a self-assured person. Her short infatuation towards Bhaskar and his advances towards her disappears when she examines her feeling and subjects herself to critical self-reflection. She is not like Vanna who is puppet in the hands of her husband. Not to speak of educated woman like Vanna and Priti, even an illiterate woman Shakutai preaches to Urmi at the end of the novel: "You can never opt out, you can never lay it down, the burden of belonging to the human race. There is only one way out of this *Chakravyuha*. Abhimanyu had to die; there was no other way he could have got out" (202). Shakutai, engaged in her daily chores, struggling with the burden of life and assimilating all pains of living with a kind of philosophical detachment, gives life-sustaining message to Urmi: "The main urge is always to survive" (203).

The analytical study of *The Binding Vine* foregrounds the notion that Shashi Deshpande is a true Indian novelist who does not encroach on the limitations. She does not go to the extremes because she knows that the "wails of anguish or thunder of curses of growls of anger do not by themselves turn into great literature (Kripalini 1968: 109). It is important to note that in the creative female world of Shashi Deshpande, all men are not villains. Urmila's husband is good to her and she is fully satisfied with him; but she realizes her responsibility to struggle for the emancipation of women who are trapped in the net of patriarchal society. She takes the cudgel to bring the truth before the society. This embodies the depths of the dimensions of personality of Deshpande's heroine.

It is not the aim of Shashi Deshpande to merely document female resistance to patriarchal ideologists, but also to focus on the strategies of readjustment for a female protagonist in order to forge an identity of their own. Her women characters struggle to learn to become "one's own refuge" and value the fellowship of other women. She creates sensitively in the female world and through modes of women's experience she gives it the main stream position. She does not isolate women's experience as her fiction consciously creates feminine sensibility. It has helped in creating a language of her own. Thus, *The Binding Vine* depicts women's experience in the Indian context hitherto unexplored and creates values and power that demand recognition.

A Matter of Time is a novel woven around human predicament. It depicts the fascinating story of three brave women representing three generations in a family. It is the saga of their pain, pleasure, endurance, suffering and love, understanding and support extended towards one another. Sumi and Gopal are wife and husband having three young daughters— Anu, Charu and Seema. In the very beginning of the novel, Gopal enters house and informs his wife that he is leaving the house. Next day Sumi tells her daughter about it, "Almost exactly repeating Gopal's words, leaving out nothing" (9). Sumi's feelings are deeply hurt by Gopal's action but she endures the pain within herself and tries to keep the thing normal for her daughters.

Sumi has a sense of estrangement due to Gopal's desertion. Her daughters blame Sumi for Gopal's action too; and she gets hurt. She says: "Do my daughters blame me for what Gopal has done? Do they think it is my fault? Why can't I talk to them, tell them what I feel, how it was? Why can't I open my heart to them?" (23). As a matter of fact, she is trying her level best to cope up with the reality, trying to come to terms with the hard painful reality and wants her daughters to do the same. Her daughters seem worried about his being alive; but "Sumi has no fears of his death, on the contrary, there is the certainty of his being alive, of his steadily pursuing his own purposes" (24). Sumi has her own question to ask him. She does not blame Gopal; but she is curious to know, how he has taken the decision to disown things and people in this age of acquisition and possession. She says:

> If I meet Gopal I will ask him one question, just one, the question no one has thought of. What is it, Gopal...that makes man in this age of acquisition and possession walk out on his family, and all that he owns? Because...it was you who said that we are shaped by the age we live in, by the society we are part of. How then can you, in this age, a part of the society, turn your back on everything in your life? Will you be able to give me an answer to this? (27)

The novelist has very skillfully revealed the inner strength to present the ladies. Sumi, unlike a traditional Indian lady, does not cry rather she faces the problems of maintaining the family boldly. It proves that a man can run away from his responsibilities; the present day educated Indian lady is competent enough to face the challenges of life. The novelist very subtly reflects the element of Indian brand of feminism and post-feminism.

The novel underlines Gopal's desertion as another dimension of betrayal and cruelty to women. His sudden decision to desert the family results in a 'swift dismemberment' of the family leaving despair-filled hurts behind. It is like a death in the family, "a death without a body". Sumi, the deserted wife, does not show any distress outwardly, but there is an apparent silence but it is no less than the cry of despair. The apparent stoicism may compel someone to get confused and treat her like an invalid person. Besides, "Gopal's desertion is not just a tragedy, it is both a shame and a disgrace" (13). It is a matter of great surprise and pity that disgrace clings not so much to the man who walks out on his family but to the wife who is deserted. The impact of the shock can be easily seen mainly on Sumi and her eighteen-year-old daughter, Aru. The reactions given by these two characters vary as the first one is matured whereas the other is standing at the threshold of her youth. Almost all the novel deals with female problems and psychology; but for the first time, an attempt has been made to understand the male psychology in general and Gopal's psychology in particular. Although Sumi reasons out that the metaphysical question of the ultimate truth of human life and the persistent search for meaning in existence is Gopal's reason, yet she questions, "...what about us, the girls and me? We are here because of his actions: how does this fit in?" (27). But she will not coerce him into coming back to her and here she exhibits her dignity. On the contrary, she explores ways of coming to terms with the painful reality and going on with life. She tries to get a job and learns to ride a scooter and above all, discovers writing talent within her and produces a play for her school children. On the other hand Aru is filled with anger and resentment against her father. She thinks that her father should not be allowed to go scot-free, and consults for bringing legal action against him.

Sumi, being matured, understands her young daughter's desperate need of the warmth and togetherness of the family.

Even though she set Gopal free without any grudge or complaint. This understanding between Gopal and Sumi makes their relationship a unique one in Deshpande's fictional world. All the men-women relationships in her novels are oppressive, strange, uncomfortable or silent. Here both Sumi and Gopal stand out uniquely in spite of the fact that Gopal leaves them for something unattainable. Sumi's daughter, Aru is rebellious against her father Gopal. She approaches Gopal not expecting sympathy for herself or her mother. She wants to unravel the strange behaviour of her father. She asks Gopal, "Why did you marry, why did you have children?" (65). Her searching question makes Gopal re-examine his motives in fleeing from the family. Aru is shocked to see the tragedies of her grandmother and mother. Credit goes to the straitjacketed laws prevalent in the patriarchal society which made Aru declare: "I'm never going to get married" (76). She has contemptuous views on the patriarchy. She is grieved to observe how women are subjected to torture—both mentally and physically. She is very much critical of Gopal—her father. She does not want to be submissive or tolerant like her mother. She wants Gopal to be punished for whatsoever injustice he has done to her mother and family. This is the reason; Aru meets a feminist, Surekha, a lawyer by profession. However, the activist lawyer does not find it a case of usual marital discord. Here the novelist also tries to draw the attention of the readers towards the drawbacks of the Indian law which are not sufficient enough to protect the Indian women from being victimized. Another aspect of this episode is that the modern educated Indian women are getting ready to revolt against the patriarchal set up of the society where they can breathe freely, think freely and live a life of their own choice.

A Matter of Time has been written reflecting an intricate pattern of relationships within an extended family spanning across generations. Manorama, Kalyani, Sumi and Aru represent four generations of the same family. All of them have their experience of life in the patriarchal society. Manorama is the typical product of patriarchal value system because she is very much resentful of the birth of Kalyani, her daughter. The reason behind it is her utmost desire to beget a son. Much against the wishes of her daughter Kalyani, she forced her to marry her younger brother Shripati. She seems so insensitive to her daughter that she holds Kalyani responsible for all her sorrows and calls her an enemy. On the contrary Kalyani is an icon of women's power of survival. She never compromises with her self-respect. She struggles silently which bears the fruits. It is the will power of survival which tides her across her mother's ill-treatment and her husband's rejection. A transition from Manorama to Kalyani is evident when Kalyani says to Aru:

> My mother didn't care for my children, either. Daughters again, she said...I'm luckier than my mother. She is the one unlucky who didn't know how to enjoy her children and grandchildren. (226)

The time Gopal deserted Sumi, it appeared to Kalyani like a reenactment of her own life, but unlike her mother, she gives emotional support to her daughter. Sumi is the only lady who struggles to learn to live alone and asserts oneself against the tide of tragedy. On the one hand, we find Sumi trying to withstand the shock and emptiness created by Gopal; but on the other hand Aru is full of the sense of injustice and protest against her father. Sumi is trying to retain her identity, but Aru fights for the rights of women.

The aim of the novelist is not only to present female resistance to patriarchal ideologies, but also to focus on the strategies of readjustment for the female protagonists. Her female protagonists try hard to forge their own identity. They come to terms with their male counterparts. They try to find the solution of their problems within the periphery of marital life rather than revolting and breaking the established social norms. They struggle to become "One's own refuge" and honour the sentiments of other women. They can succeed in getting their equal status in the society provided they develop a sense of co-operation among themselves. She recreates very subtly the female world through modes of women's experience. She is not inclined to isolate women's experience as her fiction consciously creates feminine sensibility.

Shashi Deshpande is such a woman writer who writes about the problems faced by the women in the male-dominated society. Most of her writings are the expression of her own intense and long suppressed feelings. It comes out of the experience of the difficulty of playing different roles assigned to the women. Her writings are the true reflection of her consciousness of the conflict between her ideas of herself as a human being and the idea which society has of her as a woman. Her writings are based upon gender discrimination. She believes that all her writings are committed to serve the society without any prejudice. She wants to be recognized as a writer who writes for the welfare of whole humanity.

Small Remedies narrates the tragic tale of Savitribai Indorekar, doyenne of the Gwalior Gharana. She leads the most unconventional of lives, but undergoes great mental trauma due to the partialities done with women in the Indian society. She was wise enough to understand the gender based discrimination right from her childhood. Madhu, the protagonist, was also a victim of the double standards of the society. She gets totally estranged by her husband Som after she naively discloses to him about her single act of physical intercourse before marriage. It is a matter of great surprise for the readers to know that Som himself had also a full-fledged physical relation with another married woman before marriage. He should have been tolerant to his wife. What a different mind set-up the man has.

Small Remedies bears the stamp of Shashi Deshpande's feminist writing. The manner typical to her writing is reflected through the central character. Not just in this aspect but also in her special way of looking at details, love for imagery, in her deliberately slow manner of unveiling the plot that is full of sudden twist and turns, in her ability to look into the depths of human heart and give expression to the feelings buried in there, and in the very honesty with which her central character confronts her own life, in the importance given to dreams to unravel events.

Small Remedies is a narrative of narratives. The narrative is woven of several interrelated stories mapping a larger network of relations justifying their human and existential contexts. This can be best understood in terms of the relation between character and narrative, which explores the link between desirable social structure and intelligible narrative structuring. The narrative mode is meant to liberate nemesis from memory and memory from its own shadows. The analysis of the novel in the feminist perspective will be incomplete unless the narrative frames of the novel are taken into consideration. The first narrative frame involving Madhu's proposed biography of Savitribai Indorekar living the life of a recluse in Bhavanipur. On the completion of the book, Madhu is likely to start a new life. She will then become "the writer from Bombay". For, at present it is "an identity so new, so strange, it feels like a disguise" (16). Madhu cannot begin the book, because the strands become complex and get more and more complicated. Savitribai's reputation is trapped in the social labyrinth. She also faces controversies which she tries to clear for the reconstruction of her public image. She was born in a respectable Brahmin family but without caring anything she eloped with a Muslim tabla-player and begot a daughter from him. Now she is inclined to recreate her past in such a way that the reconstructed links give greater clarity to her fading image.

Munni's story gives the second strand of the narrative. Baiji's reluctance to acknowledge this child out of wedlock forces Madhu's memory along a track that is at once dangerous. The third and fourth strands are those of Savitribai Indorekar and Leela. Each is a figural repetition of Madhu's own attempts to justify the series of exclusions from her own life. Savitribai wants her story to be recorded as she told it is a motif that repeats itself in different ways. Each is an interpreter in his/her own right and reserves the right to tell it that way.

Madhu gets quite confused at times about Bai's courage or lack of it. She had led the most unconventional life which no one could have ever imagined. But behind these acts of bravado was a woman who wanted to conform, to establish the identity of her own, to be accepted by society. Savitribai is not like a stereotypical feminist of devil-may-care attitude. She is very much concerned about the future reputation of herself as well as Munni's. This is the reason she does not mention the name of Ghulam Saab while narrating her life history to Madhu, her biographer. This incident reveals her anxiety to cover up her youthful indiscretion with the view of presenting a picture of respectability. She even disowns her lovely daughter Munni born through the association with Ghulam Saab. Madhu, who is aware of Savitribai's past and her daughter Munni, is quite surprised at the indifference shown towards her daughter. Madhu, the biographer, wants Bai to make immortal by revealing the name of her daughter. But in the Indian social set-up it is quite impossible to recognize a lady of such character as a model of feminist movement. This is why the novelist, through Savitribai, wants to convey the message that the Indian women should try to respect the norms of the established marriage institution honestly and try to find the solution within the periphery of marriage.

Leela's life is also a saga of miseries. Madhu tries to establish the identities of Leela and Savitribai amidst all the facts she has collected. She thinks:

> I've begun thinking that in writing about Bai, I'm writing about Leela as well. And my mother and all those women who reached beyond their grasp. Bai moving out of her class in search of her destiny as a singer, Leela breaking out of the conventions of widowhood, reaching out from her small room to the world, looking for justice for the weak, my mother running in her bare-feet, using her body as an instrument for speed.... Yes, they're in it together. But they paid the price for their attempts to break out. (283-84)

She thinks "that both were courageous women, that both were women who worked for and got the measure of freedom they needed, that both were ready to accept wholly the consequences of their actions" (284) and that, more importantly, whatever happened, they still went on with their lives. Madhu has now accepted the simple truth that it is not necessary to know all the answers to the questions that life throws up.

Madhu realizes that life has been simply to be lived, no matter what happens, even when things look so much abysmal.

That truth comes to Madhu not abruptly but slowly as she witnesses the lives around her. One such instance is an *upanayan* ceremony she witnesses in Bhawani temple, a ceremony that is marked with muted pain and grief. The death of the father had not meant that *upanayanam* could not take place. Life has to go on.

Madhu's troubled heart gets consoled when she listens to Hasina singing a Vachana by Akka Mahadevi, a saint poet of Karnataka. It is a night performance held in the Bhawani temple on Savitribai's guru Kashinath Buwas's death anniversary. During the first major performance Hasina sings, "I saw a dream, I saw a dream" (319) as a repeated affirmation of the vision of not only the poet but of all kinds of people through the ages. Madhu realizes: "She's speaking of my dreams too, so many of them, all woven about Adit. And Som's dreams for his son. It's all over now, there are no more dreams left for me, for either of us" (319). She knows that even if there are no dreams left for her because of Adit's death, life has to be lived. That nothing works against our morality.

> Mustard seeds to protect us from evil, blessings to confer long life—nothing works. And yet we go on. Simple remedies? No, they're desperate remedies and we go on with them because, in truth, there is nothing else. (315)

Can a man come to the conclusion that there are no remedies in life? Of course, there are so many remedies. But the remedies that are available are small remedies—an affectionate hug like the one she shares on the beach with Joe a short while after her father dies, the words of a song like the ones sung with devotional feelings by Hasina, even the aroma of hot oil and of curry leaves roasting in it, splutter of mustard seeds and so on. This revelation is what makes Madhu ask herself at the very end of the novel.

> How could I have ever longed for amnesia? Memory, capricious and unreliable though it is, ultimately carries its own truth within it. As long as there is memory, there's always the possibility of retrieval, as long as there is memory, loss is never total. (324)

This was the same Madhu who had thought, at the beginning of the story, "of the totality of loss" (5), its irrevocability.

Small Remedies clearly reflects the feminist ideas of Shashi Deshpande's writings. In the manner typical to her writing the story is revealed through the inner consciousness of one central character; life around is focused through the mind of the character. Her special way of looking at details, love for imagery, slow manner of unveiling the plot are the salient features of her feminist writing. Her ability to look into the depth of human heart and give expression to the feelings buried in there, the very honesty with which her central character confronts her own life, in the importance given to dreams to unravel events are the special qualities from the other feminist writers.

Like in her other novels, the house in *Small Remedies* reflects its inmates. "In spite of being a slapdash kind of household, there's no chaos in it" (21). It is Lata, the effervescent Lata, who is the mistress of this house, who is constantly on the move, and who by moving seems to imbibe new bouts of energy. The description of the very first night and morning which Madhu spends in the new house in Bhawanipur is so rich with details that it comes across like a miniature painting. One feels more like a spectator than like a reader. It is a book where no image, no description is superfluous. Like the path Madhu chooses out of three available ways to approach Savitribai's house.

Small Remedies is also a novel which clearly reflects the personal philosophy of the novelist. The epigraphs of the novels need to be looked at, to understand the core of Deshpande's philosophical thoughts, and to trace their development. The epigraph "You are your own refuge; there is no other refuge. This refuge is hard to achieve" (From *The Dhammapada*) of her first novel, *The Dark Holds No Terrors* indicates that the only support Saru can find is within herself. The epigraph "Father of the earth, protect us; Father of the sky, protect us; Father of the great and shining water, protect us;—To which God shall we offer our worship?" (From *Rig Veda*) of *Small Remedies* points at the futility of searching for a God to whom we can offer our homage. It tells us that there is no such homage that can protect us, that there is really no protection from life's disasters. All that we can hope for are remedies, and for these we do not have to look beyond the little acts of kindness that people around us extend to us.

Women's struggle for identity in the novels of Shashi Deshpande is the central theme. Quest for identity gets largely accentuated due to their frustrating experiences born of the prohibitive nature of the Indian patriarchal society. In her novels, the male characters—husbands, lovers, fathers and other relations—display different aspects of patriarchy and oppression. While the majority of the husbands are patriarchal in their approach, the older men particularly the fathers are broad-minded. Surprisingly, the male friends are "feminist" in their approach and sympathise with the protagonists' lot. Deshpande's male characters only serve to enable the protagonists to define their identities more clearly. Shashi Deshpande has constructed motifs of patriarchy and oppression by employing the methods of negation and affirmation. Her protagonists are victims of the Indian patriarchy and after initial submission resist the oppressive situation, thereby reflecting the author's view that a woman must assert herself within marriage to preserve her individuality.

Shashi Deshpande's view on marriage is different from those of what the most western feminists like Simon de Beauvoir, Germaine Greer and Kate Millet hold. In *The Second Sex*, Simon de Beauvoir writes: "It has been said that marriage diminishes man, which is often true, but almost always it annihilates woman" (1983: 496). Germaine Greer even goes to the extent of saying that women should not marry. Kate Millet is having the opinion that marriage reduces the status of women to a mere object of decoration and a tool of man's sexual gratification. But Deshpande never subscribes to the views of any feminist. Her ideology may not be of the type radical feminists hold but she has her own brand of feminism which, as Jaidev says, "has to be authentic, rooted and context bound" (1991: 57). She is not against the institution of marriage, as her women protagonists strive to make their marriages work in their endeavour to lead a meaningful existence.

Shashi Deshpande keeps her narratives female centered and gives an intimate insight into the psyche of the middle class Indian women who feel oppressed and hemmed in by their patriarchal socialization. She provides new ideals for a better man-woman relationship, thereby broadening the scope of woman's existence. She not only presents a feminist insight into patriarchal values, but also prescribes a balance between tradition and modernity as a working philosophy for the contemporary woman. According to Deshpande, traditions are the values of harmony and co-existence that symbolize the Indian way of life, and modernity is the assertion of the independent, individual identity. After having passively played out their socially ordained roles, her protagonists move out of their cloistered selves to assert their individuality as human beings. Deshpande feels that the woman must be true to her own self if she wants to realize herself. The straitjacketed role imposed on woman only bogs her down in mire of negation and suppression. She must venture out of the familial framework to give full expression to her individuality and identity.

Roots and Shadows comes out with its feminist approach in Indu's exploration into herself. It also moves beyond feminist boundaries into a realization of the predicament of human existence. Indu traverses the road of self-realization and her destination in the point of comprehension of the mystery of the human life. In the long run, she realizes the basic truth of human existence through self-exploration. Thus Indu's uncompromising and paradoxical feminine self finally finds its roots in the home with her husband. She sees life with the possibilities of growth. Hence the message of Indian feminism comes out in her character.

In *The Dark Holds No Terrors,* Sarita, the protagonist frees herself from the dependence syndrome. The problematic of life, in the process of search for a feminist space only brings out the inner conflict of the modern Indian woman who is trying to balance her multiple roles as a member of the family, as a professional and above all, as a human being. In the case of Sarita, the novelist seems to have made no attempt to bring her finally anywhere to accept the new feminist moral vision.

Achievement of individual identity and formal autonomy must not be the goal of feminism. After having accorded that autonomy on her, she should be brought to accept the basic human values like motherhood and responsibility of the family and society, at least on her own terms. There is a need to harmonise the man-woman relationship as equal partners.

That Long Silence portrays the sufferings and deprivation of feminine life by presenting certain characters as stereotyped representative of traditional womanhood. Jaya, the protagonist, realizes that in order to attain selfhood, a woman must transcend silence, negation and self-alienation. A balanced and purposeful life is not a utopian fancy for a woman if she liberates herself from the stereotyped conditioning of society and is not dependent on the male presence to authenticate her thoughts, emotions and deeds at every step. The character of Jaya aesthetically communicates the essence of the creed of feminism along with the contemporary realities.

The novel *The Binding Vine* opens with Urmila, the protagonist, grieving over her dead infant daughter which is sufficient enough to prove her love for child. Further she brings the incident of Kalpana's rape to the police much against her mother's wishes. It proves her boldness in order to save the women from any sort of tyranny meted out by the patriarchal society. Though Urmila is accused of being a 'traitor' to Mira and Kalpana, she is resolute to break the silence of women which come in different forms—sometimes in the name of the social taboos, sometimes in the name of family honour. Through this character the novelist conveys a message to the Indian women to be bold and self-dependent. Indian women must be ready to face the harsh realities of life and harmonize the social as well as private life.

A Matter of Time is a novel woven around human predicament. It is the story of women's pain, endurance, suffering and love, understanding and support extended to one another. Sumi, the protagonist, after a lot of suffering and self-introspection comes to terms with her present with an understanding and acceptance of her past and is now ready to march ahead with a new acceptance of life. The most striking quality in Sumi's character is that she could forgive her husband who is the root cause of her sufferings. Deshpande's feminism seems attributed in her character. She achieves freedom without transcending the social norms and values.

In *Small Remedies*, Madhu, the protagonist, is a victim of double standards being practised in the Indian society. The estrangement between Madhu and her husband Som presents the stark picture of the patriarchal mind-set of men. Once she revealed, though in innocence, her pre-marital sex relation with Chandru which gave a great shock to Som, whereas he himself was having a full-fledged extra-marital sex relation with a married woman. Through this revelation, the novelist wants to draw the attention of the readers towards the one sided sex morality. Really, the Indian society does not appreciate such things. This rule should be applicable on both the life partners. Thus essence of feminism is reflected here. At end of story, both Madhu and Som reunite. This is the indication of their mutual understanding between them. Thus, we come to the conclusion that the novelist's concept of feminism reflected in this story can be a panacea in order to save the families from disintegration and sufferings.

It is true that Deshpande is not an avowed feminist but she occupies a place of pre-eminence among the contemporary woman novelists concerned with women's issues. Her creative talent and ideology have established her as a great feminist writer genuinely concerned with women's issues and anxieties. Her protagonists are modern, educated, middle-class women who, fettered to their stereotypical roles of a wife and mother, feel smothered and helpless in a tradition-bound male-dominated society.

Shashi Deshpande's novels present the real anguish and conflict of the modern educated middle-class women. Caught between patriarchy and tradition on one hand, and self-expression, individuality and independence on the other, her protagonists feel themselves lost and confused and explore ways to fulfill themselves as a human being. Deshpande's concern and sympathy are essentially for the woman. She has given an honest portrayal of her fears, sufferings, disappointments and frustrations. Besides revealing the woman's struggle to secure self-respect and self-identity, the author lays bare the multiple levels of oppression, including sexual oppression. Deshpande's primary concern for the woman makes her a feminist writer.

It is undeniably true that Shashi Deshpande is a feminist writer but with a broad humanistic outlook. Her novels are essentially reflective of the unenviable situation of the beleaguered great artistic excellence and astounding originality. Her commendably realistic depiction of the contemporary Indian women's situation and the pragmatic solution she puts forward accord her novels an imperishable importance for their affirmative eloquent message for women and the whole humanity as well.

Bibliography

A. PRIMARY SOURCES

Novels

Deshpande, Shashi, 1980. *The Dark Holds No Terrors*. Ghaziabad: Vikas Publishing House.

——. 1982. *If I Die Today*. New Delhi: Vikas Publishing House.

——. 1983. *Come Up and Be Dead*. New Delhi: Vikas Publishing House.

——. 1983. *Roots and Shadows*. New Delhi: Orient Longman Ltd.

——. 1988. *That Long Silence*. London: Virago Press Ltd.

——. 1993. *The Binding Vine*. New Delhi: Penguin Books Ltd.

——. 1996. *A Matter of Time*. New Delhi: Penguin Books Ltd.

——. 2000. *Small Remedies*. New Delhi: Penguin Books Ltd.

——. 2004. *Moving On*. New Delhi: Penguin Books Ltd.

Short Stories

Deshpande, Shashi. 1978. *The Legacy & Other Stories*. Calcutta: Writers Workshop.

——. 1979. "The Day of the Golden Deer." *Common Wealth Quarterly*. Vol. 3. No. 12, Sept. pp. 64-73.

——. 1986. *The Miracles & Other Stories*. Calcutta: Writers Workshop.

——. 1986. *It was the Nightingale*. Calcutta: Writers Workshop.

——. 1986. *It was Dark*. Calcutta. Writers Workshop.

——. 1993. *The Intrusion & Other Stories*. New Delhi: Penguin Books Ltd.

——. 1996. "The Boy." *The Book Review*. Vol. 20, No. 5, May, pp. 21-22.

——. 2000. *The Stone Women*. Calcutta: Writers Workshop.

——. 2003. *Collected Stories*. Vol. 1, New Delhi: Penguin Books Ltd.

——. 2004. *Collected Stories*. Vol. 2, New Delhi: Penguin Books Ltd.

Children Literature

Deshpande, Shashi. 1980. *The Hidden Treasure*. Bombay: India Book House.

——. 1980. *The Only Witness*. Bombay: India Book House.

——. 1982. *The Narayanpur Incident*. Bombay: India Book House.

Non-Fictions

Deshpande, Shashi. 1974. "A Journey Towards Understanding." *The Second Writers Workshop Literary Reader*. P. Lal (Ed.). Calcutta: Writers Workshop.

——. 1984. "The Eternal Theme". *The Indian English Short Story*. Naik, M.K. (ed.). New Delhi: Arnold Heinemann. pp. 238-46.

——. 1985. "The Dilemma of Women Writers." *The Literary Criterion*. Vol. 20, No. 4.

——. 1985. "Language No Bar." *The Sunday Times of India*. Ahmedabad. 23 April. p. 10.

——. 1986. "The Dilemma of the Woman Writers." *Women in Fiction and Fiction By Women: The Indian Scene*. C.D. Narasimhaiah and C.N. Srinath (eds.). Mysore: A. Dhvanyaloka Publication. pp. 31-34.

——. 1991. "The Writing of a Novel." *Indian Women Novelist*, Set. 1, Vol. 5, R.K. Dhawan (ed.). New Delhi: Prestige Books. pp. 31-36.

——. 1992. "No Woman is an Island." *The Sunday Times of India*. May 10, p. 12.

——. 1993. "Work In Progress.... Writers On Writing: Women's Minds and Bodies." *Indian Review of Books*. Vol. 2, No. 4. Jan. 16-Feb. 15. p. 26.

——. 1993. "An Archipelago." *Indian Review of Books*. Vol. 3, No. 1, Oct. 16-Nov. 15. pp. 32-33.

——. 1995. "Waste Land." *The Statesman Festival Special*. pp. 97-99.

——. 1996. "Of Concerns, Of Anxieties." *Indian Literature*. Vol. xxxiv, No. 5, Sept.-Oct. p. 108.

——. 1997. "Where do We Belong? The 'Problem' of English In India." *Kunapipi*. pp. 65-74.

——. 1998. "Writing From the Margin." *The Book Review*. 22:3, pp. 9-10.

Interviews

Choudhory, Romita. 1995. "Interview with Shashi Deshpande." *World Literature in English* 34:2, pp. 15-26.

Dickman, Sue. 1995. "In Conversation: Sue Dickman With Indian Women Writers." *The Book Review*. Vol. 19, No. 4, April. pp. 30-35.

——. 1998. "An Interview with Shashi Deshpande." *Ariel* 29:1, Jan. pp. 129-35.

Geetha, T.N. 1995. "An Interview with Shashi Deshpande." *Indian Women Novelists,* Set-III, Vol. 4, R.K. Dhawan (ed.). New Delhi: Prestige Books, pp. 9-11.

Holmstrom, Lakshmi. 1993. "Interview: Shashi Deshpande Talks to Lakshmi Holmstrom." *Wasafiri,* No. 17, Sept. pp. 22-27.

Holm, Chandra. 2000. "A Writer of Substance." *Indian Review of Books*. Vol. 9, No. 8, May 16-June 15, pp. 5-9.

Kuortti, Joel. 2001. "Years of Silence Come to an End: Interview with Shashi Deshpande, Bangalore, 6 January, 2000." *Kunapipi*. 23:2, pp. 145-65.

Nair, Malini. 1989. "The Message is Incidental." *The Times of India*. No. 25. November.

Ramarao, Vimala. 1997. "A Conversation with Shashi Deshpande." *The Journal of Indian Writing in English*, Vol. 25, No. 1 & 2, Jan.-Jul. pp. 131-36.

——. 1998. "In Conversation with Shashi Deshpande." *The Fiction of Shashi Deshpande*. R.S. Pathak (ed.). New Delhi: Creative Books. pp. 256-59.

Riti, M.D. 1988. An Interview. "There is No Looking Back for Shashi Deshpande." *Eves' Weekly*, 18-24 June, p. 28.

Thakur, Pallavi. "An Interview with Shashi Deshpande." 2001. (21 Aug. 2001. Bangalore). *The Quest*. Vol. 17, No. 1, June. pp. 66-68.

Viswanatha, Vanamala. 1987. "A Woman's World.... All the Way." *Literature Alive*. Vol. 1, No. 3, pp. 8-14.

Viswanatha, Gita. 2005. "In Conversation with Shashi Deshpande" (3 June 2003). *Writing Difference*, Chanchala K. Naik (ed.). Delhi: Pencraft, pp. 228-36.

B. SECONDARY SOURCES

Books

Anand, Mulk Raj. 1988. "In Yama's Hell: Indian English Writing About Women." Kamini Dinesh (ed.). *Between Spaces of Silence: Women Creative Writers*. New Delhi: Sterling.

Arora, Neena. 1991. *Nayantara Sahgal and Doris Lessing: A Feminist Study in Comparison*. New Delhi: Prestige Books.

Ardiner, Shirley (ed.). 1978. *Perceiving Women*. New York: Halsted Press.

Adrey, Mukta and Viney Kirpal. 1998. *Shashi Deshpande: A Feminist Study of Her Fiction*. Delhi: B.R. Publishing Corporation.

Bai, Kalle Meera. 1996. *Women's Voice: The Novels of Indian Women Writers*. New Delhi: Prestige.

Bakka, Olive. 1981. *Face of Feminism: A Study of Feminism as a Social Movement*. New York: St. Martin's Press.

Bala, Suman (ed.). 2001. *Women in the Novels of Shashi Deshpande*. New Delhi: Khosla Publishing House.

Balachandran, K. 2004. *Critical Responses to Indian Writing in English: Essays in Honour of Dr. A.P.J. Abdul Kalam.* New Delhi: Sarup and Sons.

Baym, Nina. 1978. *Women's Fiction: A Guide to Novels by and About Women in America*, 1820–1870. Ithaca: New York Cornell University Press.

Beauvoir, Simon de. 1997. *The Second Sex*. H.M. Parshley. (trans. & ed.), London: Vintage.

Bebel, A. 1976. *Women in the Past, Present and Future.* New Delhi: National Book Centre.

Berger, John. 1972. *Ways of Seeing.* Harmondsworth.

Bhatnagar, Man Mohan K. (ed.). 1999. *Feminists English Literature.* New Delhi: Atlantic Publishers.

Bullough, V. 1973. *The Subordinate Sex: A History of Attitudes Towards Women.* New York: Penguin.

Chandra, N.D.R. 2005. *Contemporary Literary Criticism: Theory and Practice.* Vol. I and II. New Delhi: Authors Press.

Chanana, Kurana (ed.). 1988. *Socialization, Education and Women: Exploration in Gender Identity.* New Delhi: Orient Longman.

Chaterjee, Lola (ed.). 1986. *Woman/Image/Text: Feminist Readings of Literary Texts.* New Delhi: Trianka Publications.

Das, Kamala. 1984. 'Introduction.' *Collected Poems.* Vol. I. Trivandrum: The Navkerala Printers.

Das, Tulsi. 1990. *Sri Ram Charitmanas.* Gorakhpur: Gita Press.

Das, Veena Noble (ed.). 1995. *Feminism and Literature.* New Delhi: Prestige Books.

Desai, Anita. 1977. *Fire on the Mountain.* New Delhi: Allied Publication.

——. 1982. *Where Shall We Go This Summer?* New Delhi: Orient.

Dhawan, R.K. (ed.). 1991. *Indian Women Novelists.* Vol. 5. New Delhi: Prestige Books.

Douglas, Susan J. 2007. *These Times*. http: w.w.w. alternet.org./ story/13118. p. 1.

Dwivedi, A.N. 1996. "The Hub of Wheel: Some Recurrent Metaphors in Shashi Deshpande's Fiction." *Critical Practice*. Vol. 3, No. 1.

Eagleton, Mary (ed.). 1994. *Feminist Literary Theory: A Reader*. Oxford: Blackwell Publishers.

Ellman, Richard. 1959. *James Joyce: A Biography*. London: Oxford University Press.

Firestone, S. 1971. *The Dialect of Sex*. New York: Bantam.

Fitterley, Judith. 1978. *The Resisting Reader: A Feminist Approach to American Fiction*. Bloomington: Indiana University Press.

Friedan, Betty. 1971. *The Feminine Mystique*. Harmondsworth: Penguin.

——. 1981. *The Second Stage*. New York: Summit Books.

Freeman, Erica. 1971. *Insights: Conversation with Theodore Relk*. New Jersey: Prentice Hall.

Geertz, Clifford. 1973. *The Interpretation of Cultures*. New York: Basic Books.

Ghadially, Rehana (ed.). 1988. *Women in Indian Society*. New Delhi: Sage Publications.

Green, Gayle and Copelia Kahn (eds.). 1985. *Making a Difference: Feminist Literary Criticism*. London: Methuen.

Greer, Germaine. 1970. *The Female Eunuch*. New York: McGraw Hill Ltd.

——. 1984. *Sex and Destiny: The Politics of Human Fertility*. New York: Harper Colophon Books.

Hartman, Geoffret. 1980. *Criticism in Wilderness: The Study of Literature Today*. New Haven, Connecticut: Yale University Press.

Hornby, A.S. (ed.). 1985. *Oxford Advanced Learner's Dictionary*. Delhi: Oxford University Press.

Hunter College. 1983. *Women's Studies Collectives*. New Delhi: Oxford University Press.

Iyengar, K.R. Srinivas. 1963. *Indian Writing in English*. New Delhi: Sterling.

Jacobus, Mary (ed.). 1979. *Women Writing About Women*. New York: Noble Imports.

Jain, Jasbir (ed.). 2000. *Creative Theory: Writers on Writing*. Delhi: Pencrafts International.

——. 2003. *Gendered Realities, Human Spaces: The Writing of Shashi Deshpande*. Jaipur: Rawat.

Jain, Jasbir and A.K. Singh. 2001. *Indian Feminism*. New Delhi: Creative Books.

James, Muriel and Dorothy Jongeward. 1971. *Born To Win*: Transactional Analysis with Gestalt Experiments. Rpt. 1978. Chicago: Signet Books, pp. 64-65.

Jung, Carl G. 1982. *Aspects of Feminine*. London: Routledge and Kegan Paul.

Kakar, Sudhir. 1990. *The Inner World: A Psycho-Analytic Study of Childhood and Society in India*. New Delhi: Oxford University Press.

Kalpan, Cora. 1986. *She Changes: Culture and Feminism*. London: Verso.

Kapoor, Promilla. 1973. *The Changing Status of Women in India*. Sahibabad: Vikas.

Khan, M.Q. and A.G. Khan. 1995. *Changing Faces of Women in Indian Writing in English*. New Delhi: Creative Books.

Kealey, Linda. 1979. *A Not Unreasonable Claim: Women and Reform in Canada, 1880's-1920's*. Toronto: Women's Educational Press.

Lerner, Gerda. 1986. *The Creation of Patriarch*. New York: Oxford University Press.

Manu. 2005. *The Manusmriti*. Surendranath Saxena (ed.). Delhi: Manoj Publications.

Millet, Kate. 1971. *Sexual Politics*. London: Rupst Hart Davis.

Moi, Toril. 1985. *Sexual/Textual Politics: Feminist Literary Theory*. London: Mathuen.

Miles, Maria. 1980. *Indian Women and Patriarchy: Conflicts and Dilemmas of Students and Working Women*. New Delhi: Concept Publishers.

Mukherjee, Bharati. 1990. *Jasmine*. New Delhi: Viking.

——. 1990. *Wife*. New Delhi: Penguin.

Mukherjee, Meenakshi. 2001. *The Twice-Born Fiction: Themes and Techniques of the Indian Novel in English*. Delhi: Pencrafts International.

Nabar, Vrinda. 1995. "Caste as Woman." New Delhi: Penguin.

Naik, Chanchala K. (ed.). 2005. *Writing Difference: The Novels of Shashi Deshpande*. Delhi: Pencraft International.

Naik, M.K. 1999. *A History of Indian English Literature*. New Delhi: Sahitya Akademi.

Nityanandan, Indira. 2000. *Three Great Indian Women Novelists*. New Delhi: Creative Books.

Nubile, Clara. 2003. *The Danger of Gender*. New Delhi: Sarup & Sons.

Papanek, Henna and Gail Minault. 1982. *Separate Worlds: Studies in Purdah in South Africa*. New Delhi: Chanakya Publications.

Parikh, Indira and Pulin Garg. 1989. *Indian Women: Inner Dialogue*. New Delhi: Sage Publications.

Pathak, R.S. (ed.). 1997. *The Fiction of Shashi Deshpande*. New Delhi: Creative Books.

Plath, Sylvia. 1982. *The Bell Jar*. London: Faber & Faber.

Ramamurti, K.S. 1987. *Rise of Indian Novel in English*. New Delhi: Sterling.

Ray, Mohit K. and Rama Kundu. 2004. *Studies in Women Writers in English*. Vol. 1, New Delhi: Atlantic Publisher.

Reddy, Y.S. Sunita. 2001. *A Feminist Perspective on the Novels of Shashi Deshpande*. New Delhi: Prestige Books.

Rich, Adrienne. 1976. *Of Women Born: Motherhood as Experience and Institution*. New York: W.W. Norton.

Ringney, Barbara H. 1978. *Madness and Sexual Politics in the Feminist Novel: Studies in Bronte, Woolf, Lessing and Atwood.* Madison: University of Wisconsin Press.

Sandhu, Sarbjit K. 1991. *The Novels of Shashi Deshpande.* New Delhi: Prestige Books.

Sanga, Jaina C. 2003. *South Asian Novelists in English: An A-Z Guide*, CT: Greenwood Press.

Saxena, Surendranath (ed.). 2005. The *Manusmriti.* Delhi: Manoj Publications.

Sebastian, Mrinalini. 2000. *The Enterprise of Reading Differently: The Novels of Shashi Deshpande in Post Colonial Arguments.* New Delhi: Prestige Books.

Shanti, S.M. 1989. *Tradition Versus Modernity in the Novels of Shashi Deshpande.* Madurai: Madurai Kamraj University.

Sharma, Siddhartha. 2005. *Shashi Deshpande's Novels: A Feminist Study.* New Delhi: Atlantic Publishers.

Singh, Sushila. 1991. *Feminism and Recent Fiction in English.* New Delhi: Prestige Books.

Spivak, Gayatri Chakravorty. 1985. *Subaltern Studies.* New York: Oxford University Press.

Strouse, Jean (ed.). 1974. *Women and Analysis: Dialogues on Psychoanalytic Views of Feminity.* New York: Grossman.

Sunder Rajan, Rajeshwari. 1993. *Real and Imagined Women: Gender, Culture and Post-Colonialism.* London and New York: Routledge.

Suneel, Seema. 1995. *Man-Woman Relationship in Indian Fiction* (With focus on Shashi Deshpande, Rajendra Awasthi and Syed Abdul Malik). New Delhi: Prestige Books.

Surendran, K.V. 2002. *Indian English Fiction: New Perspective.* New Delhi: Sarup & Sons.

Tharu, Susie and K. Lalitha (eds.). 1991. *Women Writing in India: 600 B.C. to the Early 20th Century.* Delhi: Oxford University Press.

Tong, Rose Marie. 1993. *Feminist Thought.* London: Routledge.

Tilloston, Kathleen. 1961. *Novels of the Eighteen Forties*. London: Oxford University Press.

Walkar, Nancy. 1990. *Feminist Alternatives: Irony and Fantasy in the Contemporary Novel by Women*. Jackson: University Press of Mississipi.

Wilt, Judith. 1980. *Ghosts of the Gothic: Austen, Eliot and Lawrence*. New Jersey: Princeton University Press.

Wollstonecraft, Mary A. 1988. *Vindication of the Rights of Woman*. Carol Poston (ed.). New York: W.W. Norton.

Webster. 1996. *Webster's Encyclopedic Unabridged Dictionary of the English Language*. New York: Gramercy Books.

Woolf, Virginia. 1929. *A Room of One's Own*. London: Triad Grafton Book.

——. 1965. *Contemporary Writers*. London: Hogarth.

——. 1977. *A Room of One's Own*. Rpt. London: Granada.

——. 1979. *Professions for Women*. London: The Women Press.

——. 1979. *Women and Writing*. London: The Women's Press.

ARTICLES

Anand, Mulk Raj. 1988. "In Yama's Hell: Indian English Writing About Women." Kamini Dinesh (ed.). *Between Spaces of Silence: Women Creative Writers*. New Delhi: Sterling.

Bande, Usha. 1994. "Mother, Daughter and Daughter's Daughter: A Study of Shashi Deshpande." *Mother and Mother Figures in Indo-English Literature*. Jalandhar: ABS Publications. pp. 134-42.

——. 1998. "Tolerance or Female Altruism—A Study of Shashi Deshpande's *A Matter of Time*." *Language Forum*. Vol. 24, Nos. 1-2.

Barche, G.D. 1989. "Indu: Another Sisyphus in Shashi Deshpande's *Roots and Shadows*." *Creative Forum*. Vol. 2, Nos. 3 & 4, July-Dec. pp. 48-54.

——. 1994-95. "Facets of Feminism in Indian English Fiction." *The Commonwealth Review*. Vol. 6, No. 1. pp. 127-34.

——. 1996. "Facets of Feminism: *Roots and Shadows, Cry, The Peacock* & Temporary Answers." Feminism and Indian English Fiction. P.M. Nayak and S.P. Swain (eds.). Bareilly: Prakash Book Depot. pp. 91-96.

Bhatnagar, Parvati. 2001. "Search of Identity: A Study of Shashi Deshpande's *The Dark Holds No Terrors*." *The Quest*. Vol. 15, No. 1, June. pp. 50-57.

——. 2001. "Go Home Like A Good Girl: And Interpretation of *That Long Silence* by Shashi Deshpande." *Explorer*. Vol. 1, June-Dec. pp. 1-6.

Bhatt, Indira. 1991. "*That Long Silence*: A Study." *Indian Women Novelists*. Set. I, Vol. V, R.K. Dhawan (ed.). New Delhi: Prestige Books. pp. 156-62.

——. 1991. "Shashi Deshpande's *The Dark Holds No Terrors*: A Study in Guilt Consciousness." *Indian Women Novelists*. Set-III, Vol. 4, R.K. Dhawan (ed.). New Delhi: Prestige Books, pp. 41-50.

Bhavani, J. 1995. "Nirdvandva: Individuation and Integration as the Heroine's Quest in Shashi Deshpande's Fiction." *Indian Women Novelists*, Set-III, Vol. 4, R.K. Dhawan (ed.). New Delhi: Prestige Books. pp. 20-31.

Bhavani, Shakuntala. 1991. "Some Recent trends in Modern Indian Fiction: A Study of Deshpande's *That Long Silence*, Shashi Tharoor's *The Great Indian Novel* and Amitav Ghosh's *The Shadow Line*." *Indian Women Novelists*. Set-I, Vol. I, R.K. Dhawan (ed.). New Delhi: Prestige Books.

Biswal, Aarti. 1991. "Sound of the Silenced: Shashi Deshpande's *That Long Silence*." *Revolution*, Vol. 3, No. 1. pp. 39-44.

Brown, Penelope. 1970. "Universal and Particulars in the Positions of Women." *Women In Society: Inter-Disciplinary Essays*. London: Virago. rpt. 1981.

Chandra, Subash. 1991. "City in the Novels of Kamala Markandaya, Anita Desai and Shashi Deshpande." *Indian Women Novelists*, Set-I, Vol. I, R.K. Dhawan (ed.). New Delhi: Prestige Books. pp. 157-66.

——. 1991. "Silent No More: A Study of *That Long Silence.*" Indian Women Novelists. R.K. Dhawan (ed.). Vol. V, New Delhi: Prestige Books. pp. 147-55.

Chandra, Suresh. 1991. "Feminist Aspects of Recent Fiction: Mahip Singh's *Who Walks With Me*, Kiran Nagarkar's *Seven Sixes are Forty Three* and Shashi Deshpande's *That Long Silence.*" *Indian Women Novelists.* Set-I, Vol. 1, R.K. Dhawan (ed.). New Delhi: Prestige Books. pp. 139-48.

——. 1997. "Semiotics of Feministic Discourse in *That Long Silence.*" *Symbolism in Indian Fiction in English.* R.K. Srivastava (ed.). Jalandhar: ABS Publications. pp. 203-10.

Das, B.K. 1995. "Shashi Deshpande's *That Long Silence* and the Question of the Reader Response." *Indian Woman Novelists.* Set-III. Vol. IV. R.K. Dhawan (ed.). New Delhi: Prestige Books. pp. 125-32.

Dharkar, Rani. 1995. "Marriage as Purdah: Fictional Rendering of a Social Reality." *Margins of Erasure: Purdah in the Sub-Continental Novel in English.* Jasbir Jain and Amina Amin (eds.). New Delhi: Sterling. pp. 49-59.

Dinesh, Kamini. 1993. "*That Long Silence*: The Narrator and the Narrative." *Contemporary Indian Fiction in English.* Avadesh K. Singh (ed.). New Delhi: Creative Books. pp. 84-88.

——.1995. "Moving Out of the Cloistered Self: Shashi Deshpande's Protagonists." *Margins of Erasure: Purdah in the Sub-Continental Novel in English.* Jasbir Jain and Amina Amin (eds.). New Delhi: Sterling. pp. 196-205.

Douglas, Ann. 1972. "Mrs. Sigourney and the Sensibility of the Inner Space." *New England Quarterly* 45, June.

Dube, Leela. 1955. "On the Construction of Gender: Hindu Girls in Patriarchal India." *Socialization, Education and Women: Explorations in Gender Indentity.* Karuna Chanana (ed.). New Delhi: Orient Longman.

Dwivedi, A.N. 1996. "The Hub of Wheel: Some Recurrent Metaphors in Shashi Deshpande's Fiction." *Critical Practice.* Vol. III, No. 1.

Felman, Shoshana. 1975. "Women and Madness: The Critical Phallacy." *Diacritics*. 5, Winter.

Gaur, Rashmi. 2002. "Suffering and Desire in Shashi Deshpande's *Small Remedies*." *The Quest*. 16:1, June. pp. 33-38.

——. 2003. "Images of Indian Woman in Shashi Deshpande's *That Long Silence*—Stereotypes, Myths and Realities." *The Literary Criterion*. Vol. 38. No. 1. pp. 5-18.

Geeta, T.N. 1991. "The Story of Shashi Deshpande." *Indian Women Novelists*. Set-1, Vol. 5, R.K. Dhawan (ed.). New Delhi: Prestige Books.

Gupta, Ramesh Kumar. 2002. "Image of Woman in Shashi Deshpande's Novel *Roots and Shadows*: A Critical Study." *Poetcrit*. Vol. 15, No. 1, Jan. pp. 41-47.

Guttal, Vijaya. 2002. "Reading Shashi Deshpande in the Post-Colonial Context." *Haritham*. No. 14. pp. 73-81.

Holm, Chandra. 2000. "Potent Remedies: Themes and Techniques in Shashi Deshpande's *Small Remedies*." *The Atlantic Literary Review*. Vol. 1, No. 2, Oct.-Dec. pp. 154-61.

Indira, S. 1995. "A Bond or Burden? A Study of Shashi Deshpande's *The Binding Vine*." *Indian Women Novelists*. Set-III, Vol. 6, R.K. Dhawan (ed.). New Delhi: Prestige Books.

Jaidev. 1991. "Problematising Feminism." *Feminism and Recent Fiction in English*. Sushila Singh (ed.). New Delhi: Prestige Books.

Jain, Jasbir. 2003. "Gendered Realities Human Spaces: The Writing of Shashi Deshpande." *South Asian Reviews*. Vol. 15, No. 2.

Jandial, Gur Pyari. 2003. "Evolving a Feminist Tradition: The Novels of Shashi Deshpande and Manju Kapoor." *The Atlantic Literary Review*. Vol. 4, No. 3. July-Sept. pp. 108-28.

Khan, Nazneen. 2005. "Woman 'Made' Woman in the Novels of Shashi Deshpande." *Pegasus*. Vol. 4, Jan.-Dec. pp. 57-62.

King, Adele. 1990. "Shashi Deshpande: Portraits of an Indian Woman." *The New Indian Novel in English: A Study of the 1980's*. Viney Kirpal (ed.). New Delhi: Allied.

Kothandaraman, Bala. 1987. "Betwixt the Devi and the (she) Devil: The Feminist Dilemma in Indian Fiction." *Feminism and Literature*. K. Radha (ed.). Trivendrum: University of Kerala.

Maitra, Nivedita. 2003. "From Feminine to Female: Shashi Deshpande's *That Long Silence*." *The Quest*. Vol. 17, No. 2, Dec. pp. 46-51.

Mala, R. 1991. "Sexual Predicament and Shashi Deshpande's Women." *Indian Women Novelists*. Set-1, Vol. 5, R.K. Dhawan (ed.). New Delhi: Prestige Books. pp. 50-59.

Menon, K. Mahadevi. 1993. "The Crisis of Feminine in Shashi Deshpande's *That Long Silence*." *Commonwealth Quaterly*. Vol. 18, No. 46. Dec.-March, pp. 31-37.

Mother, The. 1978. "Women and War, The Mother: Words of Long Ago." *Collected Works*. Vol. 2, Century Edition. Pondicherry: Sri Aurobindo Asharam.

Mutalik-Desai, A.A. 1991. "Glint and Sparkle, Love and Death: Reflections on *Come Up and Be Dead*." *Indian Women Novelists*. Set-1, Vol. 5, R.K. Dhawan (ed.). New Delhi: Prestige Books, pp. 90-101.

Naikar, Basavaraj. 2001. "Joys and Sorrows of Womanhood in *The Binding Vine*." *Women In Novels of Shashi Deshpande*. Suman Bala (ed.). New Delhi: Khosla Publishing House, pp. 122-26.

Nirmala. 1990. "Shashi Deshpande's *The Legacy*: Some Feminist Perspectives." *Indian Scholar*. Vol. 12, No. 2, July. pp. 53-64.

Nityanandan, Indira. 1991. "Shashi Deshpande's *The Binding Vine*: Silent No More." *Indian Women Novelists*. Set-3, Vol. 4, R.K. Dhawan (ed.). New Delhi: Prestige Books. pp. 60-66.

Panikkar, K.M. 2003. "The Awakening of Women." *English With A Purpose*. Ramesh Dave (ed.). New Delhi: NCERT. pp. 15-19.

Pal, Adesh. 1995. "Ego-Self Crisis in the Fiction of Shashi Deshpande." *Changing Faces of Women in Indian Writing in English*. M.Q. Khan and A.G. Khan (eds.). New Delhi: Creative Books. pp. 71-80.

Palkar, Sarla. 1991. "Breaking the Silence: *That Long Silence*." *Indian Women Novelists*. Set-1, Vol. 5, R.K. Dhawan (ed.). New Delhi: Prestige Books. pp. 163-69.

Patil, Ujwala. 1991. "The Theme of Marriage and Selfhood in *Roots and Shadows*." *Indian Women Novelists*. Vol. V, R.K. Dhawan (ed.). New Delhi: Prestige Books. pp. 130-37.

Paul, Premila. 1991. "*The Dark Holds No Terrors*: A Woman's Search for Refuge." *Indian Women Novelists*. Set-1, Vol. 5, R.K. Dhawan (ed.). New Delhi. Prestige Books. pp. 60-81.

Prasanna, A. Hari. 1996. "Image of 'Woman' in Shashi Deshpande's Fiction: A Study of *Roots and Shadows* and *The Dark Holds No Terrors*." *The Literary Voice*. No. 3, Feb. pp. 36-42.

Rajan, Rajeshwari Sunder. 1993. "The Feminist Plot and The Nationalist Allegory: Home and World in Two Indian Women's Novels in English." *Modern Fiction Studies* (mfs). Vol. 39, No. 1. Spring. pp. 71-92.

Rajeshwar, M. 1991. "The Trauma of a House-wife: A Psychological Study of Shashi Deshpande's *That Long Silence*. *Commonwealth Quarterly*. Vol. 17, No. 43. Jun.-Sept. pp. 41-46.

Ramamoorthi, P. 1991. "My Life is My Own: A Study of Shashi Deshpande's Women." *Indian Women Novelists*. Set-1, Vol. 5, R.K. Dhawan (ed.). New Delhi: Prestige Books. pp. 37-49.

Rani, T. Asoka. 1996. "Feminism *Vis-a-Vis* Woman's Dignity: A Study of Shashi Deshpande's *That Long Silence*." *The Journal of Indian Writing in English*. Vol. 24, No. 1. Jan. pp. 17-22.

Rao, Valli. 1994-95. "'The Devi Entered into Her': Feminist Mythmaking in Shashi Deshpande's *The Dark Holds No*

Terrors." *New Literature Review*. No. 28-29. Winter-Summer. pp. 100-18.

Raveendran, P.P. 1997. "Beyond The Sheltering Tree: The Politics of Silence/Gaze in Shashi Deshpande's *That Long Silence*." *Critical Practice*. Vol. 4, No. 1.

Riemenschneider, Dietor. 1985. "Indian Women Writing in English: The Short Story." *World Literature Written in English*. Vol. 25, No. 2, Aug. pp. 312-18.

Roy, Evangeline Shanti. 2001. "Shashi Deshpande's *The Binding Vine*: A Quest for the Anchor of Life." *Littcrit*. Vol. 27, No. 1-2, June-Dec. pp. 75-82.

Sandhu, Sarbjit K. 1991. "The Image of Woman in *Roots and Shadows*." *Indian Women Novelists*. Set-1, Vol. 5, R.K. Dhawan (ed.). New Delhi: Prestige Books. pp. 102-10.

——. 1991. "The Image of Woman in *That Long Silence*." *Indian Women Novelists*. Set-1, Vol. 5. R.K. Dhawan (ed.). New Delhi: Prestige Books. pp. 138-46.

——. 1991. "The Image of Woman in *The Dark Holds No Terrors*." *Indian Women Novelists*. Set-1, Vol. 5, R.K. Dhawan (ed.). New Delhi: Prestige Books. pp. 82-89.

——. 1991. "The Image of Woman in the Novel of Shashi Deshpande." *Indian Women Novelists*. R.K. Dhawan (ed.). New Delhi: Prestige Books. pp. 102-10.

Sathupati, Prasanna Sree. 1993. "Conflict and Identity in Shashi Deshpande's Novels." *Scholar*. Vol. 15, No. 2, July. pp. 75-84.

Savio, G. Dominic. 2001. "A Woman's Heritage of the Commonwealth: A Study of *The Dark Holds No Terrors*." *Women in the Novels of Shashi Deshpande*. Suman Bala (ed.). New Delhi: Khosla Publishing House. pp. 59-67.

Singh, Ranjini Jyothi. 2005. "Quest For Space and Selfhood in Shashi Deshpande's *Small Remedies*." *Pegasus*. Vol. 4, Jan.-Dec. pp. 20-25.

Singh, Veena. 1995. "Woman as Portrayed by the Women Novelists of India." *The Brown Critique*. No. 10-12, Oct.-Dec. pp. 36-40.

Spivak, Gayatri Chakravorty. 1992. "French Feminism in an International Frame." *Feminist Literary Criterion: A Reader*. Oxford: Blackwell.

Suneel, Seema. 1995. "Marriage, a Compromise: A Study of Shashi Deshpande's *The Dark Holds No Terrors*." *Man-Women Relationship in Indian Fiction*. New Delhi: Prestige Books. pp. 74-122.

Swain, S.P. 1995. "Shashi Deshpande's *The Dark Holds No Terrors*: Saru's Feminine Sensibility." *Indian Women Novelists*. Set-3, Vol. 4, R.K. Dhawan (ed.). New Delhi: Prestige Books. pp. 32-40.

Tharu, Susie. 1986. "Is There a Tradition of Women's Literature?" *The Literary Criterion*. XXI, 1 & 2.

Tiwari, Shubha. 1997-98. "Women's Liberation Movement and Indian Women Novelists." *The Commonwealth Review*. Vol. 9, No. 2. pp. 16-23.

Venugopal, C.V. and M.G. Hadge. 1991. "Indian Women Short Story Writers in English: A Critical Study." *Indian Women Novelists*. Set-1, Vol. 1, R.K. Dhawan (ed.). New Delhi: Prestige Books.

Venugopalan, P. 2002. "Bildungsroman: Shashi Deshpande's Version in *The Dark Holds No Terrors*." *The Quest*. Vol. 16, No. 1. June. pp. 17-21.

Woolf, Virginia. 1977. "Speed, Manuscript Notes." *The Pargiters:* The Novel-Essays Portion of the Years 1882-1941. New York: New York Public Library.

Zare, Bonnie. 2004. "First Comes Marriage, Then Comes Emptiness: Identity Formation in Shashi Deshpande's Novels." *South Asian Review,* Vol. 25, No. 2, pp. 84-103.

Book Reviews

Abraham, Taisha. 1994. "Women's Vision". Rev. of *The Binding Vine. The Book Review,* Vol. 18, No. 2 & 3, Feb., Mar. pp. 71-72.

Anantharaman, Latha. 1997. Rev. of *A Matter of Time. The India Magazine.* Vol. 17, No. 3, February, pp. 76-77.

Bande, Usha. 1997. "How Women Cope When the Man of the House Quits." Rev. of *A Matter of Time, Indian Book Chronicle,* Vol. 22, No. 3 & 4, March-April, p. 42.

Bande, Usha. 2001. "Review of *Small Remedies*". *Summer hill IIAS Review. Summer-Winter*, pp. 27-28.

Banerjee, Bidisha. 2005. Rev. of *Gendered Realities, Human Spaces: The Writing of Shashi Deshpande. South Asian Review,* Vol. 25, No. 2, pp. 231-33.

Bhanu, Sharada. 1994. "Woman is the Victim". Rev. of *The Intrusion and Other Stories. Indian Review of Books,* Vol. 3, No. 11, Aug. 16-Sep. 15, pp. 36-38.

Bharucha, Nilufer E. 1995. "The Floodgates are Open: Recent Fiction from the Indian Sub-continent". Rev. of *The Binding Vine. Wasafiri*, No. 21, Spr. pp. 72-74.

Bhatia, H.S. 1981. Rev. of *The Legacy and Other Stories. Common Wealth Quarterly*. Vol. 5, No. 20, Spr. pp. 50-55.

Bordewekar, Sandhya. 1983. "Scenario for a Hindi Film". Rev. of *Come Up and Be Dead. Indian Book Chronicle.* Vol. 8. No. 16, Aug. 16, p. 283.

Chandrasekharan, K. 1981. Rev. of *The Legacy. Trivem,* Vol. 50, No. 1, Apr.-Jun. pp. 90-91.

Daruwalla, Keki. 1991. "An Intense Book". Rev. of *That Long Silence*. *Indian Literature,* Vol. 34, No. 6, Nov.-Dec. pp. 30-34.

De Souza, Eunice. 2004. "Writerly Skills". Rev. of *Moving On*. *The Book Review*, Vol. 28, No. 12, Dec. p. 26.

Dhar, T.N. 1990. "Portrait of a Marriage". Rev. of *That Long Silence*. *Indian Book Chronicle,* Vol. 15, No. 1 & 2, Jan-Feb. p. 7.

Futehally, Laeeq. 1993. Rev. of *The Binding Vine*. *The Literary Criterion,* Vol. 28, No. 3, pp. 89-91.

Futehally, Shama. 1981. "Catharsis". Rev. of *The Dark Holds No Terrors*. *New Quest,* No. 28, Jul.-Aug., pp. 265-66.

Futehally, Sharma. 1984. "Outgrown Flaws". Rev. of *Roots and Shadows*. *The Book Review*. March-April, pp. 29-31.

Futehally, Shama. 1989. "Of That Elusive Self". Rev. of *That Long Silence*. *The Book Review,* Vol . 13, No. 3 & 4, May-Aug., pp. 29-31.

Gerein, James. 2000. Rev. of *Small Remedies*. *World Literature Today,* Vol. 74, *NoA*, Autumn, p. 804.

Holmstrom, Lakshmi. 1993. "Of Love and Loss". Rev. of *The Binding Vine*. *Indian Review of Books,* Vol. 3, No. 1, Oct. 16-Nov. 15, pp. 52-53.

Holmstrom, Lakshmi. 2000. "Of Times Past". Rev. of *Small Remedies*. *Indian Review of Books,* Vol. 9, No. 8, May 16-June 15, pp. A-5.

Hussein, Aamer. 1993. "India's Mother Tongues". Rev. of *The Binding Vine*. *The Times Literary Supplement,* No. 4704, May 28, pp. 24-25.

Ikin, Van. 1988. "Pleasingly Gritty". Rev. of *It was the Nightingale*. *CRNLE Reviews Journal,* No. 1 & 2, pp. 164-69.

Kaul, R.K. 2000. "A Long Novel Short on Readability". Rev. of *Small Remedies*. *Indian Book Chronicle,* Vol. 25, No. 9, September, p. 7.

Khair, Tabish. 2003. Rev. of *Collected Stories* (Volume 1). *Wasafri, No A0,* Winter, pp. 68-69.

King, Adele. 1988. Rev. of *That Long Silence. World Literature Today,* Vol. 62, No. 4, Aut. p. 727.

King, Adele. 1994. Rev. of *The Binding Vine. World Literature Today,* Vol. 68, No. 2, Spring, p. 430.

Lal, Malashri. 1981."Good Luck to Entrepreneurs". Rev. of *The Dark Holds No Terrors. Indian Book Chronicle,* Vol. 6, No. 9, May 16, pp. 169-71.

Lindley, Arthur. 1980. Rev. of *The Legacy. The Journal of Indian Writing in English,* Vol. 8, No. 1 & 2, Jan.-Jul. pp. 189-93.

Menon, Ritu. 2000. "Pentimento". Rev. of *Small Remedies. The Book Review.* Vol. 24, No. 7, July, pp. 24-25.

Mukherjee, Meenakshi. 1981. "Ghosts from the Past". Rev. of *The Dark Holds No Terrors. The Book Review,* Vol. 5, No. 5, Mar.-Apr. pp. 30-33.

Mukherjee, Meenakshi. 1997. "Sounds of Silence". Rev. *of A Matter of Time. Indian Review of Books.* Vol. 6, No. 6, 16 Mar.-15 Apr. pp. 30-31.

Pande, Ira. 2000. "The Pain of Memory". Rev. of *Small Remedies. Biblio: A Review of Books,* Vol. 5, No. 3 & 4, March-April, p. 22.

Prasad, G.J.Y. 2004. "The Creative and the Critical". Rev. of 1. *Writing from the Margin and other Essays,* 2. *Collected Stories,* Volume II. *The Book Review,* Vol. 28, No. 9, Sep. p. 28.

Ramachandra, Ragini. 1986. Rev. of *The Dark Holds No Terrors, The Literary Criterion,* Vol. 21, No. 1 & 2, pp. 119-21.

Ramchandra, Keerti. 1997. "Of fate and eternity". Rev. of *A Matter of Time. Biblio: A Review of Books,* Vol. 3, No. 4, April, pp. 21.

Rao, Vimala Rama. 1992. "A Well-Articulated Silence". Rev. of *That Long Silence. The Literary Criterion,* Vol. 27, No. 4, pp. 76-77.

Rao, Vimala Rama. 1993. Rev. of *That Long Silence. The Journal of Indian Writing in English,* Vol. 21, No. 1, January, pp. 72-73.

Shankar, D.A. 1992. "You are Your Own Refuge". Rev. of *The Dark Holds No Terrors. The Literary Half-Yearly,* Vol. 33, No. 1, Jan. pp. 172-73.

Sharma, D.R. 1979. "Recent Short Fiction". Rev. of *The Legacy. Indian Book Chronicle,* Vol. 4, No. 14, July 16. pp. 244-46.

Simha, Indira Vijay. 1995. "Rainy Day Reading". Rev. of *The Narayanpur Incident Indian Review of Books,* Vol. 5, No. 2, 16 Nov.-15 Dec. pp. 51-52.

Singh, Madhu. 1993. "Intimate & Soul-Searching Portrayals of Marriage". Rev. of *Roots and Shadows. Indian Book Chronicle,* Vol. 18, No. 7, July. pp. 21-22.

Wasi, Jehanara. 1991. Rev. of *That Long Silence. Indian Horizons,* Vol. 40, No. 3-4, pp. 115-17.

Watson, C. Woo. 1995. "Some Recent Writing from India". Rev. of *Roots and Shadows. Wasafiri,* No. 21, Spr. pp. 74-75.

Yardi, Anjali. 1990. Rev. of *That Long Silence. The Indian P.E.N.*, Vol. 51, No. 1-3, Jan.-Mar., pp. 19-22.